Studies in Rhetorics and Feminisms

Series Editors, Cheryl Glenn and Shirley Wilson Logan

Other Books in the Studies in Rhetorics and Feminisms Series

The

Gendered Pulpit

The

Gendered
Pulpit

*Preaching in American
Protestant Spaces*

Roxanne Mountford

Southern Illinois University Press
Carbondale

Publication partially funded by a subvention grant
from the Provost's Author Support Fund, University of Arizona.

Library of Congress Cataloging-in-Publication Data

Mountford, Roxanne, 1962–
    The gendered pulpit : preaching in American Protestant spaces /
Roxanne Mountford
        p. cm. — (Studies in rhetorics and feminisms)
    Includes bibliographical references and index.
    1. Preaching—United States—History. 2. Women clergy—United States—
History. 3. Protestant church buildings—United States—History. I. Title.
II. Series.
BV4208.U6M685 2003
251'.0082'0973—dc21
ISBN 0-8093-2534-9 (cloth : alk. paper)
ISBN 0-8093-2650-7 (pbk. : alk. paper)   2003004527

The paper used in this publication meets the minimum requirements of
American National Standard for Information Sciences—Permanence of
Paper for Printed Library Materials, ANSI Z39.48-1992. ⊚

Dedicated to the memory of
my grandmother, Marguerite,
and my sweet muse, Duncan

Contents

Acknowledgments

Because this book has been written over a period of years, many people have contributed to the project in diverse ways. I want to begin first with an apology to anyone I may have left out of the list because of my own forgetfulness.

For providing me with both material and intellectual support for the project, I thank the University of Arizona. By providing me with research funding and a semester of reduced teaching, the university allowed me the time and critical support needed to finish the project. I thank my department head, Larry Evers, for lending me his belief when I was discouraged, providing guidance, and locating resources for me. I thank my senior colleagues in the Rhetoric, Composition, and the Teaching of English Program for taking on additional burdens so that I might focus on writing. For managing my research funds with efficiency and kindness, I thank Lourdes Canto. For providing me with a rich intellectual environment for my work, I thank all my colleagues in the English department.

I am indebted to those who have so generously given of their time to read my drafts and provide me with feedback: Susan Hardy Aiken, Elizabeth A. Britt, Gregory Clark, Adrienne Crump, D. Diane Davis, Larry Evers, Gregory S. Jackson, Nan Johnson, Shawn Hellman, Claire Lauer, Nathalie Lewis, Andrea Lunsford, Jill McCracken, Thomas P. Miller, Irvin Morris, Beverly Moss, Krista Ratcliffe, Rachel Srubas, and Tilly Warnock. For helpful discussions of ideas, organization, or sources, I thank Michelle Ballif, Laura Berry, Jennifer Bryan, Ralph Cintron, Richard L. Enos, S. Michael Halloran, Richard Hansberger, Fenton Johnson, Patricia Kelvin, Jean Kreis, Karen LeFevre, Keith Miller, Nedra Reynolds, Jack Selzer, Richard Straub, Robert Yagelski, and James Zappen. I am deeply grateful to Cheryl Glenn and Shirley Wilson Logan for their thorough and insightful feedback on the manuscript and for their encouragement and generous assistance throughout the process. I also thank an anonymous reviewer for invaluable suggestions and Karl Kageff for his wise counsel and support. For their feedback, careful documentation, and intellectual camaraderie at different stages of the project, I thank my research assistants, Marta Brunner and Stacy Day, who quite simply made this a better book.

For their dogged support of me through the peaks and valleys, I thank my parents, Richard and Marjorie Mountford, sister Janelle Roshong, and friends not listed above, including Chris Carroll, Carol Hulgus, Sally Jackson, Daniel Cooper Alarcon, Houston Smit, Suzy Dovi, Psipsinas Martha Fenn, Jill Winans, Jeanne Shirly, Susanne Kaplan, Sarah Iden, Lynn Davis, and Greta Binford. Above all, I thank Bill Endres, the pal of my heart, for his companionship, love, sacrifices on my behalf, and true intellectual friendship.

Finally, much of this book would not exist if three women ministers had not opened their doors to me. I am deeply grateful for and humbled by their generosity.

My thanks to Gregory Clark, editor of *Rhetoric Society Quarterly,* for permission to reprint an excerpt of "On Gender and Rhetorical Space" (31 [Winter 2001]: 41–71), which constitutes part of chapter 1.

The
Gendered Pulpit

Introduction

Gendered Bodies, Feminism, and Rhetorical Performance

> In speaking, the act that the body is performing is never fully understood; the body is the blindspot of speech, that which acts in excess of what is said, but which also acts in and through what is said. That the speech act is a bodily act means that the act is redoubled in the moment of speech: there is what is said, and then there is a kind of saying that the bodily "instrument" of the utterance performs.
>
> —Judith Butler, *Excitable Speech*

> [T]he condition under which patriarchy is psychically produced is the constitution of women's bodies as lacking.
> —Elizabeth Grosz, *Volatile Bodies*

My childhood was filled with preaching. As the daughter of the choir director at a small evangelical church, a part-time job my father held until I was twelve years old, I was present for Sunday school, Sunday morning service, Sunday evening service, and Wednesday evening prayer meeting. My favorite hymn was "The Solid Rock," and on Wednesday evenings, I often shouted out its title when my father asked for requests. I think my fondness of the hymn came from the chorus line, "On Christ, the solid Rock, I stand; / All other ground is sinking sand" (if you sang "rock I stand" a little slurred, it sounded like "Roxanne"). At this little rural church, I was "saved" more times than I can remember, but especially during camp meeting, when we attended services every night, Sunday through Saturday. During the summer, these revivals were held under enormous graying tents with packed earth floors and wooden folding chairs, and all the women, wearing tight polyester dresses, waved paper fans or church bulletins under their chins. The preacher stood on a platform, far away, pulling the microphone cord along behind him, his voice shouting, then whispering. Often I found myself in the position of a character in a Michael Lee West novel, who looked at the preacher "and everything fell silent, sucked up into the heat of his glare, as if he were the Lord Himself, calling His sinners home" (90). Then, on the tenth or eleventh repetition of "Just As I Am," I went forward to accept Jesus into my heart once again.

Eventually, my parents tired of the thirty-mile drive into the country three times a week, so we joined a more liberal evangelical church and became just members. At this church, the preacher was a compassionate man who never shouted; nevertheless, we listened with a piece of paper to copy down the outline of his three-point exegesis. He was called Pastor Joe. The altar calls were fewer and the guilt more diffused. I went to church camp in the summers for a week, and there my denomination served up the fierce revival sermons of my early childhood. We learned the details of what would happen after the Second Coming (if we were left behind, that is) and what aspects of "necking" were a sin. We were told the proper roles of the sexes, just in case we hadn't learned them through other institutional reinforcements. I walked to the altar a few more times, just to be sure.

Like many evangelically trained academics, I left much of my forbidding religious upbringing at the front door of the university, applying the hermeneutic skills I learned in Sunday school to graduate studies. I refocused my energies on feminist analysis, titling my first graduate school paper (for a Hemingway seminar) "Eden Without an Eve: Gender in the Nick Adams Stories." I studied religious drama and poetry in seminars on medieval and renaissance literature, but otherwise found religious subjects given a wide berth in my graduate studies. It wasn't until well into my comprehensive exams, with rhetoric my chosen field, that I realized there was something in my background that wanted to be studied. It took a Jewish friend to suggest it to me. I had been casting about for a way to study gender and the rhetorical tradition. She said, "With your background, I don't know why you don't study women preachers."

The world of preaching I knew as a child was a masculine world of rhetorical performance. Although during the 1960s and 1970s, women were increasingly welcomed into other American pulpits, in my own evangelical world such a possibility was literally unthinkable (indeed, conventional gender ideologies were so completely enforced that *I* never thought of it, even though as a child my radar was attuned to gender discrimination). The *artes praedicandi,* or arts of preaching, among the oldest of the rhetorical arts, inscribes this masculine tradition on the pages of preaching manuals, sometimes explicitly but most often through a smooth surface of universal advice untroubled by the specificity of gender. Hints of the intended reader come in sections on delivery *(actio),* the fifth canon of rhetoric, where homileticians address the performative nature of preaching: voice modulation, gestures, movement. In those sections, homileticians admonish preachers to control their bodies, otherwise they "might sound like a girl in the first grade" (Blackwood 211) or display signs of "effeminacy" (Allen 22). This anxiety over the masculinity of the preacher's body (in these examples, from the 1940s) strongly signals cultural ideologies at work. The generic preacher to whom the homileticians address their theories steps forward as male (not-woman) at such moments. And while the homiletician suggests that the advice is for all preachers, his subjectivity is revealed as gendered and partial, his intended audience a subsection of all those Americans who preach the gospel.[1]

American Protestant spaces—architecture, pulpits, and church communities—anticipate and reinforce this masculine tradition. At the most fundamental level, architects design spaces for the male body. Women, whose bodies are smaller on the whole than men's, are often dwarfed by pulpits, some needing step stools simply to see over the top. But more profoundly, church buildings themselves have a history written in stone and the social imagination that reminds even a casual passerby of the masculine authorities who dwell within. As I argue in this book, the twin legacy of a textbook tradition privileging the masculine body of the preacher and an architectural/cultural tradition that gives that body a home sustain gender bias and leave contemporary women preachers searching for ways to accommodate themselves to the physicality of preaching. Their bodies are not anticipated by the tradition; indeed, for centuries, their bodies have been explicitly excluded.

When I embarked on a study of women preachers, I did not anticipate that space, the body, and delivery would become central foci of my analysis. Like most feminist rhetoricians whom I admire, I oriented my questions toward women's use of language and to textual analysis of rhetorical treatises. Like them, my work led me to challenge rhetorical theory through two categories: a direct challenge to the logic of the theory itself, and an exploration of women's achievements and potential challenges to the theory. Those feminists who have worked to challenge the basic theoretical ground on which rhetoric is understood include Michelle Ballif, Barbara A. Biesecker ("Coming to Terms"), Miriam Brody, D. Diane Davis, and Susan Jarratt. Feminists who have worked both to explore women's achievements and to challenge the tradition include Karlyn Kohrs Campbell, Vicki Tolar Collins, Cheryl Glenn, Susan Kates, Gesa Kirsch, Shirley Wilson Logan, Carol Mattingly, Krista Ratcliffe, and Jacqueline Jones Royster. Both groups share an interest in bringing the particular experiences of women to bear on questions that concern rhetoric: the nature of the speech act; the function of communication (verbal, written, symbolic); the role of gender, race, and class in all communication; and the historical conditions (especially institutional) that underlie all these questions. In addition, postmodern feminists like Ballif and Davis are seeking lines of flight out of patriarchy and humanism by recuperating concepts in the history of rhetoric that have been repressed (for example, "sophism") or could be used in general to disrupt universalist tendencies in the humanities that lead to the suppression of women's experiences. Nearly all these feminists recognize the debasement of women's bodies and their exclusion from the public sphere, yet not through ethnographic study. It was not until I embarked on fieldwork to the three churches featured in this book that I recognized the need to focus on the materiality of rhetorical performance. I hope this book will add to the rich historical work conducted by feminist rhetoricians by focusing on preaching, a neglected art in the history of rhetoric, and by re-centering performance, space, and the body in rhetoric through ethnographic study of everyday women speakers.

Preaching is fundamentally an act of rhetorical performance, the gendered nature of that performance (voice, gesture, and movement) vitally reinforcing a congregation's beliefs. When I look back on the eighteen years I spent in church being shaped by rhetorical performances, sometimes on a nightly basis at camp meeting, it now seems obvious that the power of preaching was for me inherently associated with masculinity. The preachers moved the congregation by working our imagination: religion is based on an unseen cosmology, so the preacher's primary task is to bring this unseen world into view. Most sermons rely in part on exegesis of biblical concepts and in part on narratives, drawn both from human experience and the Bible. In Protestantism, there is an additional emphasis on effecting an emotional transformation in the congregation through the sermon, often by simulating the relationship between an unseen God and the individual listener. Preachers at the church camp I attended as an adolescent asked me to picture God peeking in the window as I sat alone with my boyfriend. What would God see as we sat there? This rhetorical strategy, called *energia* (vivid narratives), is a central feature of sermons, but especially Protestant sermons, many of which place emphasis on feeling the presence of God. Such mental images become God for the congregation, and the gender of the preacher and his point of view in the narrative reinforces a masculine view of the divine. The preacher (God) was looking in through the window at me.

The preacher effects these pictures through voice, posture, stance, and his relationship in space to the congregation. He stoops to look through the imaginary window. He becomes that which he portrays. His body tells a story alongside the story he is speaking. The provinces of rhetoric concerned with the speaking body are delivery and memory *(memoria)*, the first designating an art of gestures and vocal modulations that the orator typically composed along with the content of the speech and the latter designating the memorization of the performance. Many ancients recognized delivery as the most important canon in rhetoric. When acclaimed Greek orator Demosthenes was asked the three most important aspects of oratory, he replied, famously, "Delivery, delivery, delivery." In *Institutio oratorio,* Quintilian wrote:

> Now if delivery can count for so much in themes which we know to be fictitious and devoid of reality, [. . .] how much greater must its effect be when we actually believe what we hear? [. . .] We are therefore almost justified in concluding that he [Demosthenes] regarded it not merely as the first, but as the only virtue of oratory. (11.3.5–6)

Throughout history, rhetoricians have stressed that the body can be controlled, tamed, and brought into use during a rhetorical performance. For example, in 1644 John Bulwer published *Chirologia: or the Natural Language of the Hand* and *Chironomia: or the Art of Manual Rhetoric* to chronicle the semiotics of gestures. In 1796, Thomas Sheridan published *A Course of Lectures on Elocution,* which featured elaborate diagrams showing stances and gestures an orator might use to augment his speech. Indeed, throughout most of Western history, rhetoric has concerned itself primarily with oral discourse. Oral discourse is, by definition, performed before an audience, no matter how large, and, by definition, involves at least one body speaking to another in space. Rhetoric was understood to be an art performed in material spaces. And, of course, it was assumed that males of the ruling classes would perform it.

However, in the last two centuries, written discourse has dominated scholarly attention (as well as public life), and memory and delivery have largely fallen from view. By the close of the eighteenth century, rhetoricians such as Richard Whately had dropped memory and delivery from their treatises on rhetoric. And despite the rage for elocution in the nineteenth century, most rhetoricians in the universities refocused their energies on writing pedagogy and literature, excluding invention as well as memory and delivery from their textbooks (Crowley, *Methodical Memory;* Welch, *Contemporary*).[2] The paradigm shift from orality to literacy occurred so suddenly in nineteenth-century American universities that Robert J. Connors postulates that co-education was to blame. Writing pedagogy was more "irenic," Connors surmises, and therefore more appropriate for "promiscuous" classes than the (masculine) agon of oral debate that once dominated universities (*Composition-Rhetoric* 23–68; see also Ong, *Fighting*). Of course, such a view ignores the attempts of women to gain access to the public sphere, often through agonistic means. A more popular (and plausible) explanation for the decline in emphasis on delivery and memory in universities is simply that scholars and teachers regarded literacy as more essential than orality to public life (Welch, "Reconfiguring" 19; see also Halloran, "Rhetoric").

While the study of written discourse continues to dominate the humanities and social sciences, some fields are beginning to rediscover the importance of physicality, space, and oral performance in rhetoric. For example, outside the field of rhetoric, folklorists have long treated archived stories and songs as objects of textual study and not as rhetorically situated performances. As Richard Bauman and Donald Braid explain,

> [U]ntil very recently, oral traditions have been conceived of as textual items—collectively shaped, traditional texts that could diffuse across the landscape, persist through time, fill up collections and archives, and reflect culture. Viewed in these terms, oral traditions appear to have lives of their own, subject only to impersonal, superorganic processes and laws. But this view is an abstraction, founded on memories or recordings of tales as told, songs as sung, spells as chanted. Approached in terms of performance, symbolic forms we call oral traditions have their primary existence in the action of people and their roots in social and cultural life. The texts we are accustomed to viewing as the materials of oral traditions are merely the thin and partial record of deeply situated human behavior. (106–7)

In other words, texts that were once a robust rhetorical performance, complete with an audience, have too often been reduced to texts studied without reference to their performative nature. Jody Enders makes a similar argument for the study of medieval drama, noting that without attention to the performative nature of discourse in the Middle Ages, it is impossible to recognize the historic fluidity between such oral genres as law, preaching, and theater. While most scholars in rhetoric continue to treat texts as the primary evidence of rhetorical activity, scholars such as Richard Leo Enos, Ralph Cintron, and Elizabeth C. Britt have turned to the social sciences for methods that move them into the cultural contexts for rhetorical activity.

While textual study continues to dominate rhetoric studies, a few rhetoricians have begun to explore the rhetoric of bodies and spaces, an important starting place for a contemporary recovery of delivery. For example, in *Rhetorical Bodies,* a collection of essays growing out of the annual Penn State Conference on Rhetoric and Composition, scholars explore discourses of the body in medicine, popular culture, literature, and politics. In her study of the rhetoric surrounding infertility, Britt explores the discourses of normalcy used by women and their doctors when making decisions about infertility and family life. In *Gender and*

Rhetorical Space in American Life, 1866–1910, Nan Johnson explores the gender bias that emerges in non-academic rhetorics published for Anglo-American women in the late nineteenth century (for example, on elocution and letter writing), focusing her attention on the way in which this handbook tradition reinforced conventional (bodily) expressions of gender. Johnson's work illustrates the way in which rhetorical traditions are imbricated in cultural efforts to circumscribe a sphere of influence for women beyond the public sphere (in the privacy of home). In addition to this work on the rhetoric of bodies, Carole Blair and Gregory Clark explore the rhetoric of national monuments, moving rhetorical analysis into an appreciation of the role of space in shaping identity.

These studies illustrate the importance of recognizing physicality and space as critical components of rhetoric. As Jack Selzer argues in his introduction to *Rhetorical Bodies,* "material moments of rhetorical action [. . .] have largely remained beyond the reach of rhetoricians, who have traditionally (and understandably) been most attentive to oral and written discourses, narrowly conceived" (9). Yet there is still an important role for scholars to adopt what Bauman and Braid call "performance-based approaches," which take into consideration the fact that a rhetor, storyteller, or singer is influenced by an immediate audience, which "has a formative—indeed, a constitutive—influence on performance" (107–8). This deeply rhetorical principle would seem an obvious one, but even in the analysis of speeches, rhetoricians often analyze transcripts while neglecting the performative aspects of the speech, including the crucial aspect of rhetorical space, which I discuss in the next chapter.

An analysis of oral performance must begin with a recognition that the body is not only an instrument of expression but is also itself expressive of meaning. This perspective has long been recognized by feminists. As early as 1792, Mary Wollestonecraft argued:

> Taught from their infancy that beauty is woman's scepter, *the mind shapes itself to the body,* and, roaming round its gilt cage, only seeks to adorn its prison. [. . .] [W]ere their understanding emancipated from the slavery to which the pride and sensuality of man and their short-sighted desire, like that of dominion in tyrants, [. . .] has subjected them, we should probably read of their weaknesses with surprise. (103, emphasis added)

An early statement of the effects of racial prejudice on the bodies and minds of free blacks in the northern United States can be found as early as 1831 in a speech by Maria W. Stewart, who deplored the association of African Americans with menial labor, despite their education and ability. In her important treatise *The Second Sex,* Simone de Beauvoir articulates the association of women with the body and men with the mind, arguing that Woman (body and soul) is defined as all that is not-Man. In 1968, the first march of the second-wave feminist movement was staged to protest the Miss America pageant. Feminist protesters encouraged women to throw cultural objects that enslaved their bodies into a fire, including (famously) bras, girdles, and copies of *Cosmopolitan* (Bordo, *Unbearable Weight* 19). Summarizing this long history, Bordo writes:

> [F]eminism [has] imagined the human body as [. . .] a politically inscribed entity, its physiology and morphology shaped by histories and practices of containment and control—from foot-binding and corseting to rape and battering to compulsory heterosexuality, forced sterilization, unwanted pregnancy, and (in the case of the African American slave woman) explicit commodification. (21–22)

Feminism provides a foundation for the consideration of subjectivity as a process of "normative restraints" on "bodily beings" (Butler, *Bodies* x), including the words we hear associated with our corporeal selves (Butler, *Excitable Speech*).

When considered for what it is—an art of the orator's body—the historical gendering (and racing) of rhetoric is obvious, based in real terms on the male body. Yet without recuperating the fifth canon of rhetoric—delivery—we miss this critical connection. Of course, we inherit a sense of delivery as a system whereby just the right gesture, just the right nod here or fist pounding there, will augment the speech. This debased idea of the body (that it can and must be controlled) has become foundational doctrine for Western civilizations since Descartes, so much so that even mainstream Americans have begun to believe that they can control their body's basic functions, including immunity to disease (Martin, *Flexible Bodies*).[3] Nevertheless, as Elizabeth Grosz argues, the body plays a more formative role in subjectivity than Western culture allows:

> Human bodies, indeed all animate bodies, stretch and extend the notion of physicality that dominates the physical sciences, for animate bodies are objects necessarily different from other objects; they are materialities that are uncontainable in physicalist terms alone. If bodies are objects or things, they are like no others, for they are the centers of perspective, insight, reflection, desire, agency. (xi)

We live and learn of the world as gendered beings, our subjectivity shaped by our bodies and the discourses surrounding our corporeal existence. What this means is that despite the Cartesian world that we all have embraced one way or another, it is really not possible to think about rhetoric without drawing in considerations of the body. The body *is* the subject in both senses: it is the subject of rhetoric as well as the actor/orator/rhetorician herself. For this reason, refiguring delivery is critically important for a feminist transformation of rhetorical theory.[4]

Women's bodies are associated with natural inferiority and reproductive functions, and their confinement to the private spheres of community has been predicated in part on their sexual difference. Because preaching primarily occurs in the public sphere, women have long been banned from participation.[5] Indeed, religion has been an important site for the disciplining of women's bodies; every Catholic girl who was asked to kneel so that a nun could check her skirt length understands this point implicitly. World religions enforce chastity through restrictions on the bodies of women—where they can go, with whom they can associate, what they can say, and what they can wear in private and public. Medieval Christian mystic Margery Kempe is an especially interesting case precisely because she reports breaking so many rules of travel, clothing, and association while justifying these transgressions through divine revelation (Glenn, *Rhetoric Retold* 106–13). When women preachers have challenged these same restrictions, they have risked banishment (as in the case of the Antinomian Anne Hutchinson) or death.

Remarkably, despite these risks women preachers have emerged persistently throughout the history of Christianity. Their presence has most often coincided with the founding of new religious movements, when greater egalitarianism marks the movement as set apart from established religious traditions. An early example of this pattern occurred among the followers of Peter Valdes, who began a lay movement around 1173 in France. Known as "Waldensians," Valdes's followers apparently included a number of women. The Waldensians took vows of poverty, left their families, and traveled around Europe preaching the gospel in the tradition of the early apostles. They sought the approval of Pope Alexander III, who offered his support of their lifestyle while cautioning them not to preach without authorization. The Waldensians refused to submit to the Catholic Church, arguing as Protestants did centuries later that God could be known by laypersons outside the hierarchies of the church through direct revelation. They translated the Scriptures into the vernacular and spread the gospel in public, apparently without regard of gender. As historians have discovered in the letters and treatises published in the twelfth century, the fact that Waldensians encouraged women to preach was even more horrifying to church officials than the fact that *all* the Waldensians were defying church authority. For example, in his treatise on the Book of Revelation, Geoffroy of Auxerre singles out two Waldensian women from the village of Clermont for historical chastisement and revisionism, claiming that they themselves boasted of their promiscuity, gluttony, and slothfulness: "'After the preaching every day [we were] feasting splendidly; almost every night we were choosing new lovers,'" Geoffroy caused them to say (qtd. in Kienzle 102). In this example, it is especially noteworthy that Geoffroy focuses his attention on sins of the body: women speaking in public in ways threatening to authorities are often accused of promiscuity (the case of Anita Hill is a recent example). If women are found outside the private domain engaging in activities considered inappropriate for their sex, authorities surmise that their bodies are engaged in other unchaste activities as well.

This pattern repeats itself throughout history, although in some periods—for example, during the Inquisition in Europe—women were so persecuted for any public activities, or indeed any nonconforming private activities, that they engaged in preaching at great risk. The Inquisition began as an effort of the Roman Catholic Church to rein in its bishops and priests and thereby regain religious control over Europe. After the eleventh century, popes sought to enforce priestly celibacy, sending preachers into villages to preach "frightening sermons about the evils and dangers of female sexuality, calling the clergy to celibacy, and placing before them the choice of either losing their positions and livings or renouncing their mistresses and wives" (Torjesen, *When Women Were Priests* 226). Their rhetorical strategy was to denounce women's bodies as innately evil, the conduits of sin and damnation. The abbot Conrad of Marchtal was so convinced by this argument that he refused to assume a position of authority over a convent of nuns:

> We, and our whole community of canons, recognizing that the wickedness of women is greater than all the wickedness of the world [. . .] and that the poison of asps and dragons is more curable and less dangerous to men than the familiarity of women, have unanimously decreed for the safety of our souls, no less than for that of our bodies and goods, that we will on no account receive any more sisters to the increase of our perdition, but will avoid them like poisonous animals. (Southern 314)

By 1454, this basic theology had turned the Inquisition into a witch-hunt, which eventually led to the burning of hundreds of thousands of women at the stake for the crime of consorting with the devil. (Torjesen estimates that one million women were killed in Europe, though the number is probably lower [*When Women Were Priests* 229].)

The Protestant Reformation in Germany, England, and Switzerland did not rid Christianity of its cultic aversion to women's bodies. The Puritans' persecution of women is well known; Puritans in the Massachusetts Bay Colony harassed Quaker women, considering them "lewd" for preaching in public, and executed one—Mary Dyer—in 1660 (Pestana). They also subjected ordinary women to torture and death for suspected witchcraft. When the First Great Awakening settled upon New

England and the Middle Colonies (1736–50), female Calvinists continued to exhibit an obsession with their own bodily and spiritual pollution. Catherine A. Brekus points out that New England women converts "persistently identified their bodies, not their hearts, as the source of their corruption." For instance, in her conversion narrative, Deborah Prince lamented, *"'By Nature I am half a Devil and half a Beast; I know that in me, that is in my Flesh, dwells no good Thing'"* (qtd. in Brekus 40). In 1741, at the height of the First Great Awakening, Bathsheba Kingsley stole her husband's horse and road off to preach the gospel in neighboring towns (Brekus 23). To justify her behavior, she claimed to have been visited by God; but in their rebuke, church officials contradicted her, arguing that her "'weak, vapory habit of body'" made her susceptible to Satan's misleading (qtd. in Brekus 41). She was suppressed along with many other women who were moved to speak in public under the egalitarian forces of the revivals. Order was ultimately restored; male church authorities regained control, and arguments against women preaching in public on the grounds of their moral and spiritual inferiority continued.

However, despite the efforts of male church authorities to suppress women preachers, women have found spaces from which to preach throughout history. Their history is, as Brekus puts it, "not a continuous tradition [. . .], but a disconnected and broken one" (16). Indeed, in her study of more than one hundred women who preached between 1740 and 1845 in America, Brekus discovered that most women preachers who left records were isolated and unaware of other women like themselves. There were two key reasons for this historical amnesia. When new religious movements became formal denominations, historians (all male, Brekus notes) erased the contributions of foremothers. Forefathers of the movement who left memoirs were more charitable, and it is primarily through study of their papers that feminist historians have discovered the existence of women preachers. The case of Methodism has been well documented (Chilcote; Collins; D. Andrews 99–122; Muir). John Wesley appointed women as deacons and itinerant preachers in the early years of the movement, but when the Wesleyan Methodists became a formal denomination in the early nineteenth century, clergymen voted against allowing women to preach under any circumstances, and church authorities wrote histories that agreed with this perspective. The result is that such important Methodist preachers as Grace Murray, Sarah Crosby, Elizabeth Ritchie, and Mary Bosanquet were erased from public memory. A second problem is that secular feminists have preferred to recuperate secular foremothers rather than study women who, no matter how pioneering they were, preached a message that could not always be squared with contemporary feminism. Avoidance of religious subjects, no matter how important to cultural history, has prevailed in the humanities for much of the twentieth century, and feminist scholars are no exception to this practice.

What do we know about women preachers in American history? We know that the Quakers are the one religious denomination that consistently supported women preachers throughout American history, including a former African American slave named Elizabeth (1765?–1866). More than a thousand Quaker women traveled in the Colonies between 1700 and 1775 preaching, and in the case of such celebrated speakers as Rachel Wilson, often to enormous crowds (Rebecca Larson 7). We know that extraordinary women preachers founded religious movements in the United States, including Phoebe Palmer (1807–47), who founded the Holiness movement; Aimee Semple McPherson (1890–1944), who founded the International Church of the Foursquare Gospel and was a pioneer in radio evangelism; and M. L. Esters, who founded a black Pentecostal denomination known as The House of God, Which Is the Church of the Living God, the Pillar and Ground of the Truth, Inc. We know that while secular women speakers were often ostracized for speaking in public, women preachers often did so to great acclaim. For example, in 1827, Harriet Livermore, an evangelical preacher, was invited to preach before the House of Representatives in Washington, D.C., and more than a thousand people from the most prestigious circles came to hear her, including President John Quincy Adams, who sat on the floor because the audience had grown so large (Brekus 1–2). We also know that women like Livermore have been largely forgotten.

Many of the women who preached in the United States did so as evangelists or itinerant preachers (sometimes to avoid the prejudices against women preaching, they called themselves "exhorters") (Brekus 48). Occasionally, they did so with ordination rights, as in the case of Julia A. J. Foote, the first woman to be ordained in the African Methodist Episcopal Zion Church (in 1895). But most often they did so with the blessing of individual ministers, as in the case of Jarena Lee, authorized by African Methodist Episcopal (AME) Church founder Richard Allen to preach 130 years before the AME Church voted to ordain women (in 1948). Extending ordination to women meant admitting them to the company of clergymen and providing them with leadership of churches, something many clergymen fought (and in some denominations are still fighting) bitterly. The ordination of women was *the* denominational question of the twentieth century, and it was decided in the affirmative by almost every mainline Protestant denomination in America by 1979.[6] However, as studies by Delores C. Carpenter; Edward C. Lehman Jr.; Barbara Brown Zikmund, Adair T. Lummis, and Patricia Mei Yin Chang; Carol M. Norén; Frederick W. Schmidt; and

Paula D. Nesbitt show, there is still gender prejudice at work in denominations that ordain women, leaving many clergywomen unemployed or underemployed, underpaid, and isolated. In introducing Schmidt's study of women clergy in four major denominations (Episcopal, United Methodist, Evangelical Lutheran, and Southern Baptist), ordained minister Betty Bone Schiess writes:

> [I]n spite of much effort during the last two decades to include women in the church as full participants, women clergy [. . .] are not happy—are, in fact, limited by the churches they serve, their voices muffled by those who should be listening, their talents badly used by those who should know about sloth. (x)

In a recent review of all the literature on working conditions for American Protestant clergywomen, Mark Chaves agrees, arguing that ordination rights for clergywomen are sometimes little more than institutional window dressing. He points out that the majority of Protestant denominations voted for ordination rights in response to "normative pressures emerging from the denomination's cultural environment" and not out of appreciation for clergywomen's innate value to the organization, a situation that remained unchanged at the end of the twentieth century (33).

Nevertheless, women are effecting some change in their denominations through ordained leadership, and a few women are beginning to break through to higher levels of their denomination's hierarchy (for example, Barbara C. Harris, the first woman to serve as a bishop in the Episcopal Church, and Vashti M. McKenzie, the first woman to serve as a bishop in the AME Church). Feminist scholars in theology, homiletics, and folklore have explored some of the theological perspectives and metaphors in the sermons of these clergywomen (for example, Lawless; C. Smith). This work suggests the importance of women's preaching for the future of Protestant Christianity, especially in the articulation of a theology that includes the full range of human experience. In many ways, this book supports and extends this important work by connecting the struggles of women preachers with what Johnson calls "the role of rhetoric in the disposition of power and in what has always been in American culture a highly gendered struggle over the control of public rhetorical space and its benefits" (*Gender* 2).

This book asks several questions that are at the heart of much feminist analysis, both inside the field of rhetoric as well as outside it: What does it mean for a field of knowledge to take into consideration the experience of women? In what way is a speech act or rhetorical performance "gendered"? How does a woman earn the respect of an audience conditioned to regard her body itself as symbolic of lack (of authority, eloquence, power, substance)? I explore these questions in three ways.

I offer analysis of the rhetorical spaces in which preachers perform (considering the history of church architecture and the ways in which these spaces are gendered). Focusing on key texts in the Protestant homiletic tradition, I consider the ways in which homileticians have simultaneously encoded rhetorical performance as universal (that is, offering advice as universally applicable, regardless of the specificities of preachers and congregations) and male (through pronoun use and explicit references to the male body and conventional masculine behavior). Finally, I explore the rhetorical performances of three mainline Protestant women preachers, all of whom were the first women to lead their churches and all of whom faced skeptical congregations.

Chapters 3, 4, and 5 are based on fieldwork I conducted in 1990 and 1991. I located the clergywomen in the study through a clergywomen's association and through the religion section of the local newspaper. I was purposeful in choosing mainline Protestant congregations that varied in size, racial characteristics, and location; these factors offered interesting organizational dynamics that I explore in each chapter. Denominational differences also played a role in the study, although not in predictable ways. For example, given its longer history of women preachers, I would have predicted that the Methodist church featured in chapter 5 would have been the most accepting of its minister. But instead, the hierarchical structure of the denomination, in which bishops, not congregations, "call" a minister, formed the backdrop to the problems the Reverend Janet Moore experienced with many of the older members.[7]

There is no question that this book is heavily influenced by my own experiences and history. I suspect that most feminist scholars, like most scholars who study race, class, and gay, lesbian, and bisexual issues, come to their subject through a profound experience early in life. Feminists have argued that such experiences should be pondered and made explicit to the reader in order to give their scholarly work credibility. Although I have made this argument myself in an essay on writing ethnography ("Engendering Ethnography"), I am wary of the fine line between "reflection" and "confession." For example, in *Translated Woman: Crossing the Border with Esperanza's Story,* Ruth Behar tells of her own struggle to attain tenure in a chapter that is ostensibly about the informant, Esperanza. Behar's self-reflection helps clarify moments when the informant's life becomes a mirror for the ethnographer. But the charges of "solipsism" leveled at Behar by Daphne Patai are an important bellwether for such analysis:

> Are we really expected to take seriously—and read "generously"—
> the anthropologist Ruth Behar's claim [. . .] that her struggles to
> get tenure at an American university should be seen as parallel to
> the struggles of Esperanza, a Mexican street peddler?

Maintaining the precarious balance between reflection and confession is a difficult one, since an ethnographer is the primary eyewitness to the story she wants to tell.

Nevertheless, I agree with Patricia Bizzell that some of what is best about feminist research in the history of rhetoric (as well as the ethnography of rhetoric, I would add) is the robust emotional connection that researchers bring to their work. I have not shied away from this connection. Feminist rhetoricians need to reclaim the word "empiricism." Such a move returns researchers to the task of rigorously attending to the world around us, listening for insights that are new to us, resisting the temptation to turn our work into an opportunity for self-righteous grandstanding. There is no doubt that ethnography is a construction of events the author witnessed and words she heard, and as Clifford Geertz long ago observed, she will earn her credibility through the *ethos* she offers up as an author. While avoiding the temptation to confess, I nevertheless offer stories—both my own and others'—that bring into view the relationship of rhetorical performance and gender. When I was a child, adults around me said that the world was peopled with just two groups—heathens and Christians. So I began to listen to what others had to say about themselves, to learn other ways of categorizing experience in the world. My love of fiction and of ethnography are founded on this lifelong "formalized curiosity" (Hurston 174). I am motivated to enrich institutional knowledge through exploring the complexity of everyday acts of rhetorical performance.

As a child, I never saw a woman preach; the only women who stepped before the pulpit gave announcements, led hymns, or told tales of missionary work in Third World countries. In the evangelical churches of my childhood, the minister stood behind the pulpit in the center of our world, tall and masculine, and the Pauline Scriptures forbidding women to preach were enforced. The first time I heard a woman preach was in 1989, when I was twenty-seven years old. When I did, I found myself noticing what a difference gender makes in the rhetorical space of the sermon. This book seeks to capture something of the surprise and delight I felt in seeing a woman preacher in the pulpit for the first time.

1

On Gender and Rhetorical Space

> Rhetorical spaces [. . .] are fictive but not fanciful or fixed locations, whose (tacit, rarely spoken) territorial imperatives structure and limit the kinds of utterances that can be voiced within them with a reasonable expectation of uptake and "choral support."
> —Lorraine Code, *Rhetorical Spaces*

> Space itself has a history.
> —Michel Foucault, "Of Other Spaces"

When scholars write about "space," they most often use the term metaphorically to describe the cultural landscape of laws, customs, and beliefs that form the geographies of our lives. Indeed, Gaston Bachelard argues that spatial distinctions are the foundation for Western thought: we use "here" and "there" and "outside" and "inside" in philosophical discourse and on street corners to put ideas—and people—where we think they belong. In *Rhetorical Spaces: Essays on Gendered Locations,* feminist philosopher Lorraine Code theorizes the geography of argument in this way, noting that "the very possibility of an utterance counting as 'true-or-false' or of a discussion yielding insight" depends on one's location (x). She uses the example of women attempting to have "productive public debate about abortion in the Vatican in 1995" (x). Code calls this phenomenon "rhetorical space," which rhetoricians in turn recognize as "the rhetorical situation."[1] It is a familiar observation in rhetoric, stretching back in its most basic form to the early Greek concept of *nomos,* traditionally translated as "custom" or "law" (Kerferd 112). Aristotle suggested that a rhetor must modulate his speech for the old, the young, and for women, groups whose beliefs create an exigency that must be accounted for in the invention process. Particular traits presumed to adhere to these groups offer "cues" for how one must argue, act, or even be.

"Rhetorical space" can be made a more useful concept for rhetoricians, however, if we apply it more narrowly to the material spaces surrounding a communicative event. I am thinking here literally of rooms, lecterns, auditoriums, platforms, confession booths, and classrooms, all of which are interpreted by participants through social expectations but which also have material dimensions that affect what we do there. Rhetorical space is the geography of a communicative event and, like all landscapes, may include both the cultural and material arrangement, whether intended or fortuitous, of space. The cultural is the grid across which we measure and interpret space but also the nexus from which creative minds manipulate material space. The material—a dimension too little theorized by rhetoricians—often has unforeseen influence over a communicative event and cannot always be explained by cultural or creative intent.[2]

To illustrate this theory, I explore the pulpit—movable furniture in some traditions, an architectural structure in others, but in all an embodiment of clerical authority. As I argue in this chapter, the pulpit is a gendered location and therefore a rich site for exploring rhetorical space. To make such a claim is to argue that rhetorical spaces carry the residue of history within them, but also, perhaps, something else: a physical representation of relationships and ideas. To illustrate the dynamics of rhetorical space, I explore how four novelists adapt the pulpits of their fictional preachers to amplify their characters' gender. I then turn to real pulpits and preachers to further explore how hierarchies of gender and status are worked out in the sacred geographies of Christian churches.

A Poetics of Gender and Space

Imagine, first, the pulpit in *Moby-Dick*, a structure so high above the congregation that the preacher must climb a steep ladder to reach it. In Herman Melville's 1851 romance of masculinity, this structure is created from the imagination of Father Mapple, a former harpooner in "the hardy winter of a healthy old age," who eschews carriages and umbrellas, walking to his chapel in a "great pilot cloth jacket" despite terrible weather. His pulpit is

> [l]ike most old fashioned pulpits, [. . .] a very lofty one, and since a regular stairs to such a height would, by its long angle with the floor, seriously contract the already small area of the chapel, the architect, it seemed, had acted upon the hint of Father Mapple, and finished the pulpit without a stairs, substituting a perpendicular side ladder, like those used in mounting a ship from a boat at sea. (42)

Once aloft, Father Mapple pulls the rope ladder up behind him, his pulpit then becoming "a self-containing strong-hold" (43). As if to reinforce the masculine offices represented by this pulpit, Melville mixes his metaphors. The pulpit is a fortress but also a ship's prow (44). By extension, the preacher is a soldier as well as a sailor (and not just any sailor—a harpooner), offices associated with traditional masculinity and the absence of women.

Contrast this picture with the reader's first witness of Dinah Morris, the Methodist evangelist in George Eliot's 1859 pastoral novel, *Adam Bede.* Typical of the early Wesleyan movement, Dinah, as conceived by Eliot, is in no way ordained, so she travels from town to town as a layperson and preaches without benefit of a church or even a building. When asked by the rector of the town why Methodists allow women to preach, she responds:

> [The Society] doesn't forbid them, sir, when they've a clear call to the work, and when their ministry is owned by the conversion of sinners, and the strengthening of God's people. [. . .] I understand there's been voices raised against it in the Society of late, but I cannot but think their counsel will come to naught. It isn't for men to make channels for God's Spirit, as they make channels for the water-courses, and say, "Flow here, but flow not there." (83)

Her first sermon in Eliot's novel is preached on Hayslope Green, her "pulpit" a horse cart drawn up under a maple tree. The meadow is a transitory place, a place decidedly apart from institutions. The pastoral setting is reflected in Dinah's appearance; Eliot writes that she had "one of those faces that makes one think of white flowers with light touches of colour on their pure petals" (21). As she preaches, a stranger watching notices that Dinah is unlike the Methodists he has heard: "She was not preaching as she heard others preach, but speaking directly from her own emotions, and under the inspiration of her own simple faith" (26). The pastoral setting and the horse cart underscore Eliot's theme of the purity and strong character of the farmers and laborers of rural England. Dinah is unordained and uneducated (and ultimately rejected by the Methodists at the end of the novel because of her sex), but her relationship to God's Spirit is, in Eliot's view, as organic as a watercourse.

What these two fictional "pulpits" illustrate are the complex cultural associations of the pulpit as metonym for the Protestant Church as institution (as in the locution "the Pulpit," meaning "Church"), the pulpit as site of clerical authority, and the pulpit as emblem of the nature of God. Father Mapple's ship/fortress reinvests clerical authority with virility and masculine strength. This pulpit, high above the congregation, is one of the opening scenes in a novel about the raw power of nature and its dark extension in the face of a Calvinist God. Dinah Morris's little cart under a maple tree and her earnest countenance begin a pastoral novel in which humble labors and forgiveness are contrasted with the ills of institutional authority. The transient and provisional nature of Dinah's pulpit leaves her close to the people but far away from the institutional church. Dinah's God dwells beyond the walls of a church in pastoral settings. Her cart-pulpit is suggestive of domestic life, and that is where Dinah finds herself at the novel's end.

Because of Ann Douglas's well-known book *The Feminization of American Culture,* many scholars have assumed that the masculinity of nineteenth-century clergymen had been eroded by century's end. Douglas argues that the disestablishment of the liberal churches in the American Colonies led to a gradual "feminization" of the clergy, by which she means the turn of the stern Calvinism of the Edwardian school toward "softer" Victorian sentiments. For Douglas, the "feminization" of liberal clergy in the nineteenth century spelled the end of an intellectually oriented polis; for her, feminization and "anti-intellectualism" go hand-in-hand. However, Douglas glosses over the enduring patriarchal nature of the liberal churches and of preaching: to say that the clergymen of the late nineteenth century embraced a "softened" Calvinism does not mean that they were "feminized" in their attitudes toward women nor in their preaching style. The pulpit opened slightly to admit women in the late nineteenth century, but prejudice against women's ability to lead churches was firmly in place in the liberal church.[3] Written in a decade that saw the rise of a mainstream, ecumenical movement known as "muscular Christianity" in England and America, *Adam Bede* and *Moby-Dick* illustrate the hegemonic struggle over the public image of the pulpit.

Contemporary literary images of the pulpit have underscored the masculinity of the preacher and his office, primarily by locating women preachers in natural settings beyond the institutionalized church. Perhaps the best-known contemporary example is Baby Suggs in Toni Morrison's *Beloved,* a novel about a woman named Sethe who believes her murdered infant daughter is haunting her. Baby Suggs is Sethe's beloved mother-in-law, a preacher without training who dies near the beginning of the novel. The narrator tells us that prior to the events of the novel, Suggs attracted large crowds and was often called to preach in neighboring churches:

> Accepting no title of honor before her name, but allowing small caress after it, she became an unchurched preacher, one who visited pulpits and opened her great heart to those who could use it. In the winter and fall she carried it to AME's and Baptists, Holinesses and Sanctified, the Church of the Redeemer and the Redeemed. (87)

However, in the spring and summer she found her pulpit outside the four square walls of institutionalized churches in a secluded place called the

Clearing, "a wide-open place cut deep in the woods nobody knew for what at the end of a path known only to deer and whoever cleared the land in the first place." There she was "followed by every black man, woman and child who could make it through" (87).

According to Morrison's narrator, Baby Suggs is "uncalled, unrobed, and unanointed" and in the Clearing presides over a distinctly unorthodox service, which begins after Baby Suggs "situates herself on a huge flat-sided rock." Watching her from beneath the trees, the people wait until she puts her stick down and calls out to the children. She asks the children to laugh for their mothers. She asks the men to dance for their wives and children. She asks the women to weep "for the living and the dead" (87–88). Then she preaches.

> She did not tell them to clean up their lives or to go and sin no more.
> She did not tell them they were the blessed of the earth, its inheriting meek or its glorybound pure.
>
> She told them that the only grace they could have was the grace they could imagine. That if they could not see it, they would not have it. (88)

Suggs's unconventional sermon focuses on self-love in the face of racism: "'Here,' she says, 'in this place, we flesh; flesh that weeps, laughs; flesh that dances on bare feet in grass. Love it. Love it hard. Yonder they do not love your flesh'" (88). Indeed, she never makes reference to a deity. When she finishes her sermon, Baby Suggs gets up from the big rock that has served as her pulpit and dances with the people, moving to a song that they sing for her. The scene is reminiscent of Dinah Morris's sermon, preached from an applecart pulpit, though even further removed from institutional contexts. The scene is deep in the woods, a wild place beyond culture's edge. Indeed, Suggs's sermon is not distinctively Christian, nor is the "service" she leads. Accordingly, the pulpit is of the natural environment, not a product of human hands.[4]

Likewise, in *The Temple of My Familiar,* a novel that challenges conventional histories and includes a character named Lissie who remembers past lives, Alice Walker imagines a time and place outside the boundaries of institutionalized religion where women could lead their people spiritually. An elderly character named Hal tells the story of a time when the island where he lived (a colony of escaped slaves) had two ministers—a man and a woman. He tells the story of how he and his wife Lissie were married by the woman preacher:

> "[W]e got married on the front porch at Lissie's people's house, looking out over the bay. It was a pretty spring day, and I just itched to paint it. I never will forget we had a woman preacher to marry us, because we had two preachers on the Island, both of them called

by the spirit, and we were too out of the way things were done in the rest of the world to know the spirit didn't call women." (97)

Lissie claims to remember a time before Christianity when matriarchal religions flourished. During the wedding ceremony, Hal recalls, Lissie said "she *remembered* that women were called *first* and this calling was something men took away from them" (97). But Hal did not take her seriously until he "'was in the army and saw how all the preachers, priests, and chaplains everywhere we went—and we got as far as France—were men'" (97). But the ideal world that Lissie and Hal remember, a time from the late nineteenth century, is a culture in which spirituality is divided between a man's sensibilities and a woman's sensibilities. As in *Adam Bede* and *Beloved,* it is a world well outside the mainstream, a place that Hal discovers to be innocent of the sexist institutional practices that occur beyond the island. Walker's creation of Hal and Lissie and the island where they lived offers a brief glimpse into a world in which seeing only men in the pulpit is the oddity. Still, when the reader "sees" this nameless woman, she is performing a wedding ceremony on a front porch, looking out over a bay on a beautiful morning. The site is not a church. There is no pulpit. It is, once again, a private home, a private structure, on the threshold of nature: a domestic scene.

What are we to make of these four scenes of clerical authority? In each case, the novelist tenderly develops the scene so that the reader is drawn to notice the location where the preachers deliver their sermons and where they stand in relation to others. All four scenes ask the reader to measure the preacher's authority, credibility, and performance. The reader observes how the preachers relate to their congregations and measures this relationship across an understanding of gender. In *Adam Bede, Beloved,* and *The Temple of My Familiar,* the setting is domestic and natural, and it is from within this unusual space that each woman accomplishes her art of preaching. The pulpit of Father Mapple is also a fantastic and unusual space but for an entirely different reason: it requires physical strength to mount and is so impressively high and cut off from the congregation that the preacher himself is phallically elevated (both literally and figuratively) in stature. Eliot, Morrison, and Walker place their fictional women preachers in meadows and woods and on porches; they are of nature and of the local culture. That is not to suggest that these women preachers are without authority; in fact, Eliot, Morrison, and Walker underscore their authority from the community's perspective. However, their wisdom is associated with their gender and their liminal, fleeting position. Baby Suggs is an itinerant preacher/prophet and dies without leaving behind a church. Dinah Morris marries but is also forbidden to preach after a reorganization of the Methodist Church. The unnamed preacher in *The Temple of My Familiar*

exists only because her community has been isolated from larger patriarchal trends and prejudices in the churches of the nineteenth century.

In each case, the reader observes the preacher through the eyes of a
significant character rather than directly through the narrator. Father
Mapple is viewed through the eyes of Ishmael; Dinah Morris through
those of a man on horseback who is a stranger to the town; Baby Suggs
through Sethe, her daughter-in-law; and the unnamed woman in *The
Temple of My Familiar* through Hal, who was married by her. Through
this means, the authors offer a personal reaction to the preachers that
gathers in all the cultural meaning of the scene. Foremost in the minds
of these fictional characters is the gender of the preachers and the ways
they enact their gender as they preach. Why? For Eliot, Morrison, and
Walker, the idea of a woman preacher is presented as an anomaly and
therefore an opportunity to redefine "the pulpit"; for Melville, the
preacher's masculinity (his hardiness, virility, and physical strength) and
his sermon on God's wrath establish the masculine universe around
which the novel revolves. But in all cases, gender is important both to
the eyewitnesses and, by extension, to the British and American writers
who conceived of these scenes.

The authors of these novels also call attention to the profound effects
of *space* on the act of preaching—indeed, on all rhetorical performances—and its relationship to gender. Father Mapple's masculinity and
authority are reflected by the impressive height of his pulpit and the fact
that he must climb a rope ladder to reach it. One way to check the masculine dimensions of this structure is to try to imagine a woman climbing the rope ladder. What comes to mind here (at least from this woman's
mind) is the awkwardness in which a woman of the period might climb
in floor-length skirts, the rope ladder swinging and twisting, her boots
catching on her skirts as she climbs. Or one might imagine an Anglican
clergyman from across town climbing the rope ladder in his vestments
(floor-length ritual clothing). Others who could climb the rope ladder
(and as readers, we do not miss this point) would invite titters of laughter
and the threat of authority lost to a comedic scene. But when Father
Mapple climbs the rope ladder leading to the lofty heights of the pulpit, Melville (through Ishmael) means us to notice his masculine strength
and homoerotic appeal to nineteenth-century sailors.

In contrast, Eliot, Morrison, and Walker turn to nature in trying to
imagine a space for preaching where women might be accepted and have
influence. Dinah Morris and the unnamed woman preacher in *The
Temple of My Familiar* preach outdoors in areas within a community
but beyond the four walls of any building. Baby Suggs preaches deep in
the woods, a space far wilder and less touched by human hands than
Hayslope Green or the front porch of Lissie's people. The sermons

preached are commensurate with these spaces: Dinah Morris preaches a sermon with Methodist themes; Walker's unnamed preacher performs a familiar ritual—a wedding. But Baby Suggs, deep in the woods, preaches a sermon that is far outside the bounds of established Christian theology and ritual. Her sermon focuses on the difficulties of maintaining self-esteem and courage in the face of slavery. It is an exhortation, but far from a traditional sermon. In each case, there is no climbing of stairs or ladders. The rhetorical spaces in which their authors place them complement the themes of their sermons and their performance of gender.

Cultural and Material Dimensions of Rhetorical Space

So why turn to literary examples to explore a real-life phenomenon, the gendered nature of the pulpit? Because writers, like all spectators of life, offer a fresh lens for understanding the nature of rhetoric. As Thomas B. Farrell suggests, the exploration of public oratory goes on without the help of specialists, for through "habituated capacity as an audience," all spectators understand intuitively what moves them in a speech (12). These are not obscure matters for audiences. Who better to explain what an audience understands instinctively than a novelist? Of course, the average person is unlikely to encounter a preacher climbing a rope ladder to reach his pulpit, but they are likely to encounter pulpits with staircases, as I point out later in this chapter. Through this literary exaggeration of a common rhetorical space, Melville illustrates a profoundly important matter about the nature of pulpits: as architecture they communicate something to the audience quite apart from the sermon itself. They have communicative powers of their own. Melville demonstrates the importance of this principle by devoting an entire chapter to the description of Father Mapple's pulpit.

To develop a full definition of rhetorical space, I turn to a philosopher and several scholars of cultural geography. Let us return to Bachelard. In *The Poetics of Space,* an exploration of spatial metaphors, Bachelard writes, "Outside and inside form a dialectic of division, the obvious geometry of which blinds us as soon as we bring it into play in metaphorical domains" (211). Outside and inside are forms of negation, writ in primitive spatial dimensions, long associated with social inclusion and exclusion. These spatial metaphors make reference to material realities, but as Bachelard suggests, the vehicle is forgotten when transported into philosophical discourse. In anthropologist Susan M. Ruddick's *Young and Homeless in Hollywood,* an ethnography of homeless youth in an opulent section of Los Angeles, Bachelard's metaphors become material functions of daily life for city residents. Ruddick puzzled over the behavior of urban residents. She noted that a sense of space—"where people/things ought to be"—was related to but different from a sense of a place that comes from material boundaries. For example, when they see homeless youth, city residents believe these youth ought to be somewhere else: on an ideal plane of cultural existence, they are out of place. Ruddick calls this sense of the spatial dimensions of culture the "social imaginary." Abstract but not without "territorial imperatives," as Code puts it, this dimension of space exists in and forms the boundaries of human behavior. The "social imaginary" is, therefore, the cultural dimension of space: it is that sense of locations as having hierarchies and forming relationships between human residents.

Henri Lefebvre, whose *Production of Space* has inspired cultural geographers in their exploration of the intersection of social behavior and material space, brings the material dimensions of space into view. Lefebvre employs the term "social space" to connote both the metaphorical/cultural dimension articulated by Code, Bachelard, and Ruddick and the material dimensions of space. Like Code, he writes, "Itself the outcome of past actions, social space is what permits fresh actions to occur, while suggesting others and prohibiting yet others" (73). But he goes further, mapping the material dimensions of such spaces as nature, buildings, the space between natural and built structures, the insides of buildings, furniture. For Lefebvre, material space and the social imaginary work in tandem: material spaces can trigger the social imaginary because of the historical and cultural freight attached to the space. For example, when I see a church, I think "location for Christian worship," whether or not the church is still being used for religious purposes. When architects at Rensselaer Polytechnic Institute, a university dominated by its engineering school, converted a nineteenth-century chapel into a computer center, they created a symbolic paradox that continues to delight and perplex visitors. Students work in computer labs with cathedral ceilings and stained glass, begging the question of what in the material space (which still draws the eye upward, as to heaven) wants to be worshiped.

Lefebvre's work suggests that particular spaces can move us in two ways: by suggesting symbolic associations and by causing us to form relationships with each other and the space through its structures. Using the example of city landscapes, Lefebvre offers the following example:

> It may be said of this space that it presupposes and implies a logic of visualization. [. . .] The arrogant verticality of skyscrapers, and especially of public and state buildings, introduces a phallic or more precisely a phallocratic element into the visual realm; the purpose of this display, of this need to impress, is to convey an impression of authority to each spectator. *Verticality and great height have ever been the spatial expression of potentially violent power.* (98, emphasis added)

When one walks on the streets of the New York City financial district for the first time, one feels dwarfed by the size of the skyscrapers. Repeated over and over in Hollywood films, this scene represents the awesome power of this king of American cities. One need not make the more complex symbolic association of "phallus" with "skyscraper" to experience the material dimension of this space. One can just look up and say, "Wow!"

This is the dimension of material space that Melville counts on in developing Father Mapple's pulpit. Melville causes Ishmael to look at Father Mapple climbing that tall pulpit and express the literary equivalent of "Wow." But because it is a narrative pulpit, a second-hand experience of space, the reader has access to rich symbolic associations woven into the description. The pulpit is ship—or fortress. Melville (through Ishmael) can't decide. But regardless, it is a strangely masculine space. Eliot also uses the material dimensions of space in developing Dinah Morris's pulpit, the applecart. It is an improvised object—not something an authority would use. One is deliberately built to elevate the preacher above his congregation; the other is ephemeral, a borrowed tool of farmers. Such spaces resonate with symbolism, symbolism that is not lost on spectators and inhabitants. But they are also ordinary in their materiality: one looks up and says "Wow" because of verticality; one stands near the applecart and feels an intimacy with the preacher because she is physically close.

Spaces exercise heuristic power over their inhabitants and spectators by forcing them to change both their behavior (walls cause us to turn right or left; skyscrapers draw the eye up) and, sometimes, their view of themselves. Lefebvre writes, "In an apartment building comprising stack after stack of 'boxes for living in,' for example, the spectators-*cum*-tenants grasp the relationship between part and whole directly; furthermore, they recognize themselves in that relationship" (98). The apartment building includes one identical apartment after another; tenants are like so many drones in a hive. For this reason, Nedra Reynolds finds ironic the discrepancy inherent in rhetoric and composition scholars' representing themselves as "working on the frontier" while giving papers in palatial downtown hotels during their annual conventions. Reynolds wonders how these opulent structures inflate participants' view of themselves and mask the material conditions at home in which they work. Her argument suggests the importance of including the material dimension of space—as well as the interpretation of that space in the social imaginary—in any exploration of location ("Composition's Imagined Geographies").

Having established that rhetorical space is material as well as cultural, I turn now to a closer study of the pulpit. I have argued that the pulpit is necessarily a gendered space that makes the presence of women there metonymically problematic. I have explored the way in which gender and preaching are intimately associated with "place" in the novels of four authors, who perceive that character is evaluated in location. Mikhail Bakhtin suggests that characters in a novel are associated not only with locations but also with—and embody—an entire class within a social hierarchy. Apparently for the authors, the image of a woman preaching from a traditional pulpit cannot accomplish their poetic objective; therefore, they place their women preachers far from a brick-and-mortar church. According to the narrator, Baby Suggs had preached in a church building, but Morrison places her deep in the woods for the scene that is pivotal to her character development in *Beloved*. Dinah Morris, Baby Suggs, and the unnamed woman in *The Temple of My Familiar* are on the margins of society, and all are close to the people. If Eliot, Morrison, and Walker had placed their fictional ministers in a traditional pulpit, the poetic effect would have been far different. For as a rhetorical space, the pulpit has been associated culturally with male authority for two millennia and traditionally designed to physically separate the congregation and the minister. In the sections that follow, I explore these two points.

Sacred Rhetorical Space: The Pulpit and Gender Hierarchies

The association of the pulpit with male authority is based on a deeper ideology of gender hierarchy to which Christians worldwide have subscribed for two thousand years: "Christ is the head of every man, and the man is the head of a woman, and God is the head of Christ" (1 Cor. 11:3).[5] Given this hierarchy, the author of the First Letter to Timothy[6] warned that women were not to serve in any capacity over men:

> Let a woman quietly receive instruction with entire submissiveness. But I do not allow a woman to teach or exercise authority over a man, but to remain quiet. For it was Adam who was first created, and then Eve. And it was not Adam who was deceived, but the woman being quite deceived, fell into transgression. (1 Tim. 2:11–14)

With few exceptions, church leaders throughout Christian history have interpreted this passage as a clear injunction against women preaching or teaching mixed groups of adults in public. There are a host of examples, but this 1941 explication is representative:

> In New Testament churches a woman's place was to be taught, not to teach. A woman's place was to be silent, not to be a public speaker. A woman's place was to be in subjection, and not to be in

authority. Certainly this Scripture forbids any woman to be a preacher or pastor or evangelist. [. . .].

Pastors and preachers have a real authority from God to rule. But a woman is not to have authority over men, and so a woman could not be a pastor of a church, or a preacher of the gospel, in the ordinary sense. (Rice 43–44)

The recurring trope of location in this passage is worth noting: "A woman's *place* was to be taught [. . .]. A woman's *place* was to be silent [. . .]. A woman's *place* was to be in subjection [. . .]" (43). The trope is such a familiar part of the ideology of gender roles that we overlook its spatial dimensions. To have one's "place" be silence makes no sense unless we imagine silence attached to a rhetorical situation that necessarily involves material space: a woman sitting silently in a church pew while a man preaches. The trope of "place" makes social position and physical location interchangeable.

Of course, struggle against the ideology of gender hierarchy enforced by such injunctions has been a major theme in feminist literature since the Middle Ages. In *Rhetoric Retold,* Cheryl Glenn offers the example of Julian of Norwich, who was well known as a woman mystic in her time but was compelled to defend her right to speak as a woman: "'But because I am a woman, ought I therefore to believe that I should not tell you of the goodness of God, when I saw at that same time that it is his will that it be known?'" (qtd. in Glenn 96–97). Glenn writes that Julian of Norwich and Margery Kempe "spoke to limitations of social location and gendered identity within a culture of masculine privilege and religious power [. . .]" (116). Centuries later in her defense of women teachers and preachers, Sarah Grimké echoed Julian: "[T]here is no respect of persons with God; the soul of the woman in his sight is as the soul of the man, and both are alike capable of the influence of the Holy Spirit" (692).[7] In a 1905 apologia titled *Women Preachers,* Fannie McDowell Hunter, an evangelist in the Holiness tradition, offers scriptural evidence in the Old and New Testaments that women served as prophets, judges, and deacons and refutes with great force Pauline strictures that women keep silence in the churches. The fourth chapter of her book is devoted to a history of modern women preachers, beginning with Susanna Wesley, whose ministry to congregations of several hundred inspired her son John to found Methodism. Hunter devotes most of this chapter to the "calls" of nine women preachers (including her own) whose careers began more than one hundred years ago (48–93). She begins her first chapter with the annunciation: "That women are to take a prominent part in evangelizing the world is clearly taught in the Old Testament" (9).

Despite the astonishing number of women who have preached in spite of injunctions against them,[8] the idea that "woman's place" is not in the pulpit has had surprising resonance throughout the centuries, particularly in fundamentalist, Catholic, and other conservative Christian sects. Even groups who relaxed literal enforcements of Paul's injunctions have had a tendency to withdraw them. Despite the history of women evangelists beginning with Susanna Wesley, the Methodists voted to prevent women from preaching in their pulpits at the beginning of the nineteenth century, an event that is portrayed in *Adam Bede.* At the time of this writing, the Southern Baptists have voted on an article of faith limiting the office of preacher to men, despite the fact that their seminaries have been ordaining women preachers.[9] Since Southern Baptist Convention representatives voted in 1998 to adopt language reinforcing gender hierarchy in marriage, this move is consistent with their reinforcement of conservative gender ideologies.

The trope "a woman's place" suggests how persistently gender hierarchies are associated with geography. Throughout history and across cultures, women have been excluded from certain sacred places. Women were banned from all but the outer courtyard in the temple of Jerusalem, and Orthodox congregations continue to practice the *mechitzah,* or ritual separation of the sexes.[10] In ancient Hawaiian culture, women were prohibited from entering a range of social spaces. Sherry Ortner writes that

> in terms of ideology, [Hawaiian] men were defined as sacred *(kapu)* and [Hawaiian] woman as profane or unsacred *(noa)*. There were taboos against men and women eating together, lest women offend the gods with whom men were in communion. There were thus separate men's and women's eating houses. Young boys ate with the women, but at the age of nine they were ritually transferred to the men's eating house and never ate with the women again. There were also a large number of "male" foods, which were part of the sacrificial offerings that men shared with the gods and which women were not allowed to eat. Women were also not allowed in the temples, where male priests made sacrifices to the gods on whom the welfare of the society as a whole was said to depend.[11] (158)

In the United States, this extreme form of segregation is more commonly associated with Jim Crow laws and racism than with gender bias. Nevertheless, in Christianity throughout the Western world, sacred areas of churches have traditionally been off-limits to women of any rank. In Roman Catholic churches prior to Vatican II (1963), women were prohibited from entering the sacristy (the location of the altar, pulpit, and the host) except to perform domestic chores; for this reason, there were no altar girls in Roman Catholic churches until the 1960s. In many Protestant faiths, women were seated separately from the men; for example, the Quakers and Puritans located women in separate sections of the nave (normally across the aisle but occasionally in the balcony). In Anglican churches in England, the separation of the sexes has been theorized as the reason for the varying locations of pulpits. In his 1915 history of English pulpits titled *Pulpits, Lecterns and Organs in English Churches,* J. Charles Cox writes, "It is sometimes said that the proper place for the pulpit was on the south side, because that was the more honourable side, being the side of the men; but there is rather more to be said for the north, for that was usually the gospel side" (32).[12] Even if the pulpit were associated with the gospel side (that is, the location from which the gospel is read), it would still be associated with men in Cox's time, since only ordained ministers (a group that could not, by church law, include women) could read the gospel. Cox's exhaustive exploration of church furniture (including also lecterns, hourglasses, and organs) offers an interesting window on the relationship of gender and pulpits in England, as we shall see.[13]

These examples suggest that "sacred" spaces—that is, those places set apart for special, ritualized purposes—are marked by the ordering of objects *and* persons.

> A native thinker makes the penetrating comment that "All sacred things must have their place." It could even be said that being in their place is what makes them sacred for if they were taken out of their place, even in thought, the entire order of the universe would be destroyed. Sacred objects therefore contribute to the maintenance of the order in the universe by occupying the places allocated to them. Examined superficially and from the outside, the refinements of a ritual can appear pointless. They are explicable by a concern for what one might call "micro-adjustment"—the concern to assign every single creature, object or feature to a place within a class. (Lévi-Strauss 10)

In his gloss on this passage, Judaic scholar Jonathan Z. Smith notes that "place" here is understood in the ordinary sense of "putting things in their places" (xii). For example, the flag of the United States, in reality just a tri-colored cloth, is made sacred by the rituals attached to it. According to military protocol, the flag must be placed to the right of the speaker when displayed during a speech, and it must never be flown outside during the rain, touch the ground, or be worn as a garment. When the flag is hoisted on a pole and put into the ground during or after a battle, it is marking the ground beneath it as American territory. To an outsider unfamiliar with the symbolic importance of the flag, these procedures might seem like "micro-adjustments": Why not put the flag to the left of the speaker? Why can the flag be burned when it is decommissioned but not touch the ground when it is "on duty"? The answer is that the *rituals themselves* make the object sacred. When the sacred space is a building, such as a church, it is the placement of objects and persons within it that contribute to its sacred status.[14]

In the introduction to his 1843 biography of Salome Lincoln, a Quaker preacher of the early nineteenth century, Almond H. Davis struggles to explain to a general reader why a woman preacher should be accepted. It is clear that one obstacle is the sacred nature of the pulpit. In his apologia, he writes, "[S]ome who admit the propriety of women speaking in public conference, deny them the right of going into the pulpit, and taking a text for the foundation of remarks" (13). His solution to this contradiction is to attack the hermeneutics of space:

> [B]ut I have yet to learn, that the pulpit is a more sacred place, than any other portion of the house. And if it is right for a woman to speak in public conference, it is right for her to quote passages of scripture, and if right to quote scripture, it is also right to take a passage as the foundation of remarks; and as the desk[15] is not the *sanctum sanctorum* of God's house, it is equally right to enter that—with a text selected from the word of God. (13)

This is a rather remarkable defense! Rather than arguing that women have just as much right to enter sacred spaces as men, Davis instead challenges his readers to consider whether or not the pulpit is indeed sacred. He argues that there are *no* spaces in a church building that are more sacred than others, a democratic sentiment that protects him from making a more unpopular argument: that women are equally sanctioned by God to preach. If the pulpit is not sacred, then anyone may enter it— even a lowly woman.[16]

Feminist and postcolonial geographers have long noted that women, racial "Others," and the poor live—literally—on the borderlands, "across the tracks," as it were, from the *kapu*, the sacred or privileged people. In fact, it is geographies that often tell where each are located in the cultural hierarchies that interested Claude Lévi-Strauss. But from the eye of a person outside of the sphere, these geographies often seem arbitrary. For instance, take this description of a small Southern town during segregation, as narrated by white Christian lesbian Minnie Bruce Pratt:

> What I would have seen at the top [of the town's courthouse]: on the streets around the courthouse square, the Methodist church, the limestone building with the county Health Department, Board of Education, Welfare Department (my mother worked there), the yellow brick Baptist church, the Gulf station, the pool hall (no

women allowed), Cleveland's grocery, Ward's shoestore; then, all in a line, connected, the bank, the post office, Dr. Nicholson's office, one door for whites, one for Blacks [. . .]. I was shaped by my relation to those buildings and to the people in the buildings, by ideas of who should be working in the Board of Education, who should be in the bank handling money, of who should have the guns and the keys to the jail, of who should be *in* the jail; and I was shaped by what I didn't see, or didn't notice, on those streets. (16–17)

This compelling example of the relationships of people and buildings illustrates the seemingly arbitrary nature of social hierarchies in spatial arrangements. Why separate doors for whites and blacks? Why would one building be off-limits to women altogether? Because their status in the social imaginary must be marked by these geographical exclusions. In *Feminism and Geography,* Gillian Rose argues that the persistent geographical as well as cultural/social boundaries placed around women—especially women of color—cause feminists to write metaphorically about finding "other" spaces, spaces carved out of the social imaginary, to inhabit (155–59). Both Rose and Edward W. Soja offer bell hooks as an example of one feminist of color who has persistently looked for what Soja calls "Thirdspace" (96–105) and what Rose calls "unexplored conceptual territories" (155–56). hooks proposes to reform the center by inhabiting the margins, a paradoxical, *transgressive* move that cannot easily be made within a system of cultural taboos. Yet hooks and other feminists have persistently argued that thinking beyond the locations instituted by race and gender hierarchies requires an act of imagination—as well as many symbolic trespasses upon sacred *material* ground.

While reading Cox's history of pulpits in England, a book arranged around wooden and stone pulpits in the medieval and post-Reformation periods, further subdivided by shire, I was astonished to come across the following passage: "At Breadsall a pulpit was of recent years constructed out of early sixteenth-century bench-ends; but it fell victim, with the rest of the church, to the criminal lunacy of militant suffragists in June 1914" (58). Later, in a section of the book devoted solely to lecterns (a stand for holding books—normally the Bible—in liturgical churches), Cox repeats this rather remarkable news: there was a "double stand, for several volumes, at Breadsall, Derbyshire," he writes, but "the latter was reduced to ashes in June 1914, when the ancient church of Breadsall was burnt by militant suffragists" (201). In fact, in 1914, suffragists in England committed hundreds of acts of arson and bombing on public institutions in England and countless acts of protest, including the burning of All Saints Church in Breadsall ("Breadsall Church Destroyed"). At another church in Clevedon, suffragists succeeded only in burning all the vestments of the priest, after a bomb they threw into the window of the vestry sputtered out before entering the thousand-year-old main church building ("Attempt to Burn a Church"). The *Times* reported that the Clevedon arsonists left a calling card—suffragist tracts tied to the tombstones in the churchyard.[17]

What could be a more symbolic act of trespass than the destruction of a sacred place—and particularly an old one? Perhaps the burning of the sacred clothing associated with the priest at Clevedon. In liturgical churches, the priests wear vestments (long robes, over which they wear ornate clerical stoles) that are meant to highlight their authority and office. Deacons and lesser officials often wear robes of subtly different design, not unlike the system of academic garments in colleges and universities. To burn the vestments of a priest is to symbolically destroy the priest's authority. In Breadsall and Clevedon, women trespassed on the spaces set aside for men, a dramatic form of protest that illustrates the connection between gender and space. The Church of England did not vote to ordain women until 1994 (Nesbitt 25)—very late in the history of women's ordination, an event that was bitterly contested.[18] So while we may never know what was preached from the pulpits at Breadsall and Clevedon as well as the many other churches that were picketed in 1914, it is clear that for the suffragists who participated in the bombings, gender hierarchies were being enforced from and/or represented by the pulpit. Burning the magnificent pulpit at Breadsall, painstakingly recreated with bench-ends from the sixteenth century, was an act of trespass upon male authority. It was, for Cox, writing at the same time, an act of "lunacy"—an intermittent act of insanity associated with the phases of the moon and with women throughout history. Of course, such symbolic trespasses always are met with outrage by those who endow with meaning the "micro-adjustments" of the objects and creatures in a sacred space.

Sacred Rhetorical Space: Relationship of Pulpit to People

Thus far I have been meditating on the ritualized nature of space and its association with gender hierarchies, particularly in the case of the pulpit. But there is another sense in which the pulpit works as a space: in its relationship to the congregation. The pulpit in *Moby-Dick* separates Father Mapple from his congregation absolutely: it is structurally high, putting a distance between him and his parishioners, but then, so we do not miss the point, Melville causes Father Mapple to draw up the rope ladder behind him, cutting him off from any physical contact with the congregation. Furthermore, the pulpit surrounds his body (hence the image of a fortress), hiding all but his chest, arms, and head from the gaze of the audience. In contrast, Baby Suggs and Dinah Morris are raised up only slightly on their ephemeral platforms with no fortress to hide them from the gaze of an audience. Baby Suggs remains seated. They are close to their congregations—literally standing or sitting *with* them. Whatever distance there may be (and it is minimal) is elided by the lack of pulpit or any other physical barrier.

In a recent interview with a woman still in seminary training, I was interested to learn that she considered the pulpit to be a "shield." The large, wooden structure formed a barrier between her and the people—and she did not want to be separated from them. In the instances when she could not leave the pulpit, she preached an expository sermon, tightly focused on explication of Scripture, because the populist sermons she preferred could not be "pulled off" if she could not leave the pulpit and move in toward the people. In a church with a long, narrow nave (the portion of the church where the congregation is seated), she needed to use the pulpit to be seen and heard. Conversely, a shallow nave with pews radiating out from the sanctuary gave her the opportunity to walk out to the people and make eye contact. "The architecture of a church affects what kinds of sermons I can preach," she announced. So profound is the pulpit and its placement in space that for this preacher, her entire rhetorical performance is affected—including the content of the sermon.

This is not surprising when we consider that spaces are *productive* of meaning as well as endowed with meaning. The most familiar example of this effect is the panopticon, a design for a nineteenth-century prison made famous in Foucault's *Discipline and Punish*. In the panopticon, guards are stationed in the center of each floor with the prisoners' cells radiating out around the center. Such a design promotes the idea that prisoners are people whose every movement must be watched, monitored, corrected; "discipline," Foucault argues, "proceeds from the distribution of individuals in space" (141), and it is the structure of the prison that distributes them. The imaginary construct of "discipline" is realized (at least in part) through the space of the prison. Even in the most liberal traditions, religion also proceeds from the distribution of individuals in space; as Emile Durkheim argues, religion can be defined as the absolute distinction between the sacred and the profane (55), which includes distinctions between believers and nonbelievers, priest and people, women and men. The placement of the pulpit and its structure and design might be compared to the guard's station in the panopticon: where it is placed in relationship to others tells those others something about their status.[19]

Churches, like all sacred spaces, are designed to embody—and produce—particular religious beliefs, in part by acting as a stage for the rituals involved.

> [R]eligious beliefs are [. . .] symbolized and enacted by rituals and ceremonies, and there is often a close correspondence between the rituals and the architectural form. This correspondence is not just at a pragmatic facilitating level, but also at the deeper symbolic level, because both the ritual and the architecture are concretizations or enactments of the same existential need that has given cause for the particular myth. In other words, architecture, in addition to directly symbolizing the belief system, in essence acts as a stage that accommodates and facilitates the enactment of the myth through ritual. The myth is embodied in the form of the architecture, the act of the ritual, and their interplay. (Barrie 5)

For the seminary student I interviewed, the pulpit expressed a sense of authority, on the one hand, and a sense of profound separation from the people, on the other. To use Thomas Barrie's language, it "embodies" power and authority and "enacts the myth" that the preacher is set apart from the people as God's representative. Historian James F. White writes that "[t]he design of the pulpit can give a sense of the divine-human encounter possible in preaching. This is especially true when the pulpit is solid and substantial enough to suggest authority far higher than the preacher's personality" (46). Note White's assumption that the divine-human encounter occurs best when the human is sufficiently impressed with the authority of the preacher and his separation from the congregation, an assumption that the seminary student did not make.

One of the primary functions of church architecture is to enact the myth of the preacher as messenger from God, chosen and set apart from the people. Traditionally, this myth is played out through the creation of spaces that only the priest or bishop may inhabit: the vestry (where priests put on their vestments), the chancel (the front end of medieval churches where the host and altar are kept—a space often separated by a screen), or the sanctuary (the area in some churches that includes the pulpit, altar, and baptismal font).[20] Church historians believe that this separation can be traced back to the development of the early church in Rome, where wealthy homes were often the site of Christian meetings (White; Bieler). Developed according to patriarchal ideology, these homes contained an altar to honor the gods and a chair placed behind the altar in which the patriarch of the house sat for ceremonial occasions. For Christian meetings, the altar is thought to have been used for serving communion and the chair for the local bishop (White 52–55). An alternative view is that early churches built in Rome after C.E. 313 were based on Roman basilicas (most likely used as courthouses),[21] where an apse (a raised platform that was built onto the end of the building with a semicircular wall behind it) contained a large chair for the judge against the wall of the apse.

The bishop's throne replaced that of the judge but retained the same central spot against the wall of the apse. It might be elevated at the head of several steps. The curve of the apse on either side of the bishop's throne contained a row of seats for the presbyters (ministers). The platform of the apse might extend out into the nave (the main hall of the church). Usually it was set off by a low screen (cancellus), thus defining and separating the liturgical space of the clergy from that of the laity. The altar-table appeared at the junction of the apse and nave though at times it stood even further out in the midst of the congregation. At one side of the screen, projecting into the nave, was usually an ambo or lectern. (White 57–58)

At first the ambo was used only for reading the Scriptures—the bishop preached seated from his throne, since "[t]he seated position signified teaching authority" (59). There was no seating for the congregation, but men and women were still separated, "even to restricting the women, in some cases, to galleries over the aisles" (59). Therefore, the church building reinforced the idea that the preacher (in this case a bishop) was not just any authority, but an authority with great power, since he was seated on a throne. But in addition, the congregation and the preacher were separated by a low screen, which in the Eastern Orthodox tradition became a veil and in the Western churches became a wood screen, called the "rood" screen because of the crucifix hung from it (73). By the medieval period, the laity and the preacher were almost completely separated, "the hierarchical distinction between the laity and the clergy [. . .] unmistakable" (74).

From the Middle Ages on, the liturgical site for preaching moved to the ambo or lectern, and magnificent pulpits were built across Europe, often containing the most elaborate craftsmanship of any structure in the church. J. Charles Cox describes a stone medieval pulpit in England, built in 1475:

Staffordshire has only one medieval pulpit, but the one that it possesses is the most notable stone example throughout the kingdom. This elaborately enriched pulpit, sometimes falsely stated to be constructed out of a single huge block of stone, is attached to the pier nearest to east on the south side of the nave of the great church of St. Peter, Wolverhampton [. . .]. The plan is octagonal, and it includes the paneled enclosure of the stairs, twelve in number, on the west side. Across the coping at the foot of the staircase is the large seated figure of a somewhat grotesque lion with a speaking countenance. Each face is divided into two panels, having cinquefoiled crested heads. Below them, at the crown of the shafted pedestal, is a boldly sculptured vine trail. Above them are quartrefoils with cinquefoil central flowers; immediately under the cornice is a foliage of ivy-like leaves and small cinquefoil flowers.[22] (48)

What one notices about this pulpit is the male lion, symbol of masculine power and the risen Christ,[23] with mouth opened as to speak, an unmistakable iconographic representative of the clergy. The pulpit is on the men's side of the church (the south side of the nave). In addition, it must be reached by climbing a winding staircase of twelve steps representing the Twelve Apostles from whom all preachers are said to descend. But finally, the pulpit itself is high off the ground, cutting the preacher off from the congregation both physically (that is, in material space) as well as iconographically (that is, in symbolic space). By reinforcing the idea that the pulpit is the sacred place where godly men preach—but also by creating a physical barrier between the congregation and the people—the pulpit at St. Peter's Collegiate Church, Wolverhampton, illustrates why the pulpit is associated with male authority and hierarchy. It is, according to Calvin, "God's throne *(le siege)*" (Buttrick 28).

After the Reformation, the pulpit became an even more central part of the church, since "the pastor's personal power base" moved "from the altar to the pulpit" (Hedahl 185). The rood screens were removed during this period, and new Protestant churches were built across Europe that excluded the chancel altogether. During the sixteenth century, pulpits built in German and Scandinavian Lutheran churches were even more elaborate than their medieval counterparts; in the seventeenth and eighteenth centuries, the pulpit was moved to the center of the sanctuary (White 85–86). In one Lutheran church at Freudenstadt, the church was built in an L shape, with the congregation seated in both arms of the L with the pulpit in the middle. With this arrangement, White argues, "a fairly large number of people are brought close to the liturgical centers, but the congregation is divided into two quite distinct groups, probably men and women in this case" (86). One can imagine the difficulties for the preacher, who could not speak to one side of the congregation without turning his back to the other. In France, where the Reformation was forced underground, the pulpit was moved from home to home for worship. Remarkable for its inconvenience—not to mention danger (a pulpit is not easily hidden)—this practice is in marked contrast to worship services led by early Methodist women, who, like Susanna Wesley, preached in kitchens and backyards (Chilcote). The Reformation did not change the authority afforded "God's throne," nor did it remove the barrier between people and pulpit, as suggested by the architecture. It is no coincidence that Quaker meetinghouses were designed with pews facing one another in a rectangular building,[24] excluded a pulpit in their design, allowed members of the congregation to speak during meetings as the Spirit moved them, *and* invited women to preach.

Rhetorical space is an extraordinarily important aspect of rhetorical performance, but especially in sacred locations, where each object and participant is set in place according to the rituals performed in that space. One of the categories of "placement" employed in sacred places is gender hierarchy; another is the separation of sacred leaders and people. We might think of these two categories as axes, one marked by status and another marked by gender. In the Christian tradition, status and masculinity have been required before one may enter the pulpit, and it is, I am arguing, for this reason that Melville places Father Mapple in a pulpit, embellishing it so that the reader does not miss the association of masculinity with divinity. On the other hand, it is this same tradition that causes Eliot, Morrison, and Walker to place their women preachers in wild and domestic spaces that are unassociated with such a long and burdensome tradition. What advantages do they gain from placing their women preachers in outdoor "churches"? First, they offer us the opportunity to explore with them what place a woman might have in religious tradition. This point is especially reinforced in Walker's *Temple of My Familiar,* in which the unnamed woman preacher recalled by Hal is praised for bringing to her office the sensibilities of her gender: "'We had two spirit-called people, a woman *and* a man. It seemed right. Like you have two different kinds of parents, a woman *and* a man, you know'" (97). A rhetorical space opens here to admit other perspectives. Baby Suggs takes the opportunity that this open and unexplored "space" offers her to preach a message of self-love to poor blacks living in the shadow of the violent and repressive South.

Second, without the barriers of wood or stone structures, well outside the establishment of hierarchies embodied by brick-and-mortar churches, Eliot, Morrison, and Walker offer a scene in which the preacher is a populist—a woman "of the people." This is the central theme in Eliot's novel, and we are meant to notice the sharp contrast between Dinah Morris and the aesthete rector of the Anglican parish church in the village of Hayslope, a distinction Eliot explores at length in her character development. Adam Bede, a working-class carpenter, is the central figure in the novel; his foil is the wealthy son of the village's landlord, just as the rector is a foil for Dinah Morris. In the end Dinah and Adam marry, a plot device that is disappointing, because it marks the end of Dinah's itinerant preaching, but symbolically important: the pastoral hero—morally superior to the cultural elite—is joined to a new religious tradition through the person of Dinah Morris. It is the symbolic union of the people and the priest, the symbolic rearrangement of sacred space. The placement of Morris in an applecart, and later in the arms of Adam (the first man), suggests a world in which divinity (indeed, all that is morally fine) dwells within the domestic structures of life and not in opposition to them.

Where do such observations take us in the world of real preachers? While most preaching manuals take for granted that the preacher will offer his rhetorical performance from the pulpit, there was one notable exception: the celebrated nineteenth-century preacher Henry Ward Beecher. In his 1872 *Lectures on Preaching,* Beecher argues that pulpits inhibit rhetorical performance in a very particular way: they cause the preacher to become less "manly":

> You put a man in one of these barreled pulpits, where there is no responsibility laid upon him as to his body, and he falls into all manner of gawky attitudes, and rests himself like a country horse at a hitching-post [. . .]. But bring him out on a platform, and *see how much more manly he becomes, how much more force comes out!* The moment a man is brought face to face with other men, then does the influence of each act and react upon the other.[25] (71, emphasis added)

For Beecher, the minister earns his authority through the masculine movements of his own body—his "force," his manliness. He earns it best when the pulpit is removed and his body is fully involved in the performance. As we will see in the next chapter, the gender ideologies of preaching are reinforced in preaching manuals at the latter half of the nineteenth century. But this passage reinforces the idea that the proximity of the preacher to the people is something the preacher *enacts* through the position of his body in space. The populism for which Beecher is known in the content of his sermons is played out in his attitude toward the physical space of the church.[26]

But the pulpit also carries with it the sediment of cultural tradition, of the social imaginary. It is, itself, a gendered space. Given Beecher's emphasis on "authenticity," the pulpit is *redundant.* The preacher is already a man; his authority stands on its own. There is no need for a pulpit to reinforce his masculinity. For real women, the pulpit must be re-imagined, or quit, as for the seminary student who likened the pulpit to a "shield." In her dissertation, Margaret Ballard Hess recalls a woman in her homiletics class who preached her first sermon:

> She literally clutched the sides of the pulpit, as if she were hanging on for dear life. Her face was quite animated and expressive, but she hardly moved her body at all. She later shared that when she stepped into the pulpit, she immediately felt constricted. (147)

The pulpit surrounded the student-preacher on three sides and was two steps higher than the congregation. As she sat talking to the student about her sermon, Hess began really looking at the pulpit:

> I saw something that I had not noticed before, in all my years of teaching in that chapel. The pulpit is slightly elevated, and at the base, around the bottom, are a series of carved heads. They all seem to be the same [male] person [. . .].
> "Isn't this interesting," I mused. "When you stood in the pulpit, you were supported by all of these disembodied heads. Of course you had trouble moving your body, you were simply agreeing with the pulpit!" (147–48)

She ends the story with a caution about pulpits as rhetorical space: "Each time we enter a traditional pulpit, we encounter a much deeper reality than meets the eye. We are surrounded by layers of expectation and tradition about how we will preach. Each preacher must come to terms with those expectations" (148). But for the student-preacher, as for the authors who sought to imagine a rhetorical space for women, the pulpit was simply too fraught with symbolic difficulties to support her rhetorical performance.

What options are available to women preachers who recognize the pulpit as a space not built for them? One option is to quit the pulpit altogether, as the Reverend Patricia O'Connor, a preacher featured in chapter 3, decided to do. In full vestments, she sat on the floor halfway up an aisle during the children's sermon. She wandered around during the adults' sermon, notes written on tiny scraps of paper in her hand. She talked directly to individual congregants throughout the service. She spent most all her time in the congregants' space, not in the spaces set aside for her office—behind the altar rail, up high on the platform, or within the rhetorical space of the pulpit. When we cross-reference her intimate performance with Father Mapple's ascension to his fortress-like pulpit, we can begin to appreciate the complex relationship of gender and rhetorical space in the art of preaching. We also recognize that rhetorical space is a significant dimension of rhetorical performance deserving of further research and critical attention.

2

The Manly Art of Preaching

[A preacher] should be a manly man [. . .].
—Austin Phelps, *Men and Books*

An institution is but the lengthened shadow of a man.
—Owen E. Pence, *The Y.M.C.A. and Social Need*

The bodies and behavior of human beings are interpreted through historical, ideological processes that divide our experiences along racial and gender lines. Because we are immersed in these ideologies, they often seem inevitable and immutable. However, at moments of profound social change, "gender" and "race" emerge as unstable signs. For example, Gail Bederman opens her book *Manliness and Civilization* with the spontaneous riots that occurred nationwide in 1910 after the nation's first African American world heavyweight boxing champion, Jack Johnson, beat the former champion, a popular European American boxer named Jim Jeffries. Riots occurred in all Southern states, as well as in many cities in the Midwest, New York, and Colorado, most fomented by white men seeking revenge for this apparent challenge to their racial supremacy. Eighteen men died, and hundreds more were injured nationwide (1–3). Bederman argues that the fight promoters and the media had "insisted upon framing the fight as a contest to demonstrate which race could produce the superior specimen of virile manhood" (2). When Jeffries lost, apparently so too did white manhood. In the years that followed, Johnson was summarily punished for his "crime" (he was run out of the country), and white male superiority was restored and reasserted along other lines.[1]

Such assertions of the privilege of one gender or race over another must be bolstered by efforts to develop the qualities that supposedly *make* that gender or race superior. Such was the case of the masculinity of the preacher, which homileticians began to reassert in lectures and textbooks on preaching in the last half of the nineteenth century. There were two stress points on the status of preachers during this period: the slow disestablishment of the clergy from national life and the quiet gains made by women in education, publishing, and itinerant preaching (Douglas; Krueger). In order to make up for this loss of status, homileticians and evangelists sought to reconnect the clergy to their place in national life through their manhood. In chapter 1, I established the historical relationship of sacred space with the male preacher; in this chapter, I explore the reassertion of the masculinity of the preacher in the preaching manuals of the mid- to late nineteenth century. Written at a time when the "cult of manhood" was giving way to the more virile "muscular Christianity" of the late nineteenth century, these preaching manuals reflect a national anxiety over the status of white men as well as institutional anxiety within mainline Protestant denominations over the declining status of the minister. Couching their gender ideology in the ostensibly neutral language of "character," homileticians entreated preachers to develop themselves as *men* so that their congregations would recognize them as civic leaders in the mold of other great American statesmen.

This infusion of the cult of manhood into the training of preachers marks a shift in the tradition. Prior to the nineteenth century, homileticians argue that preachers should concern themselves with personal piety, since their behavior provided a mirror for their words. Augustine established the homiletic practice of arguing that the preacher should be a *good man,* because his life choices and character were a powerful witness to his congregation. Throughout the history of the art of preaching, the status of the preacher is not in question; Augustine argues that God can speak even through a preacher whose motives and life are ungodly. The people will listen because the preacher is a member of the clergy, sanctioned by the institution of the Church to speak to them about their eternal salvation. The preaching manuals assume the preacher's cultural status: they focus on the selection of texts, the arrangement of sermons, and the style of preaching. They divide the sermon into five parts: the exordium (or introduction), the explication of the text, the application of the message, the appeal for repentance, and the conclusion. In the eighteenth century, faculty psychology is imported into lectures on preaching to help the preacher analyze the mind of the sinner. The preacher is considered an unquestioned authority; his sermons are based in divine truth and are delivered in deductive form, applying the truth to the lives of individuals.

But in the mid-nineteenth century, homileticians turn their focus toward the preacher himself, working to build him up so that he might maintain the status that had been afforded him in previous decades. The scope of preaching manuals is greatly expanded, with character education a key component of the development of the preacher.[2] Significant for the women preachers whose ministries lay beyond the boundaries of the mainstream Protestant denominations, homileticians reinforced the idea that the preacher is a *masculine* figure. Importing the quasi-sacred cult of manhood into their treatises, preachers such as Henry Ward Beecher and Richard S. Storrs Jr. and sacred rhetoricians such as Austin Phelps and John Broadus argued that "the good man" of the pulpit should be a "manly man." Even as the Holiness tradition, the Quakers, and other dissenting groups encouraged women to preach and as African Americans were becoming renowned for their oratorical arts, the ideological work of mainline homileticians ensured that the art of preaching was formally articulated as a rhetorical art for white men.

While it is tempting to view the treatises of these preacher-scholars as quaint relics of the Victorian era, they are part of a larger trend in American culture of investing in national manhood, with the character traits attributed to leader-heroes (primarily white, but increasingly extended to heterosexual men of other races) modeled after the ideal man of the late Victorian period. Character training for men and boys is still a national calling for Boy Scout leaders, Promise Keepers, and Pop Warner coaches. The image of the preacher-pastor of the nineteenth century may be sullied by Harold Frederic's *Damnation of Theron Ware* and other novels about character flaws in the clergy, but the tender (and potentially violent) strength of a white man posited by Victorian writers has persisted in Protestant culture. This ideology of gender haunts the women preachers of this study and continues to inform contemporary preaching theory. National manhood privileges universal qualities and concerns over local politics and everyday life; embodied in preaching theory, the goal of the hero-preacher-crusader to rescue individual souls is raised above the grounded, specific needs of communities. Preaching theory projects a one-size-fits-all world, while in fact it was fitted to the Victorian man.

National Manhood

In the United States and Great Britain, the mid-nineteenth century was a period of reinvestment in the masculinity of white male citizens. Ordained ministers were regarded as part of the overall leadership structure for both nations, and therefore the overall movement toward shoring up the normative gendered behavior of male citizens also reached them. Bederman argues that American culture maintains a troubling association between masculinity, race, and civilization, with the power of white men equated with nationhood.[3] In her recent book *National Manhood*, Dana D. Nelson further develops Bederman's observations, arguing that our national identity is based on "the imagined fraternity of white men." The white male is the symbol of our strength and unity, the "brotherhood" that keeps the nation's diversity and competitiveness (the basis of our economy) from devolving into civil conflict and unrest. "Others," including white women and men and women of other races, are identified as a challenge to our nation's unity. It is for this reason that suffrage and other forms of political participation have been so difficult for a woman or person of color to achieve: they invoke the specter of our nation's dangerous diversity. While it is undoubtedly true that the barriers of race and sex to participation in public life are slowly being effaced, we have been unwilling as a nation to support someone other than a white male for president. Nelson argues that we look at the bodies of our white male presidents and feel reassured that the nation is in harmony: the white male is the symbol and substance of democracy itself. Imagining the body of another representing a cooperative democracy is literally unthinkable.

Needless to say, a nation with such an investment in its white males is a nation with anxieties about masculinity. While women of any race and men of color can afford to have many different traits, the white male at the center of our fantasy life cannot. We can look to our expectations of the character of our presidents for evidence: we want him to have served in the military (preferably during times of war and to have distinguished himself there) and to be physically healthy, married with children, religious (preferably Christian, preferably Protestant),[4] and morally pure (honest and sexually monogamous). The media engages in careful scrutiny of these categories of masculinity, and the candidates work to secure their public image: for example, Bill Clinton jogged with reporters early in his presidency to give the appearance of physical health (his weight had become an issue after reports of his frequent stops at McDonald's). He lost the support of many veterans because he not only avoided serving in the Vietnam War but also protested against it. In the end, questions about Clinton's self-control and moral purity eclipsed his presidency as the nation came to terms with his affair with White House intern Monica Lewinsky. America seemed to say that such a man could not embody the values of the nation, that he was not *man* enough. Nelson points out that it was no accident that the Harrison Ford blockbuster *Air Force One,* featuring a president who had once served in a war and therefore was man enough to single-handedly avert the hijacking of his plane, was released just as questions about Clinton's fitness for office (literally and figuratively) were reaching a crescendo (227). "The president," Nelson writes, "embodies democracy as a paradigm of national manhood's unhealthy desires for unity, wholeness, and self-sameness" (226). That is, we hold onto this deeply strange cultural commitment to white male heroes because of a desire for their *imagined qualities.*

If a country is to produce white male presidents, then the nation must offer boys opportunities to become that masculine symbol through character development. In the United States, we have seeded cartoons with hero images; we have offered frequent opportunities for boys to train for national manhood. Perhaps no organization more exemplifies the promise of fraternity and masculine achievement than the Boy Scouts of America, whose Scout Oath incorporates all the qualities of manhood required of a president in the boy: "On my honor I will do my best to do my duty to God and my country and to obey the Scout Law; to help other people at all times; to keep myself physically strong, mentally awake, and morally straight" ("Scouting's Values"). Founded in 1910, the Boy Scouts of America was based on the nature survival book *Scouting for Boys* (1908) written by British Boer War veteran Robert Baden-Powell. Baden-Powell had written a training manual for the military titled *Aids to Scouting* that he redrafted for the "character training of boys" into "true manliness" (Warren 200–201).[5] Baden-Powell wanted boys to have the training that would help them become the stuff of Kipling's (and the British nation's) colonialist fantasies. But behind his physical prowess, knowledge, and character, the scout was in some general way to be a believer "in a practical working religion," an ecumenical form of Christianity that Baden-Powell "presented as a new chivalry in which the knights appeared as the patrol leaders of the nation devoted to public service and honour" (202). As the twentieth century wore on, the Boy Scouts of America became racially integrated and inclusive of all males except homosexuals, and at the dawn of the twenty-first century, the Supreme Court upheld their right to make this one exclusion to the fraternity of men.[6]

The Scout Oath and Law descend from the mid-nineteenth century, when a large transatlantic movement was founded to reinvigorate the manliness (heterosexuality presumed) of urban youth. From the beginning, "manliness" invoked both piety and physical work. The core ideology of that movement later came to be known as "muscular Christianity," the idea that the soul of a man (and his nation) could not find salvation if his body was not made pure through physical activity. Attributed to such writers as Charles Kingsley and Oliver Wendell Holmes, this philosophy grew out of what J. A. Mangan and James Walvin call "the cult of manliness" in both Britain and America (3). It was a pervasive gender ideology that was spread through print media, schools, and religious institutions. Mangan and Walvin write:

> Well before the Great War, on both sides of the Atlantic, proponents of the ideal had securely ensconced themselves in dominant positions in society, with the result that between approximately 1850 and 1940 the cult of manliness became a widely pervasive and

inescapable feature of middle class existence in Britain and America: in literature, education and politics, the vocabulary of the ethic was forcefully promulgated. Nor was proselytism restricted to the properties and the privileged: through school textbooks, children's literature, philanthropic organizations and the churches both the image and associated symbolic activities of both Christian and Darwinian "manliness" filtered down to the proletariat through an unrelenting and self-assured process of social osmosis.[7] (2)

Providing an unrelenting cultural image of heroism, this cult of manliness is the source of the Boy Scouts and other groups that have promised to help boys fulfill their duty as members of the fraternity of men. Mangan and Walvin attribute the fall of this movement to the start of World War II, but as the Boy Scout Oath attests, muscular Christianity continues to find a home on this side of the Atlantic.

Randy Balmer traces the term "muscular Christianity" to a review of Charles Kingsley's novel *Two Years Ago,* published in 1857. The reviewer used the term to criticize Kingsley for equating heroism with Christian virtue, but the term "stuck and came to be associated with masculine expressions of piety and with various initiatives designed to make Christianity more attractive to men" (3). Of the many organizations founded to promote the new "manliness" in the period 1850 to the present, the best known are the Young Men's Christian Association (Pence; Springhall 53), the Men and Religion Forward Movement of 1911–12 (Balmer 3; Faludi 257), Campus Crusade for Christ (Faludi 232), Fellowship of Christian Athletes (Balmer 3), and the Promise Keepers (Faludi 224–88; Claussen, *Standing on the Promises* and *Promise Keepers*). Each of these organizations was founded on the idea that, as Billy Sunday put it, "'the manliest man is the man who will acknowledge Jesus Christ'" (qtd. in McLoughlin 8).

The most recent manifestation of muscular Christianity is the Promise Keepers, founded in 1990 by former University of Colorado football coach Bill McCartney. It is a nondenominational, quasi-evangelical Christian movement designed to move men back into the spiritual leadership of their families. From July 1991 to the present, the Promise Keepers organization has filled stadiums with relatively conservative middle-class men who pledge to keep seven promises designed, like the Scout Oath, to make them better men in the life of the nation.[8] The Promise Keepers movement culminated in a 1997 mass rally in Washington, D.C., called Stand in the Gap: A Sacred Assembly of Men, losing steam thereafter when the organization suffered financial setbacks (Balmer 3–4). In her 1999 journalistic exposé, *Stiffed: The Betrayal of the American Man,* Susan Faludi explores the impact of the Promise Keepers on one group of men in California. What she uncovers is the need of these men to find a greater purpose in life—that sense of higher calling endemic to national manhood, brotherhood, and the Scout Oath, which the Promise Keepers seek to fill. The men who populate Faludi's book are, in effect, failed Boy Scouts—those who were indoctrinated with the promised fraternity and social benefits of manhood but who found themselves maturing into a world with limited opportunities for heroes. Conservative, middle-class men have turned to the Promise Keepers—and continue to fill stadiums nationwide[9]—in hope of regaining lost ground on the road to manhood. And while the Boy Scouts of America and the Promise Keepers have promised to integrate men of all races into national manhood, their exclusion of gay men suggests that the greater anxiety and threat to the cult of manhood is now homosexuality. Indeed, as we will see in the work of Austin Phelps, the function of character training for national manhood is the elimination of "effeminacy," associated in the nineteenth century as now with all that is opposite the hero: powerlessness, ineffectualness, lack of piety, and physical weakness. Despite the presence of gay, lesbian, and bisexual heroes in the armed forces, these character traits are consistently associated with homosexuality. Despite some strong role models nationwide, these traits are still considered altogether absent in women, though occasionally found in anomalous cases.

When did "manliness" become synonymous with Christian piety and physical prowess? We can return to the mid-nineteenth century for some clues. In chapter 1, we see that the war of gender ideologies was played out in 1851 in *Moby-Dick,* a book that conflates masculine strength and piety in the figure of Father Mapple. In the same year, a group of evangelical men organized a Young Men's Christian Association chapter in Boston. A year later, chapters were formed in Springfield and Worcester, Massachusetts; Buffalo and New York City; Concord and Portsmouth, New Hampshire; Detroit; and New Orleans. By 1853, Providence; Baltimore; Alexandria, Virginia; Chicago, Peoria, and Quincy, Illinois; Brooklyn; Portland; Louisville and Lexington; and San Francisco had organized chapters. By 1855, there were fifty-three associations in the United States (Pence 8–9). The New York City chapter consisted of men from evangelical churches around the city. We might think of the founding of the YMCA as a nineteenth-century precursor to the Promise Keepers movement: it grew rapidly out of the felt need to train men for national moral leadership. The YMCA was an ecumenical movement, crossing the lines of denominations in order to mold the "moral and religious reflexes" (Rader 127), and it had the "cult of manliness" firmly in view. YMCA leader Luther Halsey Gulick Jr. argued that religious organizations working with young men ought to introduce Jesus in all his "'noble heroism [. . .] his magnificent manliness, his denunciation of wickedness in public places, [and] his life of service to others'" (qtd. in Rader 127). At its inception, the YMCA movement was involved in Christian character education of men and boys, but the ideology of muscular Christianity—the focus on the intersection of physical and moral fitness—eventually eclipsed its evangelical mission. Eventually the movement came to be associated more with masculine duty befitting national manhood than with any particular theology.[10]

When we turn to the preaching manuals of the nineteenth and early twentieth centuries, we discover some of the same persistent themes of manliness and morality, sometimes packaged in the "muscular" form prized by the Boy Scouts. It is clear that lecturers and homiletics writers such as Storrs, Phelps, and Broadus were invested in the character education of preachers, and the character they had in mind for their white male readers was the same one that prompted George Williams to found the first YMCA. Storrs, Phelps, and Broadus wanted preachers to work on the moral health of their congregations—to be, in Phelps's words, "manly clergy" who "make the pulpit the place where their strength [is] expended" ("Theory" 39). They were to be the spiritual leaders of their flock very much in the mold of Bill McCartney's Promise Keepers: men of vigorous physical and moral health who compelled those in their charge to become better Christians, men who, as Beecher argued, did not even *need* the masculine space of the pulpit, since they were so vigorous, morally fit, and authoritative.

The Education of Preachers

A significant "trope" in preaching manuals since *De doctrina christiana* is the figure of the minister as a morally fit leader, a "good man" whose piety underscores his words. Nevertheless, for homileticians until the nineteenth century, the office of the preacher provided a sufficient basis for his *ethos,* or personal appeal. In Book 1 of *De doctrina christiana,* Augustine writes that the wisdom of God is like the medicine that a physician applies to a sick patient. In the extended metaphor, the patient is the Church, whose "malady arose through the corrupted spirit of a woman"; the cure for the malady is Christ (15). God in Christ is the Great Physician; however, the minister, as the deliverer of God's wisdom, is God's physician on earth. This metaphor suggests both the total depravity and dependency of the congregation on the minister; the minister is both healer and authority. Following the classical trope of the "good man speaking well," Augustine argues that the preacher must take care to speak of "the just and holy and good" so that "he may be willingly and obediently heard" (140). However, he adds that God can speak through any preacher: the congregation "may hear usefully those who do not act usefully" (164). The preacher can do much in a sermon to augment his message, but his personal appeal is dependent on prayer (to bring about piety) and his authority as a minister. There is a fundamental distance between the congregation and its minister implied here, a distance born of spiritual and institutional class distinction.

As suggested by church architecture and preaching manuals, the distance and authority of the preacher has remained a theme throughout church history. The personal appeal of the minister was reduced to piety; in 1322, Robert of Basevorn includes a "statement of the purity of life demanded of the preacher" in his *Forma praedicandi*. The qualifications of the preacher are purity of life, competent knowledge, and authority given by the Church (excluding laypersons and religious, "unless permitted by the Bishop or Pope," and all women, "no matter how learned or saintly") (345).[11] The preacher was expected to gain the respect of his congregation prior to entering the pulpit, by credentials and right living, although a traveling friar should "tell [. . .] the audience that he preaches only to convert them (not to beg from them)" (349).

With its democratizing effects on Church structure and elevation of the status of laypersons, the Reformation brought renewed focus on preaching method but not necessarily to questions about the preacher's *ethos*. Royal Society member John Wilkins, the bishop of Chester, assumed the preacher's authority in his 1646 manual *Ecclesiastes, Or a Discourse Concerning the Gift of Preaching as It Falls under the Rules of Art,* a resource that appealed to both Anglican and Puritan preachers (W. Mitchell 109). On the exordium (preface)—the section of the sermon in which orators in the classical system demonstrated their fitness—Wilkins writes:

> The most general and effectual matter for a Preface, is, (that which was so commonly used by the Prophets of old) to perswade the hearers that it is the *Word of God* which is spoken to them, which concerns their *everlasting happiness* and *is able to save their souls.* That the Ministers do but *stand in Christs stead.* That our *receiving or despising of them, shall be reckoned as done unto Christ himself.* Which being believed and considered, will be a strong engagement upon the hearers, unto those three qualifications, which are the chief ends of prefacing, namely, to make them
>
> > *Favourable.*
> > *Teachable.*
> > *Attentive.* (14)

In place of a full discussion of ways for the preacher to make his hearers respond well to him as an orator, Wilkins suggests that the preacher claim authority as God's representative, remind the audience that listening to him will be profitable to their souls, and threaten them with

God's wrath if they don't pay attention. This approach is interesting, especially at a time of religious unrest when many Protestant believers were looking for other options. It suggests that the seventeenth century invested the minister with a great deal of authority; and, in fact, Wilkins saw the distance between pulpit and pew as immutable. In Section 4, amid taxonomies of items the preacher could use to create a sermon, Wilkins includes "Special Homiletic Virtues," or the qualities of good conduct between human beings; it is focused on right conduct in unequal relationships, such as keeping proper distance when among "Superiors" and exhibiting humility.[12] But in addition, by focusing the art itself on saving individual souls, Wilkins posits a generic, universal audience of sinners, implying that preachers do not concern themselves with the local needs and social concerns of congregations.

In the eighteenth century, these trends are largely unchanged in preaching manuals. The preacher continues to be a distant, benevolent speaker, speaking to a generic congregation of sinners, with the general goal of teaching and applying scriptural truths. In *Lectures on Systematic Theology and Pulpit Eloquence,* popular Scottish rhetorician and preacher George Campbell defines the congregation according to one generic model of faculty psychology.[13] Campbell argues that the sermon should be shaped according to the "faculty of mind" the preacher hoped to reach. For example, if the minister hoped to appeal to the understanding, then he should preach an explanatory sermon, devoted to explication of Scripture, or a controversial sermon, devoted to discussion of Church doctrine. If he hoped to bring about a change of heart, he preached either a pathetic sermon or a persuasive sermon, each appealing more to the passions. Campbell maintains the general purpose for preaching advocated by Augustine, Robert of Basevorn, and Wilkins— extracting principles from Scripture and teaching them to the people— but Campbell recognizes different pathways to this general purpose. Like his predecessors, he is not concerned with the personal appeal of the minister. For example, he notes that in the bar and senate, speakers sometimes win their audiences' affections by either drawing from their personal experience with their subject or by apologizing in the exordium for their lack of experience and youth. Campbell argues that such conduct is rarely—if ever—appropriate for the pulpit (160). He maintains the aura of mystery and distance between the pulpit and pew recommended by rhetoricians before him. Though Campbell delves into the psychology of persuasion, his discussions of the minister and the hearer are built on the idea that Everyman has the same psychological profile.

In the nineteenth century, two trends changed the art of preaching. The first was the disestablishment of religion from the state, which legitimized a host of Protestant movements and led to the democratization of seminary training.[14] Whereas preachers were once trained at Harvard, Yale, or Princeton, they could now find training at a multitude of new seminaries. With the building of independent seminaries, mainline Protestant denominations accepted the challenge of educating the whole man, a process that had been shared by the entire liberal arts curriculum provided at the major colleges. For this reason, homiletics texts written in the nineteenth century are, by and large, far longer and more complete than texts written in earlier ages. The struggle over what sort of textbooks to produce for the new seminarian is reflected in the introduction to the 1834 *Lectures on Homiletics and Preaching, and on Public Prayer,* written by Ebenezer Porter, Bartlett Professor of Sacred Rhetoric at Andover Theological Seminary. He writes:

> After an examination of the many books that have been written on Rhetoric in general, and the comparatively few that have been written on Sacred Rhetoric, it became manifest, that I must be called to traverse a field, to a considerable extent untrodden by any predecessor. One of the first difficulties which met me, as an Instructor of our Senior Class, was the want of any single work, that I was satisfied to put into their hands as a Text-Book on Homiletics. The best thing of the kind, as far as it went, was Fenelon's *Dialogues,* but this little work is too limited in its range of subjects, and too desultory, as to classification of the matter which it does contain, to occupy any considerable time of students so advanced in knowledge, as our Senior Class are to be. (iii)

The theories of the eighteenth century were not in question in Porter's mind, but their manner of presentation (and limited range of subjects) seemed to him inadequate for a homiletics textbook. Porter introduces his seminarians to the history of the art of preaching, making reference to Wilkins and Augustine as well as to the history of preaching, organized around rhetorical questions such as how sermons were prepared throughout the ages. Porter includes lectures on homiletics exercises for students (a unique contribution to the art), choosing texts on which to preach, the classification of sermons (doctrinal, ethical, historical, and hortatory), the parts of the sermon, the principle of unity, style in preaching, and the development of style, including hints on writing for oratory in the tradition of Quintilian's *Institutio oratoria.* Later homileticians such as Phelps developed manuals devoted to the broad education of the preacher *(Men and Books, or Studies in Homiletics),* out of recognition that preachers could no longer be expected to have had a liberal arts training.

This shift toward educating the whole man provided a natural bridge to the quasi-religious cult of manliness with its concern for the development of character in men, which emerges in lectures on preaching in the 1850s. The result is that the minister, long shrouded by distance and crowned with unquestioned authority and moral superiority, comes into corporeal view in the nineteenth century as a man. This shift has a profound impact for the women who began entering seminaries in the late twentieth century: on the one hand, the preacher is recognized as fully human, opening the door for a more populist preacher to emerge; but on the other hand, the character of the preacher is more firmly inscribed as male, moving the role of preacher out of imaginative range both for women and congregations.[15] The 1850s was the decade of *Moby-Dick* and *Adam Bede,* novels that focus on the gender of the preacher at a time when preaching manuals and popular culture projected the exaggerated masculinity of Father Mapple in the pulpit, not the more subtle femininity of Dinah Morris.

Storrs on the Character of a Preacher

On August 5, 1856, the Porter Rhetorical Society of Andover Theological Seminary invited Congregationalist minister Richard S. Storrs Jr. (1821–1900), a recent graduate of the seminary and distinguished pastor of the Church of the Pilgrim in Brooklyn, New York, to speak.[16] In a quintessential application of muscular Christianity to the education of the preacher, Storrs addressed his audience of faculty and seminarians on the subject of "Character in the Preacher." In this forty-five-page address, Storrs argues that character is the most important quality of a successful preacher. Drawing a picture of the great audience to be won by preaching, including all the sciences, the State, and every institution in the dramatic opening of his address, Storrs settles on his topic:

> I invite you to look a while to-day, [. . .] not at the special rules of this Eloquence, the particular studies or the particular practices that may help us attain it, the particular results that may help us attain it; but at that which lies back of it, indispensable to it, and which, wherever it exists and is manifested, begets such Eloquence, as suns beget light, or as flowers beget perfume; at
>
> The CHARACTER IN THE PREACHER, which shall make his words eloquent. (3)

By 1856, hundreds of American women preachers had led successful careers in such denominations as the Society of Friends and the Methodist Church and in the Holiness tradition. However, for this Calvinist minister, a preacher must be "a LIBERAL, ABLE, and MANLY CHARACTER; comprehensive, not partial; vigorous and self-reliant, not dependent on others; masculine without severity, not effeminate or weak" (4). Echoing Melville's vision of the preacher, Storrs argues that such fulness of character, such a vigorous, accomplished, and well-developed manhood, is especially needed and appropriate in the minister; who has to treat the noblest themes, who has to do the most difficult work, upon whom civilization, as well as Christianity, rests its primary hope. (4)

Melville's narrator opines, "[T]he pulpit is ever this earth's foremost part" (44); Storrs demands that the preacher be "the foremost man, in all that concerns pure personal quality, in any community in which he is placed" (4–5).

The first quality in the character of this "foremost man" is courage (what Storrs later calls "chivalry").

I mean by [Courage], what its name denotes, firmness of heart; that quality of intelligent and intrepid self-reliance, which enables a man to look dangers in the face, to look an enemy in the eye, without any vein's palpitating; which "mounteth with occasion"; and which is never so apparent, so eminent, I might almost have said so founded and so real, as when drawn out by the contact and pressure of opposition. It is the old *virtus,* manhood, of the Romans. It is that robust and hardy quality, appropriate to man, and befitting his high and spiritual forces, which the elder dramatists continually praise; to have given illustrious examples of which is the glory of the English, or of any other History; which makes its mark everywhere, wherever it is revealed; assuring of solidity in purpose and in action, of energy in feeling, and of success in endeavor. (6)

Storrs is quite earnest about the need for the preacher to be no less than the hero of a great drama: for him, the preacher's work "is for men, for heroes!" and therefore requires "the grandest fitness" (42). Coming a half-century before Baden-Powell's efforts to create the hero in the boy, this vision privileges an understanding of masculinity as chivalry, heroism in the face of opposition, sacrifice, and self-reliance.

What further underscores the remarkable connection with Baden-Powell's vision of muscular Christianity is Storrs's second quality of character: "Sympathy with Nature." Character training for Baden-Powell involved taking boys into the woods to encounter nature; the Boy Scouts are still synonymous with camping and wilderness survival training. Storrs finds a love of nature indispensable to the preacher because

[i]t is the inward response of the soul to that living, voiceful, and inspiring creation, amid which we move; which is full of lights, and tints, and sounds, and motion; full of wonder and of beauty, of the elements of power, and the pure laws of grace. Sensibility to this is always appropriate to the soul which God hath formed. It is spe-

cially appropriate and needful in the minister, who would represent the Divine Mind to men. (12)

Fully in the romantic tradition, Storrs connects this appreciation of nature with an appreciation of "the Art which represents it," arguing that the preacher cannot develop his oratorical style if he has a "deadness" to both (15). Contact with nature, Storrs argues, can bring about "a healthful, pure and natural grace, and give to his thought a manly freshness" (16); furthermore, "the general air of manly calmness, and sweet sensibility, pervading a discourse, and making it teem with attraction to the hearers [. . .] is not embraced in the logical categories; it is not learned in the lecture-room or the study" (16). Using the familiar trope of nature as a mother, Storrs suggests that nature is the parent of oratorical style, "a living form" made by God to inspire men to greatness. By transporting the image of the preacher to the wilderness, Storrs is able to contrast the "manly" preacher with the weaker man of books, who is simultaneously less physically fit, less sensitive to God, and more prone to artificial rhetorical style.

In addition to these qualities, Storrs elaborates four others: "Sympathy with Man," "Sympathetic Enthusiasm for Truth," "Conscientious Earnestness," and "Christian Benevolence." Taken together, the latter four qualities are the recipe for the chivalrous hero in the cult of manhood. Being a humanitarian, he is armed with compassion for others, contrasting him with the man of science who is dispassionate about his work. Armed with truth, he has the self-assurance that his cause is the cause of righteousness. Being earnest, he is able to persevere in the face of adversity. Having benevolence toward all, which Storrs translates as "piety," he is able "to give rest to the weary" and "to open the tidings of salvation and peace to the vagrant and the magdalen" (39). He is the epic American hero, a man of transcendent masculinity.

Indeed, in the unmistakable flavor of imperialism, Storrs argues that the office of the preacher is "to subjugate the whole earth unto Him" (42).

> My friends, do I seem to have asked too much in this series of traits? more than we can attain, in our limited sphere? [. . .] We have to conquer for God and Christ the Master-Race, on earth, in history. "Our iron sinks," said the Hindoo [sic] to the Englishman, "you build yours into ships, and yonder it swims! Our wire is silent; yours talks in the air, a thousand miles away! We have journeyed for ages on foot or in palanquins; you ride in chariots snorting fire!" To make this people, whose science [is] richer, whose passion more terrific in its heat, than any other's—to make this people obey one Law, and worship one Lord, and through them to subjugate the whole earth unto Him,—this is our office! (41–42)

Of course, it is impossible to read this passage without remembering the staggering costs of imperialism in the nineteenth century and recognizing the hubris and ethnocentrism of Storrs's vision.[17] Indeed, as John M. MacKenzie argues, the cult of manhood in late Victorian and early Edwardian times in Britain fused the character of the man with the imperialist goals of the nation. In this same period in America, many hymns elaborate what June Hadden Hobbs calls an "androcentric version of missions" (97). For example, in Will Thompson's "The Whole, Wide World for Jesus" (1908), we read

> The whole wide world for Jesus!
> Be this our battle-cry
> The Crucified shall conquer
> And victory is nigh

> (qtd. in Hobbs 98)

In Protestant churches around the nation, "Onward Christian Soldiers" (1864), with its challenge,

> Onward, Christian soldiers!
> Marching as to war,
> With the cross of Jesus
> Going on before[18]

continues to be sung with evangelical zeal, though perhaps not with the same cultural intent as Storrs's invocation.[19]

Storrs's preacher is fundamentally a man at the height of masculinity: he is bold, gallant, natural, earnest, physically fit—a Christian soldier doing battle with the secular world and conquering whole cultures for Christ, yet full of sympathy for those around him. Storrs's preacher is a manly man in the American Victorian ideal, a man who, as Beecher puts it, "bring[s] his spirit to bear upon men" through the force of his personality (*Popular Lectures* 14). While Storrs did not produce a preaching manual or a collection of lectures on preaching, the perspective he presents in his Porter Rhetorical Society address is reproduced in treatises on homiletics written by his contemporaries. At the time of Storrs's lecture, the Chair of Sacred Rhetoric and Homiletics at Andover Theological Seminary was held by thirty-six-year-old Austin Phelps, who had held the position since 1848. While we can only surmise that Phelps was in attendance that day, we do know that Phelps knew Storrs and that, in fact, Storrs was considered for the position Phelps held (E. Phelps 42). Storrs and Phelps shared the perception that in the pulpit, the preacher's manhood was his greatest asset, and they both drew on the cult of manhood to develop the character traits of a preacher. Phelps wrote several influential books on preaching, including *The Theory of*

Preaching (1881), *Men and Books; or Studies in Homiletics* (1882), and *English Style in Public Discourse with Special Reference to the Usages of the Pulpit* (1883), and gave at least one address to the Porter Rhetorical Society, titled "The Theory of Preaching" (1857), an address that was a precursor to his great homiletic treatise of the same name. His contributions to the development and training of the preacher are historically important, and his reliance on "neoclassic" theories of rhetoric make him especially interesting to historians of nineteenth century rhetoric (Hirst). Phelps's *Theory of Preaching* was popular from its first edition in 1881; the last edition was published as late as 1947 (Johnson, *Nineteenth-Century Rhetoric* 276n.21).

Phelps and the Cult of Manhood

The Theory of Preaching is a comprehensive preaching manual, taking the student through the development of a sermon from inception to delivery, not unlike some contemporary composition manuals for university undergraduates. Phelps includes forty chapters (nearly six hundred pages) covering the relationship of homiletics to rhetoric, classification of sermons, and the development and delivery of the sermon, with attention to arrangement and style. *Men and Books* is a compendium of lectures on ways the preacher can educate himself in the broad sense, particularly through the reading of literature. Both books offer a fascinating window on Phelps's view of the preacher's character, the audience, and the purpose for preaching; both books are practical and target an audience of mainline Protestant preachers, but particularly those in the Calvinist tradition.[20]

At the heart of Phelps's theory of preaching is the cultivation of character in the individual. "The great object of life, and therefore of culture, is character," Phelps asserts, "the growth, the exercise, the use, of character" (*Men and Books* 20). It is the preacher's role to cultivate character in his congregation through sacred oratory, and therefore, he must, in addition to cultivating his powers of persuasion, work on his own character. Phelps sums up the chief character trait of the preacher through the ideal of manliness, the set of character traits one finds in the soldier:

> The pulpit should be a battery, well armed and well worked. Every shot from it should reach a vulnerable spot somewhere. And to be such it must be, in every sense of the word, well manned. The gunner who works it must know what and where the vulnerable spots are. He must be neither an angel nor a brute. He must be a scholar and a gentleman, but not these only. He must be a *man,* who knows men, and who will never suffer the great tides of hu-

> man opinion and feeling to ebb and flow around him uncontrolled
> because unobserved. (*Men and Books* 29)

Echoing Storrs, Phelps regards the manly preacher as one who conquers others in part through the forcefulness of his character and the skill of his speech.

> The principle which explains, in part, the fact that an army of sixty
> thousand men keeps in subjection sixty millions of aliens in Brit-
> ish India is the same which explains, in part, the coming conver-
> sion of the world by a handful of preachers with no auxiliaries to
> speech but prayer. (*Men and Books* 10)

To be such a man, the "thoroughly trained preacher is first a man, at home among men: he is then a scholar, at home in libraries" (*Men and Books* iii). The preacher is a leader, a man of virtue, strength, and courage.

Since the cult of manhood developed around anxieties over cultural emasculation, it is not surprising to see Phelps draw distinctions between manly and effeminate uses of the pulpit. In his 1857 address to the Porter Rhetorical Society, Phelps wrote that the pulpit "must hold the place of chief honor in the policy of Christian effort, or it can hold no place in which it shall either command or deserve a pittance of respect" ("Theory" 9). His main concern was that the pulpit should lose its manly rigor through association with lesser men and religious movements. "Make it [the pulpit] subordinate," Phelps argues, "and you make it *effeminate*" ("Theory" 9, emphasis added). Among the forces that could emasculate the pulpit, Phelps singled out the following: the image of the preacher as priest (particularly in the Roman Catholic tradition), the use of "poetic sentiments" in the pulpit, preaching to social ills as opposed to individual salvation, and preaching primarily to stir the emotions. Phelps is especially critical of priests in both the Roman Catholic Church and the Church of England. Theologically, his concern is that the liturgy, with its emphasis on the Eucharist as the means to salvation, subverts the role of the clergy in Christian ministry. In such forms of worship, he argues, the altar is more important than the pulpit, and the priest's role as preacher is reduced.

> When we look for the symbol of dignity which distinguishes the
> Christian ministry, we must find it in the pulpit. A minister of
> Christ must be regarded as being, above all his other distinctions,
> a preacher. His character as a preacher cannot be submerged in
> the character of priest, and yet exist in any manly and command-
> ing form. The testimony to this effect, furnished by the history
> of the Romish church, is almost too palpable to need remark.
> ("Theory" 10)

Drawing on histories of the clergy during the Restoration period (1660–88), Phelps makes an object lesson of Anglican clergy, who, after being recalled from exile, allowed themselves to be treated as servants to the landed gentry, especially in rural England, where a chaplain might find himself working a garden or grooming a horse in order to secure his pay ("Theory" 12). "Never, before or since, has the clerical office fallen to so low a state in the English church," Phelps asserts (11). For Phelps, where the influence of the preacher is diluted by any means, the pulpit has been *feminized*.

Another diminution of the pulpit occurs for Phelps when poetic sentiments are asserted over argumentation and reason. Here, like Storrs, Phelps is wary of men who are at home only in libraries and write sermons that are works of art but that do not speak to the common person. For Storrs, taste comes through immersion in nature; for Phelps, it comes through immersion in a broad education (including books but also common opinions of the day) and theological issues. Phelps was concerned about tepid sermons that did not challenge his congregants.

> The higher classes no less resolutely than the lower withhold their spirit of obeisance from any man who is too good for it, too refined, too scholarly, too gentlemanly, or too indolent and too weak. The preacher, therefore, who has no power with the common people, has, in fact, no power with anybody. The pulpit which has no standing-ground down in the lowlands of society has none anywhere. An exclusive ministry is always a weak ministry. (*Men and Books* 69)

Powerful sermons translated theological questions to the "lower classes" while still speaking to the needs of what Phelps calls "the mature Christian mind" ("Theory" 28). He compares the preacher who can bridge the gap between the educated and uneducated and the immature and mature Christians with great secular orators (politicians and educators) who could move entire nations to act through the force of their words. For Phelps, the preacher is in the same company as other American leaders—he is in the national fraternity of men.

However, despite the preacher's membership in this national fraternity, Phelps was not in favor of preaching that focused on social issues of the day, except in moments of great moral "emergency" ("Theory" 18). Phelps argues in several texts that the preacher's primary purpose for preaching is the regeneration of individual souls ("Theory"; *Theory; Men and Books*).

> He [the preacher] must be assured that he preaches a system of truth, which in its practical relations is correlative with all forms of human life, and with history through all time. Its genius is that

of practical agitation and change. It is transforming, it is subversive, it is revolutionary [. . .].

Yet, with all this far-reaching practical energy, it is primarily addressed to the individual man; not to communities, not to governments, not to nations, not to the race as such, but to individual man. *It has to do, directly, with man singly; not with man in his organic relations.* ("Theory" 15, emphasis added)

During the great moral debates surrounding slavery, Phelps stood on the sidelines while preachers such as Henry Ward Beecher, also from the Calvinist tradition, finally were drawn into the battle over abolition.[21] It was not that Phelps disdained the abolitionist cause but rather that he defined his role in the conflict differently from Beecher: the minister, for Phelps, was engaged in a struggle to reform the whole man; focus on issues such as abolition drew time away from Phelps's larger mission of reuniting individual souls with God. Social morality would be changed, Phelps believed, when individual souls were changed. The preacher's "word is to this man and that man; it is to you, and to me, and to him; to each, *in the singleness of his identity, and in that impressive solitude in which every man is appointed to work out his own salvation*" ("Theory" 17, emphasis added). In this way, Phelps believed the word of the preacher then "will go forth to the nations" through this "channel of *individual regeneration*," and "[i]ts flow will be like that of subterranean rivers" (20). Therefore, like writers of preaching manuals before and after him, Phelps affirmed the primary goal of preaching as individual salvation and moral regeneration.

Yet because of his emphasis on the development of character in the congregation, Phelps did not believe in evangelism as the sole focus of preaching. He was critical of some of the great revivalists of the nineteenth century, whom he accused of espousing a "theory of Enthusiasm" ("Theory" 6). These preachers, Phelps argues, forgo rational discussions of theology in the pulpit, believing instead the pulpit should be used "chiefly, not for the discussion, but for the direct application, of truth" (5). They depend for their success "mainly upon the power of exhortation, and upon that magnetic sympathy by which emotion in a speaker's heart reproduces its like in the heart of an audience" (6). Far from producing individual regeneration, such practices instead gave rise to "[a]n unthoughtful piety" and "a religion of feeling, such as is most facile to undisciplined minds" (6).[22] In keeping with his neoclassical roots, Phelps instead likens pulpit eloquence to examples of great secular eloquence, "which are acknowledged by the world to be triumphs of oratory" because of "their statement and advocacy of certain great principles of truth" (25). Phelps asserts that if there is "such a thing as pulpit eloquence, which shall have a character of its own, as the eloquence of the senate or the bar has, it must derive that character from the doctrines of systematic theology" (26). The itinerant preacher and the preacher of the social gospel may not put enough time into developing these great themes, but "[t]o turn from them in search of ephemeral topics of excitement—the topics of *the day* as they are appropriately called—is to degrade the pulpit" (26). Phelps argues for a theory of preaching that is based in the development of character, rational discussion of difficult issues of doctrine and theology, and "impassioned argument" based in "stern logic" (30) with the overall goal of individual salvation.

The minister in Phelps's vision is, therefore, a man of great intellect and a paragon of masculinity—a man with membership in the national fraternity that produces civic leaders and presidents. He is an authority with "commanding form" and presence ("Theory" 10). Following from this vision, Phelps's preacher focuses his career on the regeneration of individual souls and is not distracted from this honorable profession by the social conditions around him except in times of great moral "emergencies." Phelps's theory of preaching is based on the presumption that preaching is above all a form of argument, argument based in logic and deduced from denominational doctrines, or "truths"; the preacher is the all-knowing authority on doctrine who can distribute these truths to his grateful congregation. In fact, it must be his "manliness" that makes the preacher effect this authoritative stance, for, as Phelps puts it, "The popular conception of a clergyman is that he is, *ex officio,* in respect to the knowledge of mankind, an ignoramus" (*Men and Books* 21). Acknowledging that this popular notion is probably false, he nevertheless draws on the character training emerging in his period as "muscular Christianity" to build up seminarians for their role as civic leaders, meanwhile leaving deliberately unacknowledged the women who served as pastors and itinerant preachers in nonmainstream denominations.

Character in the Twentieth-Century Preacher

By the twentieth century, the power and authority afforded the Victorian preacher on both sides of the Atlantic had dwindled, especially in the mainstream denominations that produced the vast majority of preaching manuals. Horton Davies and John R. W. Stott begin their historical accounts of preaching by contrasting the power and authority preachers enjoyed in the Victorian era with the decline thereof in the twentieth century. Of the scene in Great Britain, Davies writes:

> The English preacher of today can hardly be accused of standing six feet above criticism in a coward's castle. The censure could be more fitly directed at his Victorian predecessor, the pulpit orator. The Victorian preacher surveyed his vast congregation from his

quarterdeck of a platform, like a ship's commander, threatening the
mutinous beneath him with an eagle and authoritarian eye. The
status of the modern preacher, as befits his reduced congregation,
is humbler. E. H. Jeffs has written: "Instead of mounting his pulpit as a throne, the modern preacher is rather in the position of
being summoned into the witness-box." Even this sober estimate
might be questioned, since 80 per cent of the British people condemn the preacher unheard. (17)

Borrowing the same imagery, Stott likens the Victorian preacher in
America to Father Mapple, arguing that Melville's declaration that "the
pulpit leads the world" could never be asserted at the end of the twentieth century, with so few attending church (36). Stott and Davies agree
that the problem is the decline of religious belief in the postwar years,
and both argue that the art of preaching must change to adapt to an
increasingly skeptical public.

Nevertheless, Phelps's *Theory of Preaching* and Broadus's 1870 *A
Treatise on the Preparation and Delivery of Sermons*, a textbook very
similar to Phelps's in form and content, enjoyed widespread use in theological education until the mid-twentieth century. Both textbooks posit
the character of the preacher as of paramount importance, with Broadus
arguing that the preacher must never forget "the power of character and
life to reinforce speech. What a preacher is, goes far to determine the
effect of what he says. There is a saying of Augustine, *Cujus vita fulgor,
ejus verba tonitrua,*—if a man's life be lightning, his words are thunder"
(541). Because Broadus's text is widely considered the most successful
American textbook on preaching of all time (forty editions were published between 1870 and 1896 alone), it has been uniquely targeted by
contemporary scholars and preachers for criticism. Broadus was one of
the founders of the Southern Baptist Theological Seminary (organized
in 1859) and served as a professor of homiletics there until his death
in 1895. In his essay "Is There Still Room for Rhetoric?," Fred B.
Craddock, Bandy Professor of Preaching and New Testament, emeritus,
at the Candler School of Theology, Emory University, and an ordained
minister in the Christian Church (Disciples of Christ), argues that
Broadus, like Phelps and many other sacred rhetoricians of the nineteenth century, contributed to the deductive, three-point sermon, which
began with the explication of sacred texts, moved on to apply the text
to everyday life, and finally concluded with an appeal to the will,[23] a
pattern based on the assumption of the superior moral knowledge of
the preacher (66).

Congregations were being served sermons in three parts every Sunday (even though often the intent was not to persuade and the three

parts were not appeals to mind, heart, and will). Whatever the text, whatever the subject, sermons had three points. Sadly, as is often the case with practices born of worthy purpose and rich with history, Cicero's contribution to homiletics fell subject to jokes about "three points and a poem." (Craddock, "Is There Still Room" 67)

But more importantly, Craddock argues (in agreement with Davies) that

> the pulpit of the 1960s and beyond faced a barrage of questions [. . .] about the preacher, questions concerning authority and the right to persuade others to his or her position rather than facilitating a conversation between the community and its Scriptures. ("Is There Still Room" 67)

Craddock goes on to argue that the old assurance about the purpose of preaching is gone. "Homileticians no longer agree that the sole purpose of the sermon is to persuade," he asserts (68); the authority of the preacher can no longer be assumed.

In contrast to Broadus, Craddock develops a preaching theory based on the assumed collapse of the preacher's authority. In his book *Overhearing the Gospel,* which began as the Lyman Beecher Lecture for 1978, Craddock introduces his approach to the sermon, which begins with a narrative rather than a three-point proposition and deductive organization. Craddock suggests that the contemporary listener is best persuaded by both feeling a distance from Scripture and, paradoxically, participating in it. He advocates turning the sermon into a narrative that the congregation "overhears."

> The chronology of a narrative locates the participants in time and place. Stories are read and heard because the experience of movement through time, common to the story and all its hearers, reassures that we are alive and can enlarge our living by identifying, participating, appropriating, the experiences of others. (*Overhearing* 257)

In a sense, the minister steps out of the way, presenting no propositions, but rather causing the stories of the Bible to speak for themselves. Whereas earlier ministers like Beecher advocated warming up the three-point sermon with love and concern for the congregation, Craddock advocates distance. In this way, the credibility of the minister is earned through the skill of his narrative technique, not through the force or cult of personality. Craddock's perspective suggests that the best sermon showcases the minister and his experience the least. By placing the message of the sermon last, Craddock hopes to draw the audience inductively into their own conclusions. Quite in contrast to the minister described by Phelps and Broadus, Craddock advocates a minister who *disappears* behind his stories. But Craddock begs the question of the character of the minister, who is presumably emptied of sex, race, and any other identifying quality in the act of storytelling. Whereas Phelps, Storrs, and Broadus gender the act of preaching and name it universal, Craddock simply replaces one universal set of principles with another: the masculine preacher is replaced with a neutered preacher; story is all.

But how is it possible for the preacher to disappear? Storrs, Phelps, Broadus, Beecher, and many other post-disestablishment homileticians recognized that the preacher was a public figure who could not disappear, and they struggled to give him relevance in contemporary culture, working first to develop him into a man who would be admired by his contemporaries. Culture now as in the nineteenth century celebrates the national fraternity of manhood, even if this institution is increasingly encroached upon by women. Masculinity is ever redefined as heterosexual; white culture is ever reasserted. Without addressing the character of the preacher and the specific needs of the congregation, Craddock simply leaves open questions about how a preacher at the turn of the twenty-first century can develop a relationship with his or her hearers.

In his 1999 essay on Broadus, Steven Reagles criticizes Craddock for focusing too narrowly on sermon form, noting:

> While Broadus' homiletical method was unquestionably "prescriptive"—favoring what has been variously labeled "discursive," "deductive," "argumentative," "conceptual," "classical"—few, if any, recent writers of the inductive, story, narrative "school" have been sympathetic enough with Broadus, it seems, to notice how open he was to changing his "prescriptions." (34)

Reagles notes that Broadus supported a narrative style for the right occasion in his famous treatise and implored his students (as did Beecher and Phelps) to search for ways to be relevant to their congregations. Although Beecher also wrote in agreement with Phelps, Storrs, and Broadus that "[m]anhood is the best sermon" (*Popular Lectures* 28), he also believed that "preaching means the living power of living men upon living men" (15–16), and the search for relevance was an important part of achieving this goal. These Victorian theorists found a model for relevance in the cult of manhood, which offered the preacher a way to take his position in national life.

By neglecting to address the issue of the character of the preacher, Craddock leaves in place the long tradition of the fraternity of men and their image in the pulpit; in addition, by positing the inductive method of preaching as a universal prescription for the "anti-authoritarianism" of the late twentieth century, he merely inverts the tradition without reforming its unquestioned masculine bias. Indeed, his important work,

As One Without Authority, does not acknowledge the presence of women in the pulpit nor the fact that storytelling (animating the Bible) is a central part of African American preaching traditions (H. Mitchell, *Black Preaching* 127–47). Indeed, the fourth printing of this book, published in 1986, features a faceless male preacher on the cover, an ironic reference to the generic ideology of gender in the pages. As Reagles, Stott, and others suggest, anti-authoritarianism in an audience does not suggest that authority is no longer an issue. On the contrary—it is more at issue than ever. We can uncover the bias of this particular perspective by imagining a woman preacher "disappearing" in the act of preaching. As Elaine Lawless shows in her studies of issues facing women preachers, even the body of a woman becomes an issue for a congregation unaccustomed to seeing a preacher with breasts and hips ("Writing the Body"). In fact, as nineteenth-century homileticians suggest, Craddock would be optimistic to think that he himself could disappear behind his narrative.

In her powerful essay "Preaching as an Art of Resistance," Christine M. Smith writes:

> In the United States there are [. . .] many women and men today who understand that almost every category of religion, faith, theology, and life has been defined and proclaimed as universal truth by white Euro-American males. With contemporary social and theological awareness, we know that such generalizations perpetuate privilege and domination at the expense of human specificity and diversity. (39)

Of course, most rhetorics give a nod to the specificity of an audience, and we would go too far if we were to suggest that preaching manuals of the nineteenth century neglected altogether this aspect of the rhetorical situation. But, there is no doubt that the preacher of the nineteenth century preaching manual is unabashedly male and white, as is his congregation. Broadus wrote *A Treatise on the Preparation and Delivery of Sermons* soon after the Civil War, and he preached to a congregation that included both slaves and white citizens in Charlottesville before the war. But Broadus never suggests that the preacher address the needs and concerns of African American congregants. By strenuously turning the purpose for preaching to the individual soul, Broadus appears to have risen above criticism of racism through eight decades of acclaim for his preaching manual, although he was a popular Confederate preacher in the antebellum South (DeRemer 22). He is criticized, ironically, only for perpetuating a limited sermon form.

Nevertheless, organized religion has hitched its star to white men for the same reasons that other national institutions have done so, and so we should not be surprised to find the art of preaching, like most rhetorical arts, assuming a universal rhetor while basing the model for that orator on the specific experiences of one gender and one race. What does it mean for the art of preaching to be gendered? As with the rhetorical space of the pulpit, the art is based on the presumed authority and status of one gender, with the expectation (when taught in school) that anyone can practice its precepts. Because gendered behavior is a complex aspect of cultural life at any moment and at any given location in human history, institutional practices based in the body and experience of one sex of privileged status will in no way account for the practices of all. When a culture embraces an ideology like national manhood, and when the history of a religion has excluded women throughout all but a few decades of its history, an art of preaching based on the experiences of privileged white men will undoubtedly favor the same.

While textbooks across the field of rhetoric continue to assume a global readership and an ideal rhetor, scholarly efforts to focus on rhetorics of everyday life reveal astonishing diversity in the communicative performances of "average" people. Folklorist Elaine Lawless tracks the rhetorical practices of women preachers of the Holiness tradition, a conservative denomination in which strict gender segregation is practiced in the home but in which women preachers may earn their congregations' respect by calling attention to their status and limited authority as daughters and mothers (Handmaidens of the Lord). In Angels' Town, Ralph Cintron documents the beautiful and terrifying art of gang graffiti in a Chicago neighborhood and, like Michel de Certeau, calls attention to the mundane literacies of daily life in a large city. What makes these studies possible is the practice of participant observation and qualitative interviews, where local knowledge is privileged over universal models of communication. Because all rhetorical treatises since Aristotle, including arts of preaching, are based on observation of good practices, it is fitting that we now turn to the rhetorical arts of three women preachers, each the first woman to lead her congregation, to discover how a woman enters the pulpit with only the blueprints of national manhood to guide her.

3

Sermo Corporis

> The term action is now commonly restricted to what Cicero calls
> the *sermo corporis,* or speech of the body, including expression of
> countenance, posture, and gesture [. . .].
> —John Broadus, *A Treatise on the
> Preparation and Delivery of Sermons*

> To walk is to lack a place. It is the indefinite process of being ab-
> sent and in search of a proper.
> —Michel de Certeau, *The Practice of Everyday Life*

Motion is preordained in sacred space. The people may walk forward to the altar rail to receive communion but must then return
to their seats; the priest moves between pulpit and altar and moves beyond the altar rail only during procession. The people kneel, stand, sing,
and sit on cue; the priest raises his arms to lift the host above his head
and lowers them. These movements comprise an orderly system wherein
all move within their proper places. Transgression is about movement
outside of the proper. When British suffragists protested the antifemi-
nist clergy in the summer of 1914, they stood up in the middle of a
church service and shouted, "Votes for women!" They stood when they
should have been seated; they shouted when they should have been quiet.
When Hawaiian women protested their status as *noa,* or unclean, they
raided the *kapu* larder and ate "male" foods such as pineapples. These
protesting women were literally *out of order,* out of proper place.

During the summer of 1990, the first ordained woman pastor of an
eighteen-hundred-member Lutheran church in a growing suburban bed-
room community was "busting a move." Having spent nine years at St.
John's Lutheran Church (including the first year when she was an intern) under the control and in the shadows of a senior pastor named Rev.
Harold Mosely, the Reverend Patricia O'Connor was in the third Sunday of her emancipation when I approached her to participate in this
study. Unlike the other two clergywomen I followed, O'Connor was one-

half of a pastoral team in which she was clearly the subordinate, the daughter of a large, traditional family headed by a powerful father. Before the summer of the study, O'Connor had preached only every fourth Sunday and had never preached on a high holy day such as Christmas Eve; when she did preach, she normally did so in the presence of "Him," the honorific (and charily ironic) nickname given Mosely by the church staff. On those occasions she preached from the pulpit, she stood on a stool because of her petite stature.

During the summer of 1990, O'Connor left the pulpit for the first time in her career and began to preach from the floor. Because of the nature of her relationship with the congregation and the precarious position of her gender in that church, her ministry might best be described in terms of motion, not unlike de Certeau's description of the average city dweller's walk between spaces that serves as the epigraph for this chapter. She was, as de Certeau suggests, in search of a (new) proper location. Unlike the fictional women preachers of chapter 1, who dwelt in the habitus of their creators' own making, Rev. Patricia O'Connor was trained in institutions that had not anticipated a woman and preached in a church that had not yet changed the furniture for her. Haunted by the manly man of the pulpit, she quit his furniture and went for a walk. In the walking, she began to answer for herself a question the preaching manuals would not address: What does it mean to have good character outside the context of institutional masculinity? How could she, a woman small in stature, earn the respect of her congregation through her rhetorical performance?

Delivery and the Rhetorical Body

While contemporary rhetoricians largely neglect the fifth canon of delivery or consider it only as an afterthought, delivery is a critical element of rhetorical performance for preachers. As John Broadus argues,

> A speech, in the strict sense of the term, exists only in the act of speaking [. . .]. Whatever may be necessary for convenience in our rhetorical treatises, it is yet exceedingly important not to think of the speech and the delivery as things existing apart. (480)

Repeating the nineteenth-century dictum that the best delivery is the most natural-appearing, Broadus suggests that "delivery does not consist merely, or even chiefly, in vocalization and gesticulation, but it implies that one is possessed with the subject, that he is completely in sympathy with it and fully alive to its importance [. . .]" (477–78). The sermon is not a text; it is a performance.

Broadus and other nineteenth-century homileticians offered advice on posture, gestures, and voice, centered, of course, around the male body. Beecher recommends that clergymen preach outside the pulpit from time to time in order to feel the "force" of their bodies upon the congregation during a sermon; in case anyone should miss this obviously sexual metaphor, Beecher exclaims that a preacher is much more "manly" when out from behind the pulpit (*Lectures on Preaching* 71). Phelps argues that creation of goodwill in the audience (important in the introduction of a sermon) depends on a speaker's personal power, which in turn is dependent on stature, both cultural and physical. "[P]hysical presence is an important factor in the creation of influence with the popular mind," he writes. "Men of large frame and erect carriage have the advantage over diminutive men in competitive labors" (*Theory* 224). The cult of manhood also influences recommendations in nineteenth-century preaching manuals on exercise. In his suggestions for improving delivery, Broadus suggests that preachers take care of their general health, adding to their routines strenuous exercise, "especially *muscular exercise,* and particularly such as develops the chest, and promotes an easy erectness of position" (486). Anxiety over the masculine bearing of the preacher's body is repeated well into the twentieth century. In his 1985 preaching manual, *Preaching,* James W. Cox repeats the following story:

> I heard of a male theology student who spoke in a feminine, falsetto voice and saw that as a formidable problem for his aspirations as a preacher. A speech therapist learned that the student had affected his falsetto as a defense, from the time his classmates had laughed at him as an adolescent when his voice was changing. The therapist, by using special electronic equipment, enabled him to hear his true voice, and he was liberated. (268)

This theology student experienced a liberation *from the feminine,* a key drive in homiletic theory. Cox later repeats advice by Charles R. Brown in his 1922 Yale lecture (who in turn echoes Beecher) that a man should occasionally quit the pulpit in order to be a "whole man" (273), making no references whatsoever to what that might mean for women theology students (indeed, there is no reference to women anywhere in the book).

What might *sermo corporis* mean for women? One must begin with the fact that women's bodies are closely aligned with place, as we saw in chapter 1. A woman's body would not be expected in or near the pulpit, nor any place consistently associated with male, public spaces. Throughout history, women's bodies have been associated with the private sphere and with natural inferiority, and their participation in broader democratic culture has been restricted. Even in historical moments of greater political egalitarianism, women's bodies have been reviled. For example, during the French Revolution, femininity was associated with the ruling classes and with decay; images of heroic masculinity prevailed, and women were restricted from participating in the newly democratic public sphere (Landes, *Women and the Public Sphere;* Outram). In the United States, women were discouraged from appearing behind podiums well into the twentieth century, and as Johnson documents, rhetorical treatises clearly bolstered this trend *(Gender)*.

> [W]omen were denied access to public discourse both de facto and de jure until first-wave feminists during the late nineteenth century secured their rights to own property, legally represent their children, and vote. (The connection between their inability to own property and their inability to claim legal rights to their own and their children's bodies was not lost on first-wave feminists.) (Crowley, "Afterword" 359)

Second-wave feminists have argued that women's bodies are endlessly scrutinized and subjected to control because women's position in culture is still precarious (Bordo, *Unbearable Weight*). This phenomenon has been particularly chilling for African American women (hooks; see also Gates, *"Race," Writing and Difference*). Discourses of suspicion and images of restraint of women's bodily presence serve to reinforce their exclusions from the public sphere.

When women preach, this scrutiny follows them into the pulpit. For example, clergywomen in a regional ecumenical support group reported to Elaine Lawless that they often felt naked in the pulpit, especially when they were pregnant ("Writing the Body"). In her analysis, Lawless borrows heavily from the Catholic tradition, arguing that congregations consider their male preachers to be fundamentally asexual while women preachers are the "marked" sex. She offers the story of one of her informants as an example:

> I heard the story about a priest, when he first went to be a director of a Newman Center. It was Christmas and they were hanging things and all of that. The light bulbs needed to be changed; so he got a ladder, and someone came to him and said, "Oh, no, Father, let one of the *men* do that!" (66)

Her informant used this story to explain that clergymen were not even especially considered *men,* their bodies had been so thoroughly de-sexed. Such a story would have caused a great chuckle from Austin Phelps, who was skeptical about the masculinity of both Catholic and Anglican priests.[1] Within the textbook tradition, the Protestant male preacher is fundamentally a man, complete with all his secondary sexual characteristics: deep voice, commanding presence, and strength. In the cult of manhood, such characteristics, if absent, had to be cultivated for the character of the preacher to be established: witness the poor theology student in Cox's textbook. While it is certainly true historically that women are associated with sexuality far more often than men, since the nineteenth century, Protestant male preachers' bodies have been closely scrutinized for conventional masculinity in the pulpit, and it is their bodies around which *sermo corporis* has been theorized.[2] Women's bodies are simply not considered in the art of delivery.

As is clear in Cox's anxious narrative over the feminine voice of a male student, when homileticians assert the importance of conventional masculine behavior in the delivery of a sermon, they appear to be concerned that without such traits, congregations will infer that the preacher lacks appropriate character. Therefore, delivery involves, first and foremost, the presentation of the self in a form that will be acceptable to the audience. Classical rhetoricians considered character (understood as *ethos*) to be a malleable skill associated with the performance of an attitude toward the subject at hand. Aristotle argued that a speaker must seem to embody the attitude he hoped to engender in the audience. For example, a speaker who hoped to move a crowd to action against a perceived wrong would need to seem angry about it himself. As James Fredal explains, "Public oratory thus required not only skill at verbal composition but also skill of another sort—a performative imagination through which character could be imagined and portrayed" (253). Because orators must embody a range of emotions to win over their audiences, rhetoricians have long recognized that acting and speaking are, perhaps, the same skill in different guises.

As is well known, character acting is based on cultural stereotypes: how certain types of people act, what they look like, how they sound, what they wear. Rhetorical performance influenced theater in the Middle Ages because lawyers had become so skilled at character acting (Enders). Known as *ethopoiia,* this skill was foundational to courtroom proceedings, where attorneys "became" their clients during oral arguments in order to dramatize their clients' actions. In the Middle Ages, lawyers donned elaborate costumes and carried props to enhance *ethopoiia,* but in most rhetorical performances, including preaching, such embodiments of character type are performed with gesture, facial expression, voice modulation, and word choice. Both Enders and Fredal suggest that *ethopoiia* is, in miniature, what delivery is on the whole: that is, a presentation of the self in appropriate character.

However, in any treatment of rhetorical performance, rhetoricians must explore the ways that *particular* bodies are marked by public assumptions of character. Audiences come to expect particular behaviors from those performing public roles (as in the famous example of the café waiter in Goffman 75–76). Women who assume traditionally masculine roles face a series of double-binds, since those roles are entwined with behaviors that are, by definition, not "womanly." As Kathleen Hall Jamieson explains, throughout history, to be "womanly," (white) women must be silent or risk being viewed as gossips (*Beyond the Double Bind* 77–98). Even African American women, whose power is better recognized and celebrated within their own communities, have faced criticism that their leadership is somehow harmful to black men—and therefore unwomanly (Gilkes 174–75). When women put on vestments and stand behind the podium, they face a conflict in the art of delivery: What gendered behaviors can they show? Who can they be?

In order to refigure delivery as a central issue in feminist studies of rhetoric, it is necessary to recognize that delivery involves the physical and spatial exploration of the *boundaries* of character presentation within a cultural context. This definition expresses the fact that character presentation is necessarily bounded by cultural discourses of the body as well as by material space. In order to understand what it might mean to refigure "delivery" in terms of the female body—as well as the gay, lesbian, and bisexual body—it is necessary to consider physicality and space together in the study of rhetorical performance. For two women preachers in my study, delivery was based upon the fundamental assumption that intimacy, not distance, offered the greatest power to them in preaching. Therefore, they took their female bodies for a walk that moved them from the pulpit, "God's throne," to the floor and up the aisles to get closer to their people. Yet by hovering in the borders between the pulpit and the pew, they were "absent the proper" in their performance in more ways than one.

Background for the Study

In college, I was one of the many evangelicals who took the Canterbury trail, as Robert E. Webber has put it.[3] I spent the fall of my senior year exploring liturgical churches and, after a memorable three months of visiting Episcopal, Greek Orthodox, and Lutheran churches, found St. Paul's Episcopal Church in downtown Canton, Ohio, an old stone church with a socioeconomically diverse congregation and vibrant social mission. When it was time for me to explore the ideas that led to this ethnographic study, I went back to the Episcopal Church, a tradition that removed the roadblocks to women's ordination in 1976. The church in my new neighborhood had recently called an associate woman priest, Rev. Jennie Cox, the first woman I ever heard preach. For a year prior to my study, I explored the "habitus" of Cox's ministry in order to formulate some questions and to become aware of the factors in myself, this rector, and the congregation that would become important in an investigation of a woman minister's rhetorical performance.

As I got to know Cox, I also befriended the young male rector at this church and through him learned about Rev. Patricia O'Connor. O'Connor attended Harvard Divinity School and for one year lived in the dorm of the Episcopal Divinity School (also in Cambridge) because she lost out on a lottery for dorm rooms at Harvard. Jon Edwards was in seminary at EDS that year and got to know her. He played basketball with her and knew her husband, his classmate at EDS. My field notes to myself about a conversation with my rector include a telling (and typical) line: "He says she is really cool." So with a private recommendation of Patricia O'Connor's character, I was led to St. John's Lutheran Church. After calling to make sure O'Connor was preaching, I drove there on a scouting mission on Sunday, May 6, 1990.

The drive to St. John's Lutheran Church is a pleasant one, but especially in the month of May when the pink and white dogwoods are in bloom. The lawns of Irvington, one of the wealthiest suburbs in this Midwestern city, are deep green and well groomed, chemically induced but nevertheless a happy contrast to the straw-colored lawns of the gray-brown winter. The church is a handsome brick building, set well back from a major thoroughfare and partially hidden from view by enormous maple trees. One drives to the top of a hill, along a long sloping lawn, to reach the church parking lot. The neo-Colonial style of the homes is reflected in the white church steeple, which reminds me of the two-hundred-year-old church steeples in New England. After the church service, one could drive two blocks to a new, upscale one-story mall and drink very good coffee and window-shop at expensive boutiques. I wrote my field notes on a marble bistro table in a coffee shop there and felt unusually tony during the three months I devoted myself to understanding O'Connor's rhetorical art.

The sanctuary was very large, providing seating for over six hundred people. The pews were well padded and arranged in three sections with a wide aisle between each leading to the front of the church, where raised up on a platform was the pulpit to the left and the lectern to the right. The pulpit was typical of twentieth-century Protestant churches: wooden, barrel-shaped, and large enough to hide all but the head, shoulders, and chest of a person of about six feet in height. The choir was seated along the back of the platform behind the pulpit. The altar was on the floor in front of the first pew, centered between the pulpit and lectern. The pews were elevated, so that if one were seated in the back row, where I often sat to get a good view of the entire scene, the minister was actually down below. While large glass windows were placed along the wall in the foyer, there were no windows in the sanctuary and no adornments to speak of other than the cross on the wall behind the choir. Nevertheless, the church clearly had money: the sanctuary was less than ten years old, paneled in wood throughout, with tasteful co-ordinating earth tones on the carpet and pew upholstery.

Even from the elevation of the second-to-last pew, I could see that Patricia O'Connor was a small person. Her short black hair had a bit of natural wave, and she had a fair complexion, dotted with freckles. She looked to be athletic—or at least naturally gifted with compact form—but would have had to have real speed to play basketball with my own rector, who was a mountain at six feet four inches. Thirty-some-thing, she smiled unself-consciously, her eyes simultaneously glittering with mischief. When she gave the announcements, she teased congregation members in charge of the special events she promoted, and she laughed without a hint of artifice. She wore floor-length vestments, but she walked halfway up the aisle and got down on the floor to be eye-level with her miniature parishioners during the children's sermon. I instantly understood her connection to my rector.

That barrel-shaped pulpit was obviously not made for her—only her head and neck were visible when she stood behind it. During one of our interviews, she admitted that she had to stand upon a step stool, some-thing she had done throughout her nine-year tenure at St. John's. But during that first service she was seldom in the pulpit—just to read the gospel lesson for the day. She preached the sermon on the floor (that is, from the space below the platform in front of the first pew), with the sermon notes on tiny squares of paper in her hand. Her voice was not dramatic—she was a matter-of-fact sort of preacher whose voice modu-lated up and down only a few decibels and whose tone did not waver much from her announcement voice. In musical terms, she had the voice of a second soprano: neither as deep as an alto nor as high as a first soprano. She spoke in relatively short sentences and had the accent of a Midwesterner. She reminded me of a tomboy, a woman more at home in Converse sneakers than skirts (which she wore). I'm not sure if the impression was guided by her stature, her simple but animated features, or the fact that she plopped on the floor and illustrated a biblical prin-ciple using cartoon characters. My impression was likely built on all of these factors as well as my knowledge that she played co-ed basketball in seminary.

On that first Sunday, I picked up some essential information from the middle-aged couple sitting next to me. Rev. Patricia O'Connor was "Pat" to the people, no matter what the bulletin said—no "Reverend" or "Pas-tor" and no last name. As associate pastor, she was in charge of the children's ministry. Normally she didn't preach very often, but St. John's "main" pastor (their words), Rev. Harold Mosely, was away for the summer on sabbatical. Pat would be leading the Sunday worship until August. I later learned from Pat that Mosely had led the church during a period of rapid growth and expansion, a reflection on the growth not only of Irvington but also the city as a whole. Full of young professionals, the two-thousand-member church had outgrown two church buildings during Mosely's tenure (the current church building was the third). I was not destined to meet the Reverend Mosely, because my fieldwork ended before he came back from his sabbatical. He left Pat, his associate, in charge for one rare summer, a summer in which she could stretch into the rhetorical space of St. John's and build a preaching style that was underdeveloped from too infrequent opportunities to preach. Beginning two Sundays before I arrived for my fieldwork study, Pat had begun to explore a full-time, full-access relationship with her congregation—on her own terms.

"He"

When Pat arrived at St. John's for her internship nine years prior to my study, she quickly learned that Reverend Mosely's ministry was marked by the power of his person, which included comfortable, authoritative distance from his parishioners. He spoke in what Pat called a "stained-glass voice," a form of "forbidding authority" that she associated more with men than women preachers. His belief in his own power was evident in the structure of this very large suburban church. Pat explained, "He thinks that he is in a one-minister church." In the pastor church, one minister holds the church together, typically attending every event and being solely responsible for the community. In the staff church, this responsibility is spread out among committees, laypersons, and at least two pastors. Pat explained that many people "shopping for a church" will look for a church with good programs first and good ministers second. Persons shopping for a pastor church will not find extensive programs; their interest is primarily in the minister's personality and the community. St. John's was a staff church—many young families maintained ties with the church primarily because of the youth ministry. But it had been a pastor church for two decades, and Mosely was unwilling to make the transition. Pat was placed into a position as the pastor in charge of youth ministry, Christian education, and outreach. Churches often solve the problem of being male-centered by giving the position of director of Christian education to a woman, generally a layperson or deacon (Maitland; Nesbitt). In this way, women leaders are out of sight on most Sundays and are not in the still controversial position of teaching men. Because of her position, Pat was not completely out of sight, but her opportunities to preach on Sundays were much diminished: Mosely refused to allow Pat to preach more than 25 percent of the time and never during holidays when attendance was highest. Pat preached about every fourth Sunday, a problem, she said, in building a Sunday morning relationship with the community; in fact, she reported having more than one argument with the senior pastor about this arrangement.

During our first interview, Pat's telephone rang, and she listened to the caller, responding "Fine, fine" or "No problem" after long pauses. When she hung up, she laughed and said, "Ah, that was Harold—he misses us." Then she rolled her eyes, smiled, and told me the story of her introduction to the culture of St. John's. She served as an intern (the last step before ordination), the first woman most of her parishioners had heard preach. She quickly learned that Reverend Mosely was referred to around the church office by secretaries as "He" or "Him"— not by name. The practice was as odd to her as nurses referring honorifically to doctors as "Doctor" when speaking to patients, as in the phrase "Doctor will see you now" as opposed to "*The* doctor will see you now." Soon she learned that this practice was not used by the secretaries without a hint of irony, and so she took on the language as a kind of humorous defense against his masculine aura. Whenever Pat referred to Reverend Mosely in our interviews, she maintained this pronoun-referenceless game, always punctuating "He" with higher voice pitch, a pause, and raised eyebrows as though the word were capitalized and in bold print.

While I did not meet Reverend Mosely, everywhere there was evidence of his leadership style. For example, I was in the habit of attending the adult Sunday school class and both services that Pat led each Sunday. On the first Sunday I attended the adult class, Pat was still struggling to move the class beyond the lecture format that Mosely favored when he led the class. The class was studying the Lutheran Church, and the issue that day was the ordination process, a topic in which Pat had plenty of experience. The class met in a large multipurpose hall with a kitchen set up in the back where several class members served coffee and donuts to participants. Approximately seventy chairs were set up theater-style, with a lectern set up for Pat in the front. Thirty-seven people were present. After everyone was seated, Pat began the class by explaining the schedule for the next few weeks and then introduced the day's topic. She added, "Now then. Last week I talked too much. So this week I am going to make you talk." Then, after joking around a bit about the rain-out of a local golf tournament, she asked a question to get the ball rolling. There were long, uncomfortable pauses between questions, so Pat gave a brief presentation followed by more questions. The class seemed to perk up when they could ask Pat the questions, putting her back into the position of the One-Supposed-to-Know. The class pulled Pat into a hierarchical relationship, protesting the opportunity to enter into a full dialogue by reluctantly participating or refusing to answer when Pat asked open-ended questions.

Because Pat clearly had far greater experience with the process of ordination than anyone in this group, I wondered if the class was perhaps being pragmatic by waiting on Pat to offer them her wisdom. But in an interview the next day, she explained that this adult Sunday school class was "Harold's class" (eyebrows, punctuated voice pitch) and that she had had trouble getting discussions going from the beginning. Before he left, Mosely told Pat that he had "good discussions" with the class; however, during one visit, she noticed that in fact "He" did all the talking. She said, "Harold perceives more goes on than really does," which became clear to her by their attitude toward discussions: "They aren't used to speaking," she said. However, she knew that many people in the congregation wanted alternative formats to adult education. In her capacity as the director of Christian education, she had sent out surveys to find out what kinds of programs the congregation was looking for; adults wanted more topics on spirituality and some classes devoted entirely to "sharing and discussion." Pat wanted diversity in Sunday school programs; she said, "I want more folks to come to Sunday school and find a place for themselves." However, such a system introduced in "Harold's class" met with discomfort and resistance: the adults wanted a lecturer.

The stoicism of this class was reflected in other interactions I had with the congregation. During the time I studied the church, I was never greeted by anyone other than an official greeter at the end of the service and during the sharing of the peace during the communion service (an obligatory handshake followed by "Peace be with you," part of the liturgy in the Lutheran Church only on the first Sunday of every month when the Eucharist is celebrated). On the seventh Sunday I attended the church, I was finally greeted by members sitting around me in the first service, but this never happened again. One day when I attended "Harold's class," I stood in line for coffee and found myself in the midst of a conversation carried on by a huge man who looked over my head to the woman behind me. Though I was in their way and visible to both, they did not acknowledge me—it was as though I were nonexistent. When I mentioned my observation that her congregation members were reserved, she said that that was a legacy of the size of the church (approximately eighteen hundred members, with an average attendance of six hundred on Sundays) but also a larger problem with this congregation's view of its position relative to Reverend Mosely. They did not act as a community because the church revolved around the cult of "His" personality. Put another way, they considered themselves self-sustaining individuals working on their private relationship with God through the authority of their clergy.

But was Reverend Mosely's style of leadership a generational or a gender issue? When I first asked this question, Pat postulated that it was both. For example, in one interview Pat explained the importance of preaching from your own personal experience. She reported that Mosely and men of his generation (women were not ordained in the Lutheran Church until 1970) were trained to not expose their personal lives in the pulpit. Once she attended a seminar titled "Preaching from Commitment" in which half the seminar participants were from the older generation of preachers. They were being taught to use narratives—not necessarily personal stories, just stories. But the older preachers (all male) wouldn't do it; they were too uncomfortable with the style. Nevertheless, after recalling this example, Pat paused and reconsidered. She remembered the sermon of a guest preacher at St. John's—a young man in his twenties who had grown up in the congregation and preached one Sunday while home from seminary. The congregation knew of harrowing personal tragedies in this man's life, including an accident that left him partially paralyzed. There he was, she said with exasperation, sitting in his wheelchair, preaching about God's comfort in times of trouble. But instead of offering his own life to illustrate the text, he chose to tell a story about how *he* had comforted a woman who was dying, therefore placing himself in the position of being God's instrument. Pat disagreed with his choice of illustration on two grounds: that he set himself up as the hero of the story, which was "a typical male way of doing it," and that he neglected an opportunity to provide a more poignant and meaningful illustration based in his own experience of suffering. Pat lamented, "Even the younger guys aren't using their own experiences. You don't get this sense that sin, feeling grace, etc., is talked about as something *they've* experienced."

She contrasted this story with her own practice of telling stories about herself that put her at the same level of the congregation.

> People will say, and I think you will find in my sermons, too—it seems to be a gender-specific thing—that when we [women] preach, we will use "we" or "I" when we say, you know, "I have a difficulty sometimes" or "Sometimes I find it difficult to pray and find God near and you might, too." I think it's just a different way. We'll do that. We'll see ourselves as part of this whole group and part of this whole process that's going on. And I think also we're more willing to use some—not entire stories—but some things about our own lives that make people feel like, "Oh, yeah, that's the same experience I had that the pastor's describing. That relates to *me*." *They can feel the back-and-forth.* I've had a number of people tell that to me. And they say it's different as opposed to other people, and it's not like other preachers. Men, especially older men, are just like—or younger men say it, too—"This is how you feel." There's

a little bit of remove. A distance, a space between male preachers and the congregation. For the most part. And female preachers— and me, I don't know about the rest of them—and the congregation have less distance.

It was not so much that the young men she knew didn't tell stories; the problem was they tended to tell stories that placed themselves in the position of authority. In the process, they set themselves up in a position to tell others what they feel, by using the second person: "This is how *you* feel." By preaching this way, she suggests, there is "[a] distance, a space between male preachers and the congregation."

We can return to Austin Phelps for the precedence for this rhetorical approach. Despite living and writing in a romantic era that privileged the experience of the individual, Phelps argued that "[t]he general habit of the pulpit respecting things personal to the preacher must be that of silence" (*Theory* 226). In accordance with his overall view of character, Phelps continues:

> [The preacher] needs the power of person which personal introductions are aimed at; no man needs it more: but he has certain advantages for gaining it which lie back of the pulpit. His personal character is known to his hearers: it may be presumed to be favorably known. His reputation for intellectual ability speaks for him. His known history as a man of culture, as an *alumnus* of literary institutions, speaks for him. His reputation for piety precedes and introduces every sermon that he utters. Fortunately for every individual of the clerical order, the order as a whole has an accumulated history of qualities which commends it to the respect of men. That history is a common fund from which each one may draw, for his own use, of the power of person, till he does something which proves him unworthy of it. (*Theory* 226–27)

The theory of rhetoric underlying this approach is that offering personal stories from the pulpit cannot *improve* the relationship that one forms with the audience. On the contrary, personal experience may do a great deal to harm the "power of the man," which is essential to remaining in the community of "the clerical order." Another way of looking at Phelps's logic is that a preacher who fits in with the congregation's imagination of "the clerical order" may have a great deal to lose by revealing the self, whereas the preacher whose reputation is in question may not.

The young man about whom Pat expressed exasperation made a brief reference to himself in order to show himself to be authoritative—the Physician, the Comforter—in times of trouble. But for Pat, what was needed in this case was greater *intimacy*—drawing the congregation nearer by revealing himself to be like them. Her argument reversed

Augustine's famous metaphor: the preacher should not consider himself to be the *Physician* but rather the *Patient* when searching for illustrations. She was so adamant about the young preacher's missed opportunity and the implications of gender in it that I realized that for her, the development of character in the pulpit was closely related to the ability of the preacher to "stand with" the audience through strategic personal revelation. Her theory of preaching was based on a form of populism: gaining right of entry to leadership through revealing similarity to the people, not difference. It was an act of seeing herself "as part of this whole group and part of this whole process that's going on," an act of standing-with.

I will dwell more on the nature of "story" in feminist preaching in the next chapter, but to give some idea of how Pat translated her theory of preaching into action, I will focus on her use of the personal in two sermons: "The Dark Side of the Force," the first sermon she preached at St. John's, and "From Cradle to Grave," preached several years before the study, both of which were preached from manuscripts. In "Dark Side," Pat includes a long story about her difficulties with a supervisor of a work-study opportunity in seminary, whom she and some fellow students had nicknamed "Darth Vader," and her growth in learning to appreciate him. Near the end of this long personal narrative, she reveals, "I, for one, was startled by this turn of events. I preferred neat, definite lines to this blurry, messy situation. [. . .] I tend to, and I am more comfortable with, putting things into neat categories, polarizing, drawing up strict dichotomies." This admission in her opening sermon for this congregation, preached while she was merely an intern (student) preacher, directly contradicts the advice of George Campbell, who cautioned young preachers not to compromise their authority by drawing attention to their deficiencies. Yet it is a strategy that draws the congregation nearer to her, because she reveals herself to be much like them.

In "From Cradle to Grave," Pat used her experience with pregnancy to underscore her personal struggles with death.

> I found that I have thought more about death in the past year than I have at any other time in my life. Oddly enough, awaiting the birth of my child was the occasion for thinking about death. I would count the months, the weeks until my due date, and then try to estimate how long after that it would take me to get back into shape (literally and figuratively).
>
> As I made my calculations it struck me, really almost with the force of a blow, that I didn't have that much time to keep getting back into shape. That chasing some ideal of physical fitness would in the end prove futile. I was getting older and not younger. And as I patiently counted the weeks and months to my due date (In-

dependence Day I called it—how little I knew), anxiously waiting for them to go by, I realized that these were weeks and months I would never see again. It was sometimes a bitter place to be. Death. That meant me, too.

Like the story in "Dark Side," this recounting of personal experience meets Pat's criteria for the use of personal experience in the pulpit: the experience should not display the preacher's moral and spiritual distinction from the congregation but rather reveal the preacher's *struggle* and therefore her participation in the everyday world to which she and they are a part. Both "Dark Side" and "From Cradle to Grave" also suggest that the great passages of a preacher's life (schooling, birth, and death) are strong sources of material for preaching, although the homiletic tradition discourages such use of personal experience.

Quitting the Pulpit

"Dark Side" and "From Cradle to Grave" were sermons that Pat preached from the pulpit, reading word-for-word from a manuscript. Yet they show a strong tendency toward populism in Pat's preaching that was finally fulfilled when "He" took a sabbatical in 1990. As soon as Reverend Mosely departed, she changed her delivery of the sermon. Setting aside the manuscript, she wrote notes to herself on tiny squares of paper that could be kept out of sight, and with these aids in the palm of her hand, she quit the pulpit. At first it was an experiment, a brainstorm born out of the exigency of the moment. Pat explained that there had been a tragedy in the congregation: several mothers lost their children in a traffic accident just before Mother's Day. She decided that focusing on the traditional themes of Mother's Day would be too painful for her congregation, so she focused instead on the importance of the community becoming a "home" in a broader sense. Titled "Better Homes and Gardens," the sermon was a great success. Women in the congregation told Pat that they were grateful to her for avoiding a narrow focus on mothers and families because of this tragedy. Pat explained to me that her original impulse to preach from the floor was born out of two rhetorical goals: to be closer to the people at a difficult time and to break down the lines of formality, which she found more appropriate for a sermon that involved a great deal of storytelling. She realized that moving out of the pulpit and standing with the people suited her style far more than remaining on her step stool in the pulpit. Thereafter, she returned to the floor each week.

In his section on delivery, Broadus dwells on the strengths and weaknesses of preaching from manuscripts, from memory (recitation), and extemporaneously (with or without notes). Like most homileticians,

Broadus favors extemporaneous preaching, on the premise that it affords the least amount of artifice: "As to the delivery itself, it is only in extemporaneous speaking, of one or another variety, that this can ever be perfectly natural, and achieve the highest effect" (462). But it is also very difficult to learn to do well, so Broadus offers many caveats to those who would try it (464–70). Moving from manuscript to "free preaching" involves a greater risk of failure but a greater reward because the preacher can gauge the effect of his words on the audience by seeing "the fire of his eyes [. . .] reflected back from theirs" (460).

I asked Pat why she made such a dramatic change in her method of delivery. She said:

> It allows me first of all to get out from behind the pulpit. And I've gotten a number of comments—this has been an interesting sort of experience. And people say they like that because they don't feel like I'm dictating from on high. But, I'm one of them—but not in the sense that we're all "buds" and that kind of thing—but that I'm like them. So I'm able to do that. And that's become real important to me. I never thought that this would be something I would enjoy. But I get to be right there with the people. So it's like we're kinda in this together, like brothers and sisters talking about the good news. The impact that our common Lord has had on our life. Not, "Well, hey, let me tell *you!*" So that's been fun. That's the first thing. The second thing is that I can look at people. I look at them when I'm talking. And I think that makes it a lot better. A third thing—and this has been kinda fun, too, and I don't mind—I'm able to, instead of having this formal presentation, I'm able to say, "Well, don't you think so?" or "Beth, were you here for that service?"

Looking her parishioners in the eye so that she could see herself reflected back, as Broadus suggests, is not the reason for Pat's departure from the pulpit. Such a focus puts the emphasis on the performance of the sermon, in gauging the effectiveness of one's words on an audience. Instead, Pat is interested in fundamentally changing the nature of her relationship with the congregation—and therefore the relationship of members of the congregation with each other—through the act of preaching.

As I began to settle into my routine of attending both services and Sunday school at St. John's, I learned to rely on the church's audiotape for the sermons but on my field notes for everything else. Because the church did not have a tape ministry, as so many other churches do (providing a way for shut-ins to participate in the services), Pat slipped the tape into the church recording system sometime before the sermon began. In my field notes for June 10, 1999, I wrote, "Baby crying during announcements. Pat says, 'Ah, Jeremy, it's OK. He feels like I do—it's *early.*'" The next entry in my notes refers to the children's sermon, which Pat had titled "Teenage Mutant Ninja Turtles."

> Pat says, "Do you want to be a disciple—a Teenage Mutant Ninja Turtle? We are already disciples—Jesus's army of Teenage Mutant Ninja Turtles! Let's have an experiment—let's spread the love of God." She makes everyone—adults included—shake hands and say, "Good morning." She explains to the children that they are practicing being disciples.

These attempts to break down the formality of the service and to emphasize the responsibility of people for each other were carried over into her sermons for adults. But the delivery of her messages, which consistently relied on crossing a series of boundaries between pulpit and pew, was expressing a more complex message to her congregation.

In one of our interviews, I asked Pat to explain her method of delivery. She mentioned a moment in which she had asked a child during the children's sermon to explain what "geeky" meant. She laughed and said that she tried to get "a little bit of interaction" into every service. When I explained that I had seen her interact with individual members of the congregation in every sermon, she said:

> I try not to scare people out of their seats, but that's like fun. So I figure that's the one way it must have been in the beginning in some sense, when the disciples would get together and with a smaller group or whatever or even in larger churches with a pastor you'd have the faithful sitting there together. And you'd sit almost like you would for Bible study group or something like this, and you would talk. I like to teach, and people say I'm pretty good at that. That's the feedback I've gotten. So I got my sermons to be more of a blend of teaching and PROCLAMATION [says in a formal voice and then laughs]. *And it's* way *different from the way I was taught.* (emphasis added)

For Pat, "teaching," though associated with the discourse of authority, was fundamentally based on the seminar, in which a few students would "talk together" with an authority about their lives. Fundamental to that process was dialogue. This method of delivery was contraindicated by her training, which involved one homiletics class at Harvard. Her professor focused on the content of the sermon (preached from the pulpit), assuming that the sermon would be a proclamation based on the gospel message ("Christ died and risen to pay for our sins," as Pat put it). There was no emphasis on developing relationships with the congregation through the sermon, beyond the admonition to not "get down on people" during the holidays.

A good example of this practice of dialogue occurred in her sermon titled "The Priesthood of All Believers," excerpted here:

> *Pat:* We must stop thinking about the Christian vocation as something that's done exclusively by professionals and begin to think of every aspect of our lives, no matter how mundane, as the arena for ministry in the world. For example, in a few moments we're about to receive the offering that will be brought forward by ushers. We'll present it to God and then following that we will celebrate Holy Communion. Now let's see. Dale, how do you make your money? What do you do besides fix the church all the time? That's not for pay. What's your job title?
>
> *Dale:* Engineer.
>
> *Pat:* OK. He's an engineer. He builds things. Anita is a physical therapist.
>
> *Anita:* Lab technician.
>
> *Pat:* Lindsay, what do you do to make money?
>
> *Lindsay:* Pediatrician.
>
> *Pat:* She's a pediatrician. OK. How about you?
>
> *Man:* Account executive.
>
> *Pat:* Account executive. OK. Don't these sound like noble Christian vocations? Beth, what do you do?
>
> *Beth:* Nothing.
>
> *Pat:* You're a student, aren't you?
>
> *Beth:* Yeah.
>
> *Pat:* Who else can we pick on here? This is getting to be fun. How about guests? What do you do?
>
> *Guest:* Insurance secretary.
>
> *Pat:* Let's find another guest. Someone who doesn't work outside of the home. You've got a job already, Katie. Do we have any people who only work inside the home here? What do you do, Barb?
>
> *Barb:* Take care of children.

While an extraordinarily simple example, this dialogue takes place *within* the sermon form and therefore breaks the monological structure of the sermon. Pat performed this question-and-answer format while walking up one of the great aisles of the church, moving even closer to the people than she had in the opening part of the sermon. If we think about the dialogue in terms of delivery, we discover the preacher transgressing a sacred boundary in space with her body: she has not only refused to use the furniture set aside for the purpose of preaching but also moved in the midst of those from whom the space has been designed to separate her. She "violates" that sacred order even further by inviting the speech of others to mingle with her own during a time in which most mainline European American congregations are used to the practice of polite silence.

In rhetorical terms, the dialogue itself is working on two levels. First, it is a verbal acknowledgment of what Pat's body is expressing—that she is standing *with* the people and is fundamentally a part of the greater whole. This is an explicit part of her own art of preaching that she attributed to gender. But second, by interacting with members of the congregation and getting them to talk about themselves, she is building local knowledge of the community, which is an important part of drawing the members into greater relationship with each other and the community as a whole. In such a large congregation, with approximately three hundred in a single service each week, guests like me were virtually anonymous. Naming members of the congregation, bringing attention to them, built a mythos upon which the community could begin to form a sense of itself. Rhetoricians who study the role of stories in small and large group interactions have recognized that communities are built upon recurring stories about individuals and/or events; without such stories, which are passed along from individual to individual and retold at gatherings, groups have a poor chance of forming cohesion.[4]

Pat began building this mythos each week at the beginning of the service. The first event in the service was a ten-minute musical prelude, during which congregation members took their seats and quietly said hello to their friends. During that time, Pat stood on the floor greeting and talking to members as they took their seats. When the pianist or organist ended the prelude, Pat gave the announcements, a time in which her relationship with the congregation, which preaching manuals say must be earned *outside* the formal boundaries of the service, was both in evidence and being earned. In addition to announcing what was coming up that week at church, she shared stories about what had happened to her and to other members of the congregation during the previous week. If the service was particularly celebratory, Pat set a celebratory mood at that moment. For example, on First Communion Sunday, Pat acknowledged all the children and their relatives and explained to the rest of the congregation how hard they had worked in their catechism class (which she had taught). These announcements set the focus on the children and began a dialogue with them that was sustained throughout the service.

Like "Better Homes and Gardens," the sermon Pat preached on First Communion Sunday had its genesis in events centered around the community—in this case, the fifth-grade catechism students. The first event was the attendance of the Jewish father of one of the catechism students. Knowing he would attend, Pat decided to emphasize in her sermon the historic relationship between Christians and Jews, which for her meant emphasizing that unlike the Jewish people, whom God chose from the beginning to be God's people, Gentiles must be adopted by God through the act of baptism.

> Every one of us started out this life as a kind of orphan. In fact, we didn't belong to anyone and couldn't claim anyone as father or mother. We're sort of adopted in. God made the promise of cho-sen-ness. He called his people Israel and we're kind of Johnny-come-lately to this whole situation. It's our good fortune that God sought to include every one of us in this family and he has done that—adopted us and made us sons and daughters through bap-tism. Now I know that every one of you fifth graders and one sixth grader, Amy—she's right here [points to Amy]—have been baptized and it is through that action of baptism that you have become a part of the family of God [. . .].

Pat wanted the Jewish father in her congregation to know that the church considered him one of the original members of their family. Of course, no one but Pat and I were aware of this fact, but her hope was that this gesture of inclusivity would encourage a connection between his faith and his daughter's.

The second major event—and the one that gave Pat the idea for the sermon—was the answer one of her catechism students gave to the ques-tion, "What does baptism mean to you?" In the middle of the sermon, she stops and gives the student credit for his idea:

> There is another dimension that you fifth graders discovered, and this profound theology was in these three classes that we had with these kids: that baptism does something to your family. Not only do you have your own brothers and sisters, cousins, aunts, and uncles, but you've got a huge family out there and you could look around and you told me these are all of your brothers and sisters. This is a marvelous sense of the presence of God in all of the community of believers which you are a part of and are taking part more fully in today. I asked Rob before the service—where did Rob go? [pauses and looks around]—if I could quote and he gave me permission and this is perhaps the most profound theological thought about bap-tism that I've heard in a long time. [Walks over to Rob and his family and stands next to them.] I asked the kids what does bap-tism mean to you, and Rob says, "Look, I've got all these brothers and sisters." So for him baptism means that he is no longer an only child. Huge family. [Looks at Rob's mother, pauses, and smiles.] Don't worry, Margaret, we won't be over for dinner. [Laughs]

In addition to naming Rob, his mother, Margaret, and the lone sixth-grader in the catechism class, in this sermon Pat also refers to Bobby Jones, who was baptized in the early service, and a man named Wilson, who joined the church when he was in his seventies. She also returns again and again to the fifth graders, who are the explicit audience for much of the sermon, often with a touch of humor, as when she suggests later in the sermon that communion reminds Christians of sacrificial love: "Now hopefully I don't want to ever have to see any of you fifth graders in the news as going up in some big puff of smoke or being burned at the stake. God forbid that should happen!" By centering the sermon around the community and by naming individuals and groups at many points in the sermon, Pat draws the congregation and the message of her sermon into close relationship. The intimacy that is created by references to members of the congregation and by Pat's delivery reinforces the theme of the sermon, which is the nature of the relationships (between members of the congregation and between the group and other Christians across time and space) that are symbolized by the ritual of communion.

The Populist Preacher

Pat's tendency toward populism and intimacy with the congregation comes more into focus when we consider her overall purpose for preaching: to develop a consciousness of community in her congregation. For her, the community was the local congregation, acting as a family with responsibilities and concerns for its members. At the same time, the community was connected with the "priesthood of all believers" that was neither bound by time nor by place. She taught the children this principle in "No More Orphans" and the adults the same principle in "Better Homes and Gardens." It was the main or secondary theme in all the sermons I heard her preach during the three months I spent at St. John's. The message is perhaps nowhere better illustrated than at the end of "No More Orphans":

> I have to admit, parents, we had a talk and we plotted before we came here today that one of their first acts of self-giving was that they decided that they were not going to hassle you about what they were supposed to wear today and they were simply going to go along with whatever the parents wanted. [Scans the congregation for the parents.] How did it go this morning? Pretty well? [A few parents nod.] I know for some it was pretty good. Now in fifth grade, that's a mighty big act of sacrificial love. But it's those kind of things where you fifth graders but also you parents and the rest of us give way to one another so that we can know the peace that

God wants. *And one final thing: never, never live your life just for*
yourself. You will never know the wholeness or the joy or the ful-
fillment that God wants for every one of us if your life is only de-
voted to yourself. (emphasis added)

By itself this theme is not unusual in Christian doctrine. But as the *pri-*
mary theme for a preacher who is not associated with social reform (as
in the sermons of nineteenth-century abolitionists), it is quite unusual.
The art of preaching throughout the centuries has concerned itself with
the private salvation and regeneration of individuals, not with the relationship of congregation members with each other. The audience for the
sermon throughout the tradition is characterized theologically as sinners
or saints, with the focus of preaching centered on salvation and right conduct. Nevertheless, for Pat, the primary focus of all her work was the
creation of Christian community at St. John's. For her, this primary goal
would bring about the regeneration of individuals in a far more powerful way than a focus on a private relationship with God.

This emphasis on community is most apparent in two sermons: "Back
to the Future" and "Three, Two, One." Arranged inductively, "Back to
the Future" announces the main point near the end of the sermon: "I
think that we need to let God's Spirit shake us awake and bring us back
to God's future." The rest of the sermon turns on a series of stories. The
first two stories are about one of Pat's college friends who used to dress
up every Sunday as though he were in "Charles Dickens's England" in
order to preach. The next story is about Pat's nostalgia for the late nineteenth century in western Europe. These three stories are then followed
by a dramatic retelling of the Scripture text about Pentecost. The apostles
were sitting around longing for the good old days when Christ was
among them, and they longed for a future day when he would return
and "take care" of the Romans and place Israel in its rightful place
among nations. But then came Pentecost, and suddenly they realized that
they were the future, that the kingdom was already at hand among them.
Pat announced the problem: their longing for the past made them unable to live out the dreams God had given them.

The next story was about the St. John's community. Pat and a group
of fifth- and sixth-grade students from the church went to a food pantry to clean. The children were very enthusiastic, but an older man at
the pantry told them they shouldn't bother with the work because it
would be dirty again within a few days; he punctuated his remarks by
adding, "People don't give a damn around here." Pat said, "They [the
children] were simply pitching in where they needed to do work, and I
thought, if the dreams and visions of these young people could only
rekindle the fire in that old saint." Her last thought was that the community was the future that God had in mind (and implied was the idea

that some people in the community—like the old man—needed to get back to the future for which they had abandoned hope). Pat's stories built toward and illustrated her main point, but the effect was interesting insofar as the sum total of the stories added up to far more than what she stated in her conclusion. For instance, she never said anywhere in the sermon that she and the children were an example of what the community should be, a point that was more powerful because it was left unstated. The children were a nonthreatening example of this principle of community at work.

In "Three, Two, One," Pat parlays her emphasis on community into a message about the fundamental equality of the sexes. Throughout our conversations together, Pat shared with me her exasperation over the Lutheran Church's failure to validate women's experience. At one point, she pulled off her bookshelf a recently published book on Lutheran doctrine and read from it advice on inclusive language.[5] The author wrote that inclusive language shouldn't be a problem in the churches, because men are ontologically inferior to women. Pat was furious with this eliding of the issue, explaining that it was simply the flip side of the essentialism men had used for centuries: that because women bear children they are closer to the earth, and because men don't, they are closer to God. While Pat advocated the use of "Father" to name God in corporate worship, "because that's what Jesus taught us to say," in catechism class she taught children to use whatever form of address would remind them of a kind authority figure. She noted that the term "Father" doesn't fit for children whose fathers have left home, don't pay child support, or abuse them; for them, she suggests, "Mother" or "Teacher" is sometimes better.

Throughout her sermons, Pat used stories of women, emphasizing equality and women's unique experiences, often drawing on her own experiences. "Three, Two, One," which Pat preached on Trinity Sunday, emphasizes the nature of community within a sermon emphasizing basic Lutheran theology.

Today is Trinity Sunday and probably one of the more difficult to apprehend concepts in the Christian faith. Jonathan and I have really good friends. In fact, they're the godparents of Anna and Lucy [O'Connor's children]—even went to my divinity school but decided not to go into the ministry but to pursue the greener pastures of a real estate brokerage in Chicago. Now his wife Carol, or soon to be wife Carol, had been a child of a naval officer and spent her youth traveling from place to place and hadn't had a lot of foundation in Christian teaching. We'd had them standing up here for Anna's baptism and reciting the creed as we do at our baptisms, and only a year later when it came time for us to do their wedding did we discover the awful state of Carol's theology. She said she had some problem with the marriage service. It was an Episcopal service, so I could understand that [smiles ironically]. I thought, what could it be? She's a fairly liberated person. Could she perhaps have problems with sexist language? But no, the Episcopalians are just as trendy as we are. I'm sure they had inclusive language. So what could it be?

So we sat down the night before the wedding, Jonathan and I with Carol and Jeff, Jeff looking real nervous, saying, "Well, Carol has a few things to ask about," and Carol in her straightforward way said, "I just have a problem with all this language about the trilogy. I just don't understand the trilogy." At which point my jaw hit the table, because she didn't want us to use any of this trilogian language during the wedding service. I'm not the best or calmest apologist for the Christian faith, and I just said, "But we have to!" and that was my whole argument for the Trinity. Jonathan being a little bit more calm was able to explain it so that she could understand it. And yes, we did perform a Christian marriage using the name of God in the Trinity. But I'll bet that she is not the only one who has spent time in church or who has difficulty with this concept of God the Father, Son, and Holy Spirit. It's one of the major things that divides us from the Muslims in fact. We all have the same God. They revere Jesus as a prophet in the faith. They just can't understand why we get into this polytheism. And it's one of the things that makes it most difficult for our seventh graders, and we run up against this in catechism when we try to explain this idea of the Trinity. You have to admit, it's almost more than we can wrap our minds around. It's probably one of the most difficult doctrines of the Christian faith, but the Trinity Father, Son, and Holy Spirit is the name we Christians have for God, and it is the way that God has made himself known to us, especially in Scripture, so we're kind of stuck.

The lessons for today, all three of them, are very helpful when we talk about God as Trinity, and they help us to understand how we have experienced God and how God comes to us. I won't go verse by verse through each of them, especially since the Genesis lesson is pretty long.

[Turning to a member of the congregation] You didn't fall asleep through it, Lou, as you threatened to do. That was very good.

But the Genesis lesson is really a beautiful one. It's not the oldest account. That comes in chapters 2 and 3 when we hear about Adam and Eve and all that sort of thing, but this first chapter of Genesis was probably written when the people of Israel were already hostages in Babylon. They were far from their home. Far from Jerusalem. Far from their Promised Land where they had known God and known God's promises and way off in Babylon surrounded by these pagans who had defeated them, this is where they came up with this beautiful poem about God and about creation. It says something really different about God and about creation than any other world religion, and certainly far different from the Babylonians' understanding of gods. The Israelites believed that there was one God who was in charge of everything, and this God was the Creator God. This God was not himself created but had created everything else, and this Creator God had created everything out of nothing. Nothing existed before God. Everything that does exist now only came into existence because God spoke the word. So simply by saying the word, God brought everything into creation.

We hear that wonderful story where God says "Let there be light," and it says with that marvelous economy of language, "And it was so." Beautiful, wonderful, powerful creative words that God speaks, and we have this tremendous and mind-boggling creation around us. And what was it that God created? Well, it is our witness and testimony that God brought order out of chaos, and in fact that God can be understood as a God who brings order out of chaos. God is a god who wills harmony for all his creation. Or maybe if we leave musical terms, if we go to something in the textile arts, God made creation into a kind of tapestry, where each strand is also linked to all others. Beautiful in itself, but made more beautiful as part of the whole. That is how the creation works—in harmony as a tapestry.

And then we hear on the sixth day as the crown of creation that God created man or humankind in his image: "Male and female created he them." So here right away we have God putting together the absolute smallest unit of human community—a man and a woman. In that small unit we have everything upon which we build a greater community. There is all the diversity. Sometimes I'm not sure God knew what he was doing putting creatures so different as men and women together, but he must have. So we have diversity in this community. At the same time, we have mutuality. Male and female complement one another, and we have the beginning of responsible dependence, for these two depend upon each other and together they make one unit, and finally at the very end of the story it says that God saw everything he made, and "Behold, it was very good." This is far different from any other doctrine of creation in any other religion at that time and different from most every other doctrine of creation now. God looked at the material, spiritual world, and saw it as a whole, and said that it was very good.

We cannot split off the material from the spiritual and somehow say that one is better or superior to another. And we see when we do this, we get into all kinds of problems. This kind of division of the material from the spiritual is often used to create a hierarchy of human beings. Luther put it—his grasp of anatomy and philosophy was amazing, breathtaking! He said that men have wide shoulders and narrow hips, and therefore they're made for thinking, and women have narrow shoulders and broad hips, and therefore we're made for bearing children. So we can sort of divide our work that way. Where are men's brains in that case? I don't know. But this was used for centuries to say that those more closely tied to the earth are somehow less valuable or less worthy or not as close to God as those who spend their time in spiritual endeavors. God says, "No." All of it was good. The creation was good, and we can see the harm that we do to God's creation when we exploit it or see the material as only something for us to manipulate or use to our own ends. No. The earth is also a creature of God, and it is also good, and we need it as much as it needs us.

Well, now we have this understanding of God who created everything out of nothing, who brought order out of chaos. Who made male and female to be a mutuality in his image. Who created a tapestry of interdependence. Who blessed the material and said that it is part of the whole. We also have a God who works in history. That makes us a people with a history. We have a beginning. Everything has a beginning, and we say that that beginning is in God the Father, God the Creator, and this beginning is a continuity. It has something to say about our present, and it has something to say about our future, and when we look at all of this, we can see the whole—it is very good.

If we take a look at the second lesson, we can learn some important things about the way God acts in his creation, too. We have the Second Letter to the Corinthians that Paul writes and the part that we have is kind of tame. We skip over a lot of it. We have Paul referring to these people as his friends. He is saying, "Mend your ways. Take our appeal to heart. Agree with one another. Live in peace." It just really sounds like something you could almost put into a greeting card, but if you don't understand the way those people operated in Corinth, we miss a lot of the power where Paul was trying to get across to these people. Corinth was a wild town. Corinth is situated on the narrowest part between the two seas in this little wedge between the northern part of Greece and the southern part, and in those days, there was no isthmus. There was no canal through Corinth, so they would put these boats on logs and roll them across this narrow passageway and put them in the water on the far side. The problem was it took three days, so every time a boat came, there was a three-day shore leave for the crew. I mean, this would make Amsterdam look like a Sunday school picnic. It was an amazingly cosmopolitan town. People were there from all over the Roman Empire. These people found themselves very sophisticated. Very much in the know. Very much in control. They were very difficult people to talk to, and Paul has spent three chapters before this passage trying to reassert his authority to these sophisticated Corinthians who doubted that he, this itinerant Jewish tent-maker, could have anything to say to these people, the crown of Greek civilization.

It seems that these people in Corinth, like any other human beings, were impressed with power and performance, and they just didn't see Paul meeting the standards that they set. A lot of slick preachers had come through Corinth, and they were turning people away from the gospel that Paul had brought them from Jesus Christ. Kind of these button-down folks with blow-dried hair. [Gestures to a man in the front row in a button-down shirt.] Got to watch those people sometimes. [Winks.] [Chuckles from the congregation.]

I heard an interesting thing—we'll see if this holds true. There is a sports commentator who says there are too many baseball managers who are "sit-down media types." We need more baseball managers with names like "Stump." We'll see how well Stump Merrill lasts with the Yankees. I give him another week if he doesn't do any better. But here was Paul, kind of a Stump Merrill of preachers in Corinth, and he wasn't getting any respect. But Paul was trying to help these people understand that the power and the performance with which they were so dazzled was not the power and performance upon which they could depend with their very lives. And then he points to Jesus. How did Jesus act? How did he come into the world, first of all? God the Creator came as a tiny baby. God the Creator acted like a little boy.

We had a preacher at the Synod convention yesterday who reminded us that Jesus probably had his ears washed by his mother. Probably his father said, "Keep your hand off that saw, or I'll show you what it's used for, if you're not careful." Jesus was a human being, and how did Jesus end his life? Not by calling in legions of angels but by giving himself up. How did Jesus leave us? He was crucified. He was obedient unto death. He humbled himself. He was the perfect expression of God's self-giving, life-giving love. That is God as Paul wanted those people in Corinth to understand him. Not this slick, powerful, high-performance kind of preacher but a God who comes to us where we are and takes on our flesh, our condition, and redeems that through sacrificial love.

And then we get to the gospel lesson, which we almost didn't get to today, but fortunately we did. We get to the gospel lesson, and we have Jesus gathering his disciples. He's got them all together for one last meeting here, and he's telling them, Now, look, I want you all to go out there and tell the good news, and I want you to baptize people in the name of this God, who is Father. We have experienced this Creator. God the Son you've experienced as me. God the Holy Spirit who I give you and then we have the Spirit coming into our understanding, our apprehension, our experience of God. The Spirit which we know, as Luther says, calls, gathers, unites, and sanctifies the whole Christian Church on earth and keeps us united with Jesus Christ our Lord. That is the action of the Holy Spirit. We can't just have a relationship with God our Creator and be content with that. We can just understand ourselves as redeemed sons and daughters of God the Father, but we have to go out there and start building the community. That's what the Spirit does. It sends us out to tell more and more people this good news about a Creator God, a Father God, about Jesus who was one of us. That's what the Spirit gets us to do. So we're not worshiping three gods. We're not worshiping two gods but one God who comes to us in a number of different ways, always seeking us out to save us.

After we go 3, 2, 1, there's a way for us to go 1, 2, 3 to understand our relationship to this triune God. First of all, God respects our individuality and our uniqueness so much that he makes himself known to each of us in a personal way. Every one of us can say, "Yes, I have a personal relationship with God through Jesus Christ," and there is nothing wrong with it. In fact, if we don't say that, we're missing a whole lot. God wants each one of us individually, personally, to be in relationship with him, so God finds us. God creates us. God comes to us and God calls each one of us by name, especially in baptism. And salvation has come to each one of us individually.

[Puts hand on a woman's shoulder in the aisle.] Jesus died to save you, Ruth.

[Looks to someone else.] Jesus died to save you, Libby and Helen.

Jesus died to save every one of us, but it doesn't stop there. Jesus died to save the person sitting next to you today. Jesus came to call people who are sitting halfway around the world who we will never meet. Jesus calls us into this marvelous community of brothers and sisters all together, and so it's not just each of us but each other together who know and respond to God. And then we have each other and then God. It's the third part. This is what happens to us in baptism. We now share a common past. We now experience a common present. And we can look forward in hope to a common future. We understand that the Trinity used in the creed in baptism was one of the oldest ways for people to understand and be incorporated into the family of God. Now we baptize little babies. We can't reasonably expect them to make any kind of declaration of faith. That's why all of us as baptized brothers and sisters speak up for these little people when they're being baptized. We speak up on behalf of them and say we with you affirm that we believe in God the Father, God the Son, and God the Holy Spirit. And we make those new members part of our past, part of our present, and part of our future, just as God has made all of us.

That's our life in the Trinity. Relating to God individually. Knowing

each other as brothers and sisters and seeing the whole community relating to God as he promises to come to us and so we can be strength-
ened every day with this hope, with this assurance, with this constant
presence. And we can go out saying that the grace of our Lord Jesus
Christ and the love of God and the communion of the Holy Spirit is with
all of us all the time. Amen.

This sermon is interesting on a number of levels. Pat focuses her attention on the three lessons for the day, making clear she intends to teach
Lutheran theology. The personal story she offers at the beginning illustrates the difficulty of trinitarianism, a central Protestant doctrine. Because the story discloses Pat's failure to explain the concept adequately
to her friend, it also serves to connect her with the congregation. She is
going to teach, but she does not consider herself in hierarchy over them.
She offers historical background to gloss these passages, some rather
long and heavy with detail. In the middle of the sermon, realizing she is
losing her audience, Pat stops to make a joke about the Corinthians,
whom she says had been swayed by "slick preachers." She comments
that they are "button-down types," whom you have to watch out for,
and she gestures to a man in the front row who fits the image. After the
congregation and man in question chuckle at this joke, she goes on to
make an extended sports analogy, a move that renews her image as a
populist for those in the congregation who, like her, follow baseball.

The sermon confirms the evangelical roots of the Lutheran Church,
with its focus on the personal nature of religious belief. To underscore
this doctrine, Pat, who has been walking up and down the aisle throughout this sermon, stops to put her hand on the pew next to a parishioner
and applies this doctrine to her and to the women seated next to her.
This gesture and inclusion of dialogue personalizes the message, bringing it home to the representatives of the St. John's community in the
pews. But Pat is not satisfied to leave it at that. Pushing the message of
community that was central to her ministry, she affirms that to be
"saved" is only the first step in the life of a Christian. Salvation is not
more important, she suggests, than being part of a global community.

That being part of such a community demands justice and equitable
relationships is confirmed in an earlier passage, in which Pat stops to
dwell on the first creation story in Genesis. This powerful segment of
the sermon attacks the idea that the Bible sets up a hierarchy of men
over women, of the spiritual over the material world, of humankind over
the earth. Pat attributes these hierarchies to men like Martin Luther,
whose biblical interpretation was clouded by cultural prejudice. At the
center of the first Genesis story is the idea of community: "the absolute
smallest unit of human community—a man and a woman."[6] Commu-

nity is built upon the foundation of "responsible dependence," which is the alternative to hierarchies; men and women are mutually dependent upon each other, as are the spiritual and material worlds and human beings and the earth. In this passage, she offers a critique of the ancient equation of women's reproductive role with their debasement spiritually and intellectually, which has been so central to models of sexual difference (Laqueur). One is reminded of the words of Hal, the character in *The Temple of My Familiar* who was shielded from such doctrines on his island of escaped slaves: "'We had two spirit-called people, a woman *and* a man. It seemed right. Like you have two different kinds of parents, a woman *and* a man, you know'" (97). For echoed in Pat's doctrine is another hierarchy from which she was in the midst of walking away during the summer of 1990: the hierarchy of Reverend Mosely's "Him" over Pat's "her" and the distance between pulpit and pew that "He" embodied.

The Question of Character

In the end, a populist gains authority through reversing hierarchies and bringing unity and a sense of purpose to his or her people, and it was through this means that Pat was beginning to define what it might mean for her to earn a reputation as a "good woman preaching well." Her central goal was to create a sense of community at St. John's Lutheran Church; her overwhelming obstacle was the culture of individualism that Reverend Mosely had created in the congregation through twenty years of hierarchical leadership. It was not until the summer I attended St. John's that Pat had discovered the importance of walking away from the pulpit in order to find a better place from which to develop a relationship with the congregation. As this chapter witnesses, Pat was walking far into the spaces occupied by the congregation in the course of delivering her sermons, making her *sermo corporis*—her body's speech— tell the story of what she hoped would become of their relationship together. The intimacy created by her dialogues with individual members and by the proximity in which she spoke to those sitting in the pews powerfully underscored the message of community that she preached throughout the summer.

While this chapter is fundamentally about delivery, gender, and rhetorical space, it is also a case study of character. In the early days of my twelve weeks at St. John's, Pat told me that she did not consider herself to be a powerful person. She said, "It's impossible for me to believe that anyone would be intimidated by me. I don't have any aura of power or authority; I'm not a powerful kind of presence." And indeed, as my initial impressions of Pat suggest, I did not think of her as having what homileticians called "the power of person"—at least not in traditional, masculine terms. But later in the study, she admitted that her experience of leading the church by herself had changed her sense of her own authority.

> It's become clear to me in fact I do have an impact on people. Not that they're cowering, but I have some sort of power. It sounds weird, but I have a presence that they recognize that I would never accord myself. And I think that that's been real helpful to me, because I have no illusions about myself and can't imagine that anyone would put me on a level somewhere other than their own. I don't act that way. I don't know how other women preach, but that's one thing I think about my college chaplain, that she had a profound impact on my life and on the lives of other people. [. . .] But that was never a part of the way she saw herself operating with other people. And I'm pretty convinced that's how it is with me.

Pat's only model for how to preach as a woman came from the example of her college chaplain, who, like her, worked with students in her community "on the ground," at the same level. Pat was surprised to learn that her preaching was earning her a kind of power, although she was not seeking it and was explicitly moving away from the authoritative style of her senior pastor.

What Pat was experiencing was the general assessment of her congregation that her *character* was persuasive, interesting, and "good." She was well liked by everyone I spoke with, all of whom described her as "funny," "down-to-earth," and "unpretentious." Nine years after the start of her ministry there, they were beginning to accept her leadership and her agenda. Particularly for the families of the church who interacted with Pat over the years through her work with their children and who had the most direct "out of pulpit" knowledge of her character, Pat's venture into a more populist preaching style was welcomed as a delightful change. She knew their names and their children's names, and she emphasized an idea that they were endeavoring to teach their children: self-sacrifice and communal life focus. Her summer-long experiment ended, however, and Reverend Mosely resumed his monopoly over Sunday morning preaching at St. John's. Pat resigned a year later to assume the leadership of a church of her own in another part of the state. Nevertheless, she had momentarily changed the congregation's sense of themselves each Sunday morning as she transgressed the comfortable boundaries to which they had grown accustomed.

4

Engendering the Black Jeremiad

She don't preach like no man in a dress [. . .].

—congregation member

What the map cuts up, the story cuts across.

—Michel de Certeau, *The Practice of Everyday Life*

Narration is a form of spatial strategy. A storyteller creates new boundaries in old spaces, or builds skywalks between existing spaces, or razes buildings to create new frontiers. At its core, preaching is an act of storytelling. The preacher's narrative rearranges sacred space, removing barriers to form an enlarged "here," setting the barriers to a new "there." When the Eastside United Church of Christ called the Reverend Barbara Hill to lead them, narrative was a key strategy in her efforts to make a place for herself within the church and to make a place for the church in the world. Located in a lower-income neighborhood on the southeast side of town, many miles away from the affluent suburb of Irvington, the seventy-member African American congregation hadn't wanted a woman minister and called her only after the clergyman they had called abruptly quit less than two months into his ministry. Like many African American churches, Eastside was led by strong women members who were comfortable with the gender dynamics of a church headed by a man.[1] Immersion in Reverend Barb's early ministry at Eastside was a lesson both in the gender dynamics and distinctiveness of African American preaching. Reverend Barb set out to engender one of the central narratives of African American preaching, the black jeremiad, thereby creating a space for her dynamic ministry.[2]

The black jeremiad reverses a familiar trope in (white) American culture. Many European Americans have embraced the idea that they are God's chosen people and the New World is the Promised Land. In 1856, when Richard S. Storrs Jr. stood before the assembly of students at Andover Theological Seminary and declared, "We have to conquer for God and Christ the Master-Race, on earth, in history" (41), he drew upon this familiar jeremiadic tradition to rouse his audience. Wedding evangelism with imperialism, Storrs reminded the Andover seminarians of their clear superiority over all other races and civilizations and their obligation to take their faith and culture to the far corners of the world. Of course, to African Americans, the jeremiad is a hollow and hypocritical trope. America is not the new Israel but rather the new Egypt, and African Americans have compared themselves to the children of Israel, awaiting their deliverance. In her 1831 address, Maria W. Stewart predicted this event, arguing that the "ten plagues of Egypt" would rain down on the United States for persecuting African Americans (Raboteau 34–35).[3] The black jeremiad offers a different worldview, one in which the central narrative event is justice and deliverance from evil.[4]

At the time Storrs gave his address, the superiority of the white race was patent even to many white abolitionists, whose efforts in the American Colonization Society (founded in 1817) to repatriate freed slaves to Africa was resisted vigorously by a large number of black clergymen (Logan, "We Are Coming" 30; Raboteau 26–27). Acts of discrimination against free blacks in the North and the brutalities of slavery in the South were consistently surrounded by the discourse of white Christianity. So it is not surprising that beginning in the eighteenth century, African Americans began founding their own churches, alternative religious institutions, private societies, and oral traditions. The founding of the African Methodist Episcopal Church is a representative example of this history. Until the end of the eighteenth century, black and white parishioners worshiped together peacefully at St. George's Methodist Church in Philadelphia. However, the white members of the congregation voted to move all black parishioners to the balcony, including a distinguished member named Absalom Jones, then in his forties. During the service, while Jones was on his knees in prayer, white ushers sought to move him to the back of the balcony. He asked the ushers to wait until the prayer was over, but instead they forced him to his feet. In response, Jones and the rest of the black parishioners walked out in disgust. In 1794, under the leadership of Richard Allen, the black parishioners of St. George's organized Bethel African Methodist Episcopal Church and built the church building with their own funds. When local Methodist authorities claimed ownership of the property and white ministers demanded control, Allen and the church fought them all the way to the Pennsylvania Supreme Court—and won. In 1816, other black Methodists sent delegates to a conference in Philadelphia, and the African Methodist Episcopal Church was formally organized as a separate and distinctively African American denomination (Raboteau 23–24).

The experience of black women—both as congregants and preachers in black churches—has been mixed. On the one hand, scholars argue that the African cultures of free blacks and slaves were not, on the whole, as denigrating to women as European cultures. Women in West Africa operated within what Kamene Okonjo calls a "dual-sex political system," with a separate economic and political base that gave women power within patriarchal structures. There were many African queens in antiquity whose legacy of military and economic power are celebrated by womanist scholars as a separate tradition of African women's leadership (Gilkes; McKenzie). There is much evidence that in the slave quarters, women served as religious leaders, and many were highly valued for their skills in healing. Drawing on this evidence, Thomas Webber argues that there was a "remarkable lack of sexism" in the slave communities in the thirty-five years before Emancipation (149–50). After Emancipation, some freed African American men attempted to model the patriarchal family structures they observed among antebellum white families, but Freedmen's Bureau agents reported that they were vigorously resisted by their wives (Sterling 338–40). Cheryl Townsend Gilkes and Evelyn Brooks Higginbotham argue that this tradition of presumed equality and strength led black women to form separate, highly influential religious organizations even within denominations that refuse to ordain women, including the Church of God in Christ (an independent black Pentecostal denomination) and the National Baptist Convention, USA, Inc. (the largest independent African American denomination in the United States).

On the other hand, black women preachers have faced persistent discrimination from within their own communities. An early famous case of a woman who faced these prejudices was Jarena Lee, an itinerant preacher associated with the AME Church. Her 1836 autobiography is widely considered to be one of the first African American women's autobiographies and an early feminist statement on spirituality (W. Andrews, Introduction 2). Around 1811, Lee approached Richard Allen and asked for the right to preach, but Allen refused her, arguing that the AME Church did not permit women to preach. Eight years later, Lee was present at Bethel when a visiting preacher faltered in his preaching, and she took up the text and preached in his place. Allen publicly recognized Lee's calling to preach at that service, and Lee embarked on a long career as an itinerant preacher. The first African American woman to be ordained by any denomination was Julia A. J. Foote, a preacher in the African Methodist Episcopal Zion Church. She was seventy-one years old in 1895 when her lifelong career as an itinerant preacher was finally acknowledged by her denomination (Collier-Thomas 59). In her autobiography, *A Brand Plucked from the Fire* (1879), she makes a plea for women's equality and fundamental right to ordination at a time when first-generation white feminists and preachers such as Lucretia Coffin Mott worked for the same goals.

Black women have faced especially stiff resistance to ordination by black clergymen in many denominations, and the situation has not greatly improved, even though the AME Church finally called its first woman bishop, the Reverend Vashti M. McKenzie, in 2000. As Gilkes argues:

> The refusal of African-American churches, particular Baptist churches, to include women in ordained and authoritative leadership directly excludes women from participating in the decision making process affecting the communities in which they comprise the majority population. (205)

Gilkes blames the sexism of many black clergymen on the influence of European American gender roles in the black community (73). Why do we find such discrimination in a tradition that is otherwise invested in a narrative of liberation? Gilkes and Bederman argue that mainstream (white) culture creates a path of cultural supremacy for men that can be applied across class and racial boundaries. Bederman argues that in the nineteenth century, "African American [men] all understood that the only way to obtain civic power was through gender—by proving that they, too, were men" (21). They argued for their "manhood rights" (liberty, the right to own property, and suffrage) and encouraged each other to be "men" in their fight for freedom in the period before the Civil War (20–21). In organizing the AME Church, the Colored Methodist Episcopal Church, and African Baptist and African Pentecostal organizations, clergymen followed their white Protestant counterparts in banning women preachers; as Bettye Collier-Thomas puts it, "The right to preach was for many clergymen the last bastion of male privilege to be relinquished" (30).[5] Full rights of ordination came for women in African American churches about the same time they came for women in European American churches, which meant that at the end of the twentieth century, many churches had never heard a woman preach.[6]

Black Preaching

During the Civil War, homileticians such as Austin Phelps and John Broadus demurred on the issue of abolition or refused to address the issue altogether. In his address to the Porter Rhetorical Society, Phelps argued that sermons should be addressed to the individual and "not to the race as such" ("Theory" 15). Given the legal and social discrimination that faced both African Americans free for generations and those newly freed in the year that Phelps spoke these words, one rightly wonders what individuals Phelps had in mind. European American preachers and homileticians firmly mapped the course of preaching theory down a wide, white highway, far from the African American Protestants who founded independent denominations beginning in the late eighteenth century and who practiced an independent tradition of preaching. The white Victorian male who was at the center of the cult of manhood was sometimes magnanimous about cultural difference but still believed in his racial superiority and privilege. Homileticians to the present day have largely written for white audiences. "The most segregated hour in America"[7] has given rise to perhaps the most segregated rhetorical art in America: preaching.

Developed in the oral tradition and passed down through practice, not schooling, African American preaching has been called the central literacy event in many African American communities (Moss, *Community Text*). Although practiced by lesser-known African American women, the art has been monopolized and made famous by African American men. As an art, it has been associated with a far different rhetorical context than white preaching: it has always been organized around the needs of believers in persistent distress from daily oppression; as a result, it has been called "liberation preaching" (González and González). The theme of populism and the instinct for intimacy with the people that we see in the preaching of Rev. Patricia O'Connor is a documented part of African American preaching. As in the fictional example of Baby Suggs's preaching in chapter 1, it is also a tradition with deep instincts for the emotional needs of congregation members.

Although the importance of African American preaching had long been acknowledged, the components of African American preaching were not articulated in print until 1970, when Henry H. Mitchell's famous book, *Black Preaching,* originally his master's thesis in linguistics, was published. Mitchell traced the roots of black preaching in America to the influence of white revivalists such as George Whitefield as well as to West African culture, from which both slave and free blacks primarily descended. Mitchell attributes the singsong quality of some African American preachers[8] as well as the high emotionalism of most to the preaching of Whitefield and revivalists like him during the First Great Awakening (1726–50).[9] He attributes the dramatic storytelling that is the hallmark of African American preaching to West African culture (especially the Yoruba people). As Zora Neale Hurston, Melville J. Herskovits, and Arnold J. Raboteau have all pointed out, evidence of commonalities among New World Africans, from Brazil to New England, suggests that they melded their African traditions to the environments in which they found themselves. Especially influential were black preachers converted in the First Great Awakening. Among the first black congregations in the United States was an African Baptist church, organized in Silver Bluff, South Carolina, by Andrew C. Marshall and Shubal Stearns, both converts of Whitefield, just before the War of Independence (H. Mitchell, *Black Preaching: The Recovery* 33). Former Congregationalists, Marshall and Stearns were known for their highly passionate and emotional style, which became "the bridge over which [Protestantism] could travel to a spiritually hungry and brutally oppressed people from Africa" (34).

If it began as a hybrid of revivalist preaching styles and West African culture, African American preaching has become an art of its own. In his introduction to Mitchell's first book, C. Eric Lincoln writes:

> Preaching—good preaching—is vital to the traditions and to the satisfactions of the Black church. It is the spiritual *élan vital* around which the Black church is organized and from which it draws the peculiar nourishment by means of which it flourished and sustains a determined and long-suffering people. Preaching is also an art, and *Black* preaching is a *unique* art peculiar to the Black church. (*Black Preaching* 17)

According to Mitchell, there are two important principles of the art in the African American church. First, the preacher must declare the gospel to the community in the "language and culture of the people—in the vernacular." Second, the gospel must be articulated in such a way that it is relevant to contemporary African American culture (*Black Preaching* 29). For these reasons, the minister must closely identify with the congregation and the larger African American community (103). The context for preaching, Mitchell argues, is freer than in the white church, for "it accords a high importance to the feelings of the individual" (43). In religious practice, the minister and the congregation move in a dance of dialogue, the congregation "shouting" in a pattern of call-and-response to high moments in the sermon (45–50).

The sermon in black preaching has a formulaic structure, though a "free" one. Three components are important to the sermon: storytelling (especially dramatic narrative of a biblical event), African American idioms and language, and an emotional climax. The point of the sermon, suggests Mitchell, is the climax, "but the routes by which climatic utterance is arrived at are as many and varied as the preachers themselves and the various dialogues which comprise each of their sermons" (*Black Preaching* 178). A popular component is the animation of a biblical event, which Fred B. Craddock borrows to create his "narrative preaching." Mitchell traces the dramatic retelling of Bible stories to the oral tradition, arguing that the stories were made memorable for the people in part because many could not read those stories for themselves. By dramatizing the stories in idioms and situations, the preacher made them relevant to the congregation. This was the skill that drew Rev. Barbara Hill to the ministry; she said of her favorite preacher (an AME minister), "He made the Scriptures seem like Jesus was just sitting next to you. You could taste the dust in your mouth." The use of idioms, phrases, and language of the people (often called "code-switching" when intermingled with mainstream language) constitutes a form of dialogue that is reinforced in moments when the congregation lifts the preacher into the climax of the sermon through verbal feedback, often encouraged by the preacher through the pattern of call-and-response.

But there is little question that black preaching is a male art. Gilkes argues, "Preaching is the most masculine aspect of black religious ritual. Despite the progress of women in ministry, preaching remains overwhelmingly a form of male discourse" (129). Indeed, this point is reinforced by Mitchell's own discourse, which was not edited for the use of the presumptive masculine pronoun when Mitchell republished the book with a new introduction in 1991. In her preaching, Hill struggled against this tradition overtly, calling her congregation to a new identity that transcended both the racist environments around them but also the sexism within. She accomplished this task through a homiletics based in what I came to understand as a womanist narrative strategy—that is, a rhetorical emphasis on vivid narratives *(energia)* that reframed core beliefs about the self and the Other around the experience of black women.[10] Hill used her own experience in the application section of her sermons to reinforce her hermeneutics. To gain the assent of her congregation for her populist message, she often engaged in the frank speech *(parrhesia)* of the prophet outsider.

Background for the Study

I learned of Rev. Barbara Hill through the religion section of the local newspaper while doing fieldwork in St. John's Lutheran Church. Accompanied by an informant who coincidentally had known the large staff church where Hill began her ministry, I attended Eastside United Church of Christ on June 24, 1990. The church was located in a strip mall near a federal-assistance low-income housing development, across town and beyond the cultural imagination of the congregation at St. John's. The church was founded in 1975 after the United Church of Christ (UCC) determined there was a need for a predominantly African American church in the area. The first minister hired by the national church organization formed a children's ministry and a youth group; soon after, the denomination helped the congregation purchase a party house in the strip mall to serve as a meeting place. The party house had originally been built for a nearby apartment complex. In this space, the congregation set up a chapel with folding chairs in the one main room of the building, with offices and a fellowship hall in the basement below. During the summer, volunteers served lunches to children who qualified for a federal-assistance hot lunch program; this social ministry formed the core of the church's outreach to the neighborhood.

Sitting on folding chairs that first Sunday, I was struck by the size of the church: about twenty people were in the congregation, and only three of them were men. The congregation was a mix of ages and backgrounds, with many children and younger adults. Later in one of our interviews, Reverend Barb, as she was known to her people, said that she thought of the children as the "faithful members" who would eventually bring their parents. The youth choir sang with the adult choir, both of which were led by Reverend Barb down the aisle in a joyful procession at the start of the service. The first time I saw Reverend Barb, a tall woman with light skin and long braids, white vestments, and a kenté cloth clergy's stole, she was singing and clapping as she led the choir to the front of the church. There were no hymnals; the congregation stood and sang the processional gospel song by heart. In the middle of the service was a formal event called "Welcome to Visitors/Ritual of Friendship" in which visitors were asked to stand, the congregation clapped, and the chairs emptied out. I was greeted by everyone in the room, as were all the visitors. There were songs about perseverance: "I don't feel no-ways tired / I've come too far from where I started." During a spiritual called "Trampin'," Reverend Barb walked with the microphone through the congregation and asked individual children to sing the verses.[11] They were shy but Reverend Barb said, "Come on!" until they sang the verse in question.

The sermon was an extraordinary experience. Coming after a long pastoral prayer that brought the needs of individuals in the congregation into focus, Reverend Barb stood at the small wooden pulpit and read the biblical text that was the focus of the sermon. After she read, she said, "Pray with me for a few moments on the subject I'm defining," and then explained the context for the sermon. The sermon was built on a series of stories designed to illustrate her point. She preached the first part in her quiet, alto voice, talking in a matter-of-fact tone, behind the pulpit, reading from a manuscript but managing not to lose eye contact with the congregation. But as she preached, she became more animated, her voice speeding up and slowing down to emphasize points, her arms in billowing vestment sleeves gesturing to punctuate her thoughts or to animate a part played by someone in a story. Fifteen minutes into the sermon, she abandoned the manuscript and began to walk—first out from behind the pulpit, then in front of the pulpit, then slowly down the center aisle of the party house. She ended the sermon at the highest emotional pitch right in the center of the congregation, and then asked, "The doors of the church are wide open. Who will join the church today? Is there one?" The congregation members were already on their feet and clapping. She preached for thirty minutes, but the congregation was with her, one or two members shouting their approval at the end. It was one of the most powerful sermons I had ever heard, fulfilling the old rule to appeal to the mind and heart and to move the will with great power, yet the focus was not the individual and his or her private salvation but rather lifting up pride and hope through community identity—African American and Christian.

I did not realize it at the time, but that first Sunday marked the fourth week since Reverend Barb had been installed as the pastor of Eastside. She told me how that happened in our first interview. She started at the beginning, when she was a little girl: "Someone had died of cancer in [my] neighborhood, and I gave a little sermon on this lady—I laugh about it now. It was something that was in me that I didn't know, didn't acknowledge. But I think it had to have always been there." As an adult, Reverend Barb was a television reporter for several years until the station for whom she worked asked her to get rid of her braids. Never one to back down from her convictions, Reverend Barb instead quit her job and applied to Yale Divinity School. Her first job was as associate pastor at a large staff UCC church in the Midwest. When Eastside UCC needed a new pastor, they called the senior pastor of this church to ask for suggestions on job candidates, and he recommended Reverend Barb, his associate pastor. Eastside's search committee sent for her resumé and sent her a church profile but soon after sent her a letter indicating that they were not interested. "I had literally taken Eastside's profile out of my file and tore it up, and said, 'I don't need these people,'" Reverend Barb said. "When you are a woman looking for a pastorate, you get a lot of doors slammed in your face." And indeed, Eastside's predominantly female search committee decided that they did not want a woman.

But the man they hired for the position left after only two months, so the search was reopened. The search committee called Reverend Barb's senior pastor once again. He gave the same answer to Eastside: "You called me last year, and I gave you a name. It is the same name I'm going to give you this year: Rev. Barbara Hill. She's the best candidate I know." So reluctantly, the committee called Reverend Barb for an interview. But this time Reverend Barb had other options, including a large church in the South that had offered her a large salary to lead them (Reverend Barb said, "It was just like butter and bread, you know, it was a great, great bond"), and she was in no way interested in Eastside. Her senior pastor urged her to go to Eastside for an interview; he said, "Don't be like Jonah. God might be telling you to go." She flew in for the interview, was polite, but had already decided to take the other job. Nevertheless, the Eastside committee called her back for a second interview, and Reverend Barb reluctantly agreed. On the way to the airport,

> [i]t was early morning, and the sun was just shining on one part of a sign, and it said, EASTSIDE. I'd never seen that sign before! And it shook me up so bad, I almost ran into the overpass! And I said, "Well, I'll just be damned!"

She took the job.

While she was telling me this story, Reverend Barb invited Georgia, the church secretary and a member of the hiring committee, to join us to describe her first month at Eastside. I had just recalled a moment during her "back to school" sermon titled "What Are We Teaching Our Children?" when Reverend Barb had said:

> If you don't say anything about being African American, then nobody will notice, and in fact you know when you start listening to people and start talking about heritage and you have somebody that is brown as brown can be or blacker than the blackest bear, I mean *beautiful* black, they'll stand up and say, "Yes, my great-grandmother was Irish"! [Laughs.] "I belong to the First United Methodist Church and my great grandmother was Irish and my grandfather, he was pure blood Cherokee." Nothing about the African heritage. What is your little girl or your little boy who is standing there looking at you learning as you talk that stuff? And you're standing up there with your beautiful black self, [saying] "Yes, I'm half Irish." What is your little kid supposed to think with her beautiful black self and her nappy hair?

As usual, I had been the only white person in the room,[12] and at that moment a little girl turned around to look at me with wide eyes and pulled on her mother's sleeve and whispered. I told Reverend Barb I thought she must have said, "Momma, there's a *white* lady in this room!" Reverend Barb just smiled and began telling me about how uncomfortable it made the people when she talked about white people and how they shouldn't be like them.

When Georgia came into the room, Reverend Barb said, "Georgia, I want you to sit down here. I was giving a proposal."

> *Reverend Barb:* I was telling her how I talk about the white people, like I did on Sunday, and the little girl Latisha is worried and looked back at her with big eyes. I was telling her how I think the congregation, I think, is beginning to get more at ease with the way I am, because I can't change what I say, you know. I looked out and saw her and said, "Well, Roxanne, here you go!"

'Cause you know, I cannot change what I think the people need to hear. And I think most of the white people need to hear it, too.

Roxanne: Oh, yeah.

Reverend Barb: But I was telling her when I first came here I was really scared, I think after my first or second sermon—how many people said they were going to leave?

Georgia: Oh, about five.

Reverend Barb: We didn't have but about ten here!

Roxanne: So half the congregation wanted to go? What did you preach on?

Reverend Barb: What did I preach? It was—I don't remember. The first sermon was "I've Got a Feeling," and that wasn't, they weren't paying attention.

Roxanne: Ah.

Reverend Barb: "I've Got a Feeling" was on a Wednesday night. But on Sunday, it had to have been, I don't know what it was. But I know they were up-*tight.* And you know Bob? Our little white member? He was just sitting there. And Georgia was the one who called me. She said, "Now, I, I, I (you know how she talks), I, I, I just want you to know, well, ah, ah, that, ah, some people say they're gonna *leave!*" And I said, "Oh, God!" [. . .] And I was real nervous, because I thought, "Oh, God, they'll come back one more Sunday to, like, give me a chance, and then they'll be gone!" So the following Sunday, I only preach what the Spirit dictates to me. And the following Sunday, I'm not sure if I begged the Spirit to let me preach something else or what, because I don't think I preached anything, um, racial. You know, anything heritage or something like that. But the following Sunday, I was right back into it! [Laughs.] And I thought, "OK, here we go!"

Roxanne: So what was the turning point?

Georgia: I think it was the sermons.

Roxanne: Which ones?

Georgia: "Introduction of Myself."

Reverend Barb: "By Way of Introduction."

[. . .]

Roxanne: What did you do?

Reverend Barb: I introduced myself! [Laughs.] I basically said, "That's who I am. And in case you were wondering how it's going to be, let me tell you how it has to be, how I feel like. In order to be true to my God, this is what I have to do." I don't remember the Scripture or whatever. But I remember I prayed a very long time before I did that sermon. And I thought, "So here it goes." And then I did it.

Georgia: And it backfired, so whenever I would talk to people, and Lydia [another prominent member], too, and you know we would say to them, "If you've got a problem then you need to face yourself. You aren't where you should be. We need to be educated. And if you've got a problem with parts of the sermon, especially the part about your heritage or your blackness, then you need to begin to search your soul."

Roxanne: Hmmm!

Georgia: And you know, I said that to several women because I'm close to them, and I guess they kinda opened their eyes. Because it would appear that if I left I don't know who I am. You know, or I'm not willing to accept who I am. Also, the very positive way that Reverend Barb related her sermon was that this is who I am and I dare not let children grow up and not know who they are, you know. And you know, that just kinda touched people.

Reverend Barb: A lot of those sermons I don't remember what I said, I just remember the end [of "By Way of Introduction"], I just went around and shook hands with people and said, "Hello, this is who I am!" [All laugh.] I do remember that! I thought this might be the last time I'll ever shake anyone's hand!

The mass exodus that Georgia feared did not occur. At the end of each sermon, Reverend Barb invited people to join the church, and since then two or more members had joined each Sunday. From ten members in that first month, church attendance at Eastside on Sunday grew to between thirty-eight and forty-four members and visitors by the end of the four-month study.

Reverend Barb had two key character issues to work out during the beginning of her ministry. First, she had to overcome the prejudices of the community against calling a woman. In this African American church, the prejudice was complex. In a sermon titled "Defining the Church," preached three months after her arrival, Reverend Barb elaborated on the nature of this prejudice:

We need for the preacher to wear a clerical collar during the week and the right kind of robe on Sunday. If I were to preach in here without a robe, many of you would become uncomfortable. I daresay pretty soon somebody would start saying that I wasn't no preacher because I didn't dress right and that's not to mention the fact that God didn't call no women no-how. Many of us believe that a church is only a church if it has a male preacher and that male preacher has to preach right. I mean he's got to have his thing together. He's got to have the cadences and the move and the right tone of voice. Never mind if he never gets you to want to know

Jesus a little better. Never mind if he uses the same clichés over and over and over. Never mind if you can just about tell when he's about to holler and do his dance.

Later she came back to the differences in her style of preaching and that of the preferred African American male style:

Many of us don't believe we've got church unless the preacher fits the mold. When you go into these conversations with these male preachers, the question is does he hoot, and I don't hoot and I just be standing up there, I be listening to them, and I mean they do be doing it. [But I preach] my own little quiet talk—I never [preach like them] because that's not me. I just be practicing it because I think it's wonderful. Yeah, listen to them on the radio and they just be doing it, and I practice it because I think it's an art, but I ain't doing it.

In this sermon, Reverend Barb is painting a picture in frank language of all the preferences that go into "some people's" idea of church, including not only the sex of the preacher but also all the gender related, cultural stereotypes about his style of preaching. As Mitchell observed in his study, the cadences, shouting ("hooting"), and dancing are an old part of the tradition. Reverend Barb believed in producing an emotional "release" in the people during the sermon and occasionally shouted a "Glory, hallelujah!" at the end of her sermons. But she characterized her style as "talk" as opposed to what the tradition called "preachin'."

In addition to overcoming gender prejudice, she had to overcome the tensions created by calling the members to become educated about their African American heritage. When she wrote "By Way of Introduction," she realized that she had to start over and address the issue of her own character in order to build confidence in the community. In our interview, a tension arose between Georgia and Reverend Barb over how it was that Reverend Barb finally managed to win the character issue. Georgia took credit for calling people into account for their discomfort, but later she admitted that it was the honesty and self-disclosure in the sermon that "touched people." Georgia's relationship with Reverend Barb was a good one (Reverend Barb called her "my mama," though the women were not far apart in age), but ultimately Georgia was one of the strong women who served as a gatekeeper for Reverend Barb at the beginning (and later throughout) her ministry. After first opposing her, Georgia became a strong ally, protecting Reverend Barb and often expressing criticism of Reverend Barb's husband for not doing enough to help her. Nevertheless, in the end, Reverend Barb had to win over her congregation herself by taking on the character issue in her sermons.

"By Way of Introduction"

"By Way of Introduction," the sermon Reverend Barb preached on her fourth Sunday at Eastside, addresses criticism over the "heritage" messages she had preached the first three Sundays. The context was quite dire: down to ten members, Eastside could not afford to lose any more members. Nevertheless, Reverend Barb stayed on message, as we see in the following transcript of the sermon.[13]

Pray with me for a few minutes on the subject, "By Way of Introduction." There are two things which serve as the motivation for this sermon today. First of all, you will notice that I have returned at least partially to the Scripture we used last week from Isaiah, the Scripture which reminds the Israelites that not only should they not be afraid because of God's ever-abiding presence, but also which reminds them that they are precious in God's sight. That phrase stuck in my mind even as I preached last week, and I couldn't let go of it.

The second thing which is behind today's message is that this is the first Sunday, it happens to be the first Sunday in Pentecost, but it's also the first Sunday when we not only take in new members but we acknowledge publicly that we are *unashamedly black and unapologetically Christian*. Lord, didn't that phrase get some of y'all nervous the first time I used it. I got phone calls. People were ready to leave the church. People were concerned about me and worried that I might be offending some people who sat in here who are not African Americans. I've gotten other phone calls any time I've preached anything having to do with African Americans and Christians simultaneously, which, by the way, is what we are. I've been advised not to preach that stuff too often. I've thought about those things quite a bit, and I've decided to really introduce myself to you just so you understand who I am and what I have to preach, and I sincerely hope that you will not be offended and that you will understand and want to be a part of this ministry, which has to be African as well as Christian.

Let me start by asking you a question. Have you ever wondered—I know I have—but have you ever wondered how there could be a church on every corner in the city and still be so many lost souls in the world? How there could be a church on every corner and still be people who do not understand who they are or whose they are? Have you ever wondered how there could be a church on every corner and still be people who do not understand the power that we have within us to beat the odds in our lives and to be walking testimonies of his power?

Haven't you ever wondered how it is and why it is that Christian community so often pales in comparison to the Muslim's? When it comes to motivating African American boys to achieve and African American men to boldly walk towards the barriers put up for them in this Euro-centric world? It's almost as if there were a conspiracy going on to keep us weak and to ignore the real problems of the world. To ignore African American manhood or womanhood and to scoff at the special sensitivity there needs to be to and for an injured and oppressed people.

There is plenty of white bashing that goes on in those pulpits, but there is no attendant message of empowerment. The message that we hear in church is primarily eschatological, which means that people here will be better by and by. That things will be better one of these old mornings and that's true, that's true. When we die it's going to be fine, but I happen to believe that even as Jesus is a by-and-by God, he's a here-and-very-here God. That he's a God who can take you by the hand in your mess today and lead you out of it today so that while you're still walking and breathing today, you can feel pretty good. That's what I believe. But everybody is afraid to talk about God and his power and what he'll do while we're here. Everybody is afraid to talk about black folks and empowering black folks. We're afraid of being controversial or losing members because they talk about that "black stuff."

I don't know why all that stuff is. I've wondered those questions myself, but I need to tell you this morning in introducing myself that I'm not afraid of being controversial nor am I willing to stop talking about us and how important God is in our struggle. I cannot and will not divorce our history and ethnicity from our theology. My message to you has to be the beauty of us as God's chosen people, precious in his sight, or I don't believe I'm doing what God has called me to do.

Let me give you some reality to help you understand why I have to be this way. *Time* magazine wrote recently that "signs of crisis are everywhere." We get those reports about once a month about a crisis in the black community. You've heard the grim statistics before, and this particular article said that one in four black men ages twenty to twenty-four are either in jail, on probation, or on parole. Black men, the article said, are less likely to attend college than are black females, and once they enter they're more likely to drop out. Among our black males ages fifteen to thirty-four, homicide is the leading cause of death. Black men still find it more difficult to get jobs than do black or white females and of course white males. While in elementary and high school, black males account for 80 percent of the expulsion rates, 65 percent of the suspensions, and 58 percent of the nonpromotions even though they only make up 43 percent of the entire student body. The book *Conspiracy to Destroy Black Men* says that there is a conspiracy to destroy the black male and it would seem that this allegation is true. It would seem that the world spends a whole lot of time concentrating on the negative aspects of African American life, doling out horrible statistics which only serve to make a low self-esteem even lower, and that society still looks at African American males and decides that they ain't about nothin' and are never going to be.

In introducing myself to you, I have to explain that I cannot sit inside church and pretend that I don't have the opinion that God would want me to be silent about all of this. In schools, black children are still marked as failures. In the world, black beauty is still not recognized or appreciated. In the legal system, there is still one kind of justice for white folks and another kind for black folks. The killers of Yusef Hawkins, I've talked about him before. The young boy I've talked about who was killed when he went into a white neighborhood to look at a used car. One of his killers was actually acquitted of murder and another one was convicted, but the case is so shot full of holes that it will probably go to appeal, and that young man will probably be let off.

I'm telling you there are still two systems of justice in this country. In college, white students are harassing black students already struggling to make it in a world which says they don't belong there. In the music and dance worlds, there is still the belief that one must be white to dance with the American Ballet Theater or play with the New York Philharmonic. There is still an underlying belief that African Americans just don't have what it takes no matter how hard we've worked or how good we are, and if they simply cannot find a lame-brained excuse to dismiss us, then they still say that the reason we're good must be because we have some white blood in us. I don't know if you've ever been in a dance class and seen little African American boys and girls doing ballet, but they're wonderful. But many of them cannot get into the dominant culture's ballet companies. You know why? 'Cause our feet are flat and because when you turn sideways, you have to have the right kind of profile. You've got to have a certain kind of chin and your nose has to be pointed a certain way, and when you do all these positions here you have to look a certain way. The angles have to be the same, and it doesn't matter how bad you are as a dancer. You could dance rings around Baryshnikov and Margot Fonteyn. That doesn't matter. If you don't look right, if your feet are too flat, and your chin is in too far, then you can't be a member of the ballet company.

I'm telling you there are still big problems in this world. It's still a reality that even though we're good in sports that we're still staying in our place as far as some people are concerned. Don't you kid yourself. Even though we make millions and millions of dollars, we are still being manipulated and controlled by the powers that be. They still draft us with the underlying belief that we cannot make it in college. They pay us money we've never seen before. Buy us cars and clothes to draft us into college, and then they let us go while they make us make money for the college and they leave us to go to the dogs.

Do you know that no matter how successful you are that you are still labeled a "nigger" in many of the hallowed halls? Patrick Ewing, a star player now, was a star player for Georgetown University and a good student as well, but do you know that even though he was electric on the court that white folks up in the stands would hold up signs, pictures of monkeys, calling the monkeys "Patrick," pointing to the monkeys and insinuating that the monkey was Patrick and showing him eating bananas and would actually throw banana peels on the floor to their star player, who was bringing in thousands and thousands of dollars for Georgetown University? Oh yes, there are still big problems in this world. Don't you think that things like that do not exist. Don't you think that the world has changed so much that that stuff has disappeared, and because I know the odds our children are up against, I have to preach what I have to preach.

Do you know that black mothers when they get angry are still calling their children names relevant to their African-ness? I was taking my kids for a walk the other day, and I cringed because a mother was mad at her child and all I could hear was "Get your black you-know-what over here." It's always a really big put-down. Your black this, and your black that. Making them feel like they're dogs and dirty and ugly. Do you understand that that does more to undermine the confidence of our children than does anything else? Do you understand that those mothers do it because they hate themselves and that's the way they look at themselves? I'm telling you that there are problems in this world, and because I know that those things exist, I have to talk about it.

Do you know that if you claim your history or speak out against overt racism such as that practiced by the Roman Catholic Church that you can be ostracized by the religious community? I don't know everything I need to know and want to know about Father George Stallings, but I do know that I like what he's done in his church. I like it that he took that old, staid, dry old Roman Catholic Church and decided that he was going to claim his heritage and make up sermons that we could relate to. I don't know about all this stuff that they try to pin on you. When you do something wrong in the government, they call you a communist, and if you do something wrong in the religious world, they call you a faggot. I don't know about all that, and it really doesn't make a difference. What makes a big difference is that he has gotten people close to the Lord, and I like that. I like it that he has instilled in his people a sense of pride. And I want you to be what you want you to be.

God doesn't want everybody to look the same. God doesn't want everybody to act the same, and he didn't want everybody to look the same. In his eye there was all kinds of beauty, and all he wanted to do was understand that in his image were you created, not in your image but in the image of God, and he made us. That's what he did, and so he had to teach that lesson to the Israelites because they didn't understand that they were chosen just like all of us are chosen, but they weren't chosen in the eyes of the world, just like we're not chosen in the eyes of the world. Pharaoh's people didn't like them. Neither did the Hittites or the Amorites or all those people who attacked them. Oh, they talked about them and put them down. You've read about all the enemies they had.

God felt their misery, and so in Deuteronomy he reminded them that they had to recall a fact, and that fact was that God loved them. It didn't matter to God that the world didn't love them. God loved them and God had chosen them to be a special people—not because they were worthy or more worthy. God has chosen them because it was his prerogative to do so. As God's chosen people they were recipients of a special mercy and a special faith. He chose them. They would and could accomplish all things and survive in his sight. Not ugly; not stupid; not low-down. Not any of those adjectives. But they were precious in his sight and he told them himself, "You are precious in my sight, so don't throw that away." Because when you are in exile you kind of forget who you are. He had to remind them again because they were in exile again, and when you are in a strange land, a land that has a different culture, you are apt to be put down and held down. You want to hold onto the alien culture and ignore your own. You are apt to want to worship their god, play their game, and die their deaths, but God reminded his people that they couldn't do that because being in exile can make you crazy.

We can change our names all we want. You can go on and change your name, but you're still going to go out with your brown face and your kinky hair. We can straighten our hair and we do. We can straighten our hair all we want, but when it is all said and done, we still be African Americans. We can't hide what we are. Sometimes in the light of that fact, when we see all the people who are getting all the press, then we just want to sit down and die, but I have to tell you as a preacher of God's words that even though it gets hard and even though it will be harder, that you cannot stop moving forward, because you are precious in his sight.

So you see, as a preacher I have to remind you that B. B. King was a black man and was black on top of that, but that didn't stop him from writing good old music because he was precious in God's sight. I have to remind you that Paul Robeson was one of the very best singers in our history, and they tried to push him down because they said he was a communist, but that didn't stop him from moving forward. I have to remind you that Oprah Winfrey is one of the wealthiest women in television, but when she was a reporter in Baltimore, they tried to change her nose and tried to change her hair so that she would look white, and she didn't do it, because she was precious in his sight. I have to remind you that Mary McCleod Bethune went ahead and built her college on top of the garbage heap. I have to remind you that Patrick Ewing went ahead and finished Georgetown University even though they called him names. I have to remind you that our people—our people built the pyramids. They have not figured out yet how they did it. Don't let them tell you that you're stupid.

We come from royal stuff, and I have to remind you of that. I have to remind you that although the world says our children are not achievers, that that is a bold-face lie, and I have to motivate you if the schools are not doing what they're supposed to do because they don't want to. I have to remind you that that's okay. If the schools don't want to do for us what we need done that we can build our own schools and teach our own children. I have to remind you of that. I have to make sure that in this place called the church that we begin to strip away the years of low self-esteem and non-belief in ourselves and walk out in this world with a sense of self and a sense of love that can't nobody take away. I have to make you know what's going on in South Africa and in Liberia as well as what's going on in West Virginia and right here. If I don't do that, I'm not doing what God's calling me to do. I have to remind you that if you know who Robert Frost is and all them white folks is, then you'd better know who Malcolm X is and Nelson Mandela. I have to remind you.

I know some of you get uncomfortable. Some of you think that's the only reason you come to church is to hear about the love of Jesus, love of Jesus, and you do hear about the love of Jesus but it is the love of Jesus that *propels*. I don't know about your mama, but my mama and her mama's mama went through the baddest, worst times in history, and it is somebody named Jesus that got our ancestors reading by candlelight so they could get us to where we are today. It is nothing but Jesus that got us here today, so yes, it's about the love of Jesus, but the love of Jesus that is alive today and not some Jesus that you have to wait until you die to see. That's what I have to do. You have to understand that the world could not kill our ancestors. Slavery couldn't kill them. AIDS virus couldn't kill. Nothing can.

Can you understand that hope, even up underneath a piece of concrete, this thing called hope that God gives his special people will keep pushing up until one day after you think you've stomped it all down and killed it you look and see a little green shoot pushing all through the cracks in the sidewalk. That's what we are because we are precious in his sight. So I just came to tell you today that I'm pleased to make your acquaintance. I'm here to tell you that I just love you. I'm going to be here awhile. I'm here to tell you that in seventeen years, when Eastside United Church of Christ is down the street, I'll be standing right there. Glory! Glory, hallelujah! I'll say, they know their history and their culture. They're going to know what apartheid is. They're going to know who Nelson Mandela is. They're going to know what Africa is. They're going to know! Oh, I'm so happy to get to know you today. You cannot keep me quiet, you understand, because God told me to do this. Even if my mother made me do certain things, God makes me do this. And I'm through. Amen.

Afterward, Reverend Barb invited visitors to come forward and join the church community: "When we open the doors of the church, we ask that those of you who don't have a church home, who are looking for a church home, to come forward and give me your hand and give the Lord your heart. Is there one? Praise God. Is there another today?"[14]

In what way does this confrontational sermon help Reverend Barb earn her congregation's trust and allegiance? Given the title—"By Way of Introduction"—we might expect to receive an autobiographical introduction to Rev. Barbara Hill. We catch a glimpse of the power her mother had over Reverend Barb when she draws a distinction between being compelled to do something by her mother and being compelled to do something by God. But otherwise, there is very little about the private life of Reverend Barb in this sermon. Instead, this sermon is an introduction to Reverend Barb's hermeneutics: that the local needs of this congregation are related to the socioeconomic position of African Americans in the dominant culture. This position makes it difficult for them to achieve their potential, which is the hope of a life in relationship with God and with other believers. Instead of introducing herself by offering her own story or testimony, Reverend Barb introduces her people to her vision of who she thinks *they* are through the black jeremiad: they are a people in exile, subject to the slurs of the larger culture, just as the Israelites were when in exile in Egypt. She offers this picture in frank terms—through the rhetorical strategy of *parrhesia,* or reproaching her people when they expect her to placate them (*Rhetorica ad Herennium* 4.36.48).[15] The sermon echoes Baby Suggs's fictional sermon, discussed in chapter 1, which is also based in the hermeneutics of self-love for a people in exile: "'Here,' she says, 'in this place, we flesh; flesh that weeps, laughs; flesh that dances on bare feet in grass. Love it. Love it hard. Yonder they do not love your flesh'" (88). Like Baby Suggs, Reverend Barb is asking her people to recognize their fundamental equality, value, and distinctiveness in the eyes of God. She reproaches them for not wanting to hear the truth about their heritage. If there was any doubt of the source of this message, Reverend Barb ends by saying that she was directed by God to speak it, an old trope in the history of preaching.

What sort of character did Reverend Barb set up for herself in this sermon? In "Prophetic Preaching Now," Samuel D. Proctor argues that the African American preacher is in the unique position to call the nation to greater social justice:

> The Black community learned early how to find its strength and inspiration by transcending its immediate, historical situation, and learning how to live in lofty places. [. . .] And the one who led them in this experience was the preacher, the one called to stand between their travail and their God. (154)

After detailing all the gains made by African Americans in the nation, Proctor offers some of the same dire pictures painted by Reverend Barb of "a large, growing Black underclass" (155) and asserts that it is the African American preacher who must take responsibility for leading the people to higher ground. To do so, he argues that a prophetic preacher "must first call our Black communities to restore our original quest for racial uplift from within, emphasizing ethnic pride and resourcefulness" (156), "reach deeper than the culpability of those who are victims of oppression themselves, and probe the political order that protects and perpetuates the status quo" (157), and finally to find ways to "break the bonds of poverty and isolation" by effecting institutional change (158).

Years before penning these words, Proctor was Reverend Barb's homiletics teacher at Yale Divinity School. Though she reports she had no formal requirement in homiletics, Reverend Barb took an elective class in African American preaching and learned from Proctor that the most important element in preaching is "to ask a relevant question." For Proctor and for Reverend Barb, an African American preacher must ask the deeper questions about the cultural conditions of their people as the fundamental first step in the development of the sermon. In stark contrast to the history of the art of preaching, populated by learned white men, Reverend Barb and Samuel Proctor argue for a homiletics that is fundamentally grounded in local needs and the social and political climate of the nation. The preacher's role is exactly the opposite of the one suggested by Austin Phelps, who argued that preaching be addressed "to the individual man; not to communities, not to governments, not to nations" ("Theory" 15). It is, contra Phelps, fundamentally about the community in its "organic relations."

Reverend Barb's position is a risky one: that of prophet. If she were a man, Storrs might have praised her for her "conscientious earnestness." But she is not a man; these qualities are part of her *ethos* as a *woman* preacher within a congregation that did not want to call a woman and did not want to hear about "heritage." Yet the role of prophet has some advantages. Rarely welcomed by those who hear them, prophets stand on the margins of society while calling for fundamental change. According to Old Testament tradition, a prophet need not fulfill the culture's ideals, need not be the right gender, need not be willing, and indeed need not even be human (in one memorable story, God spoke through the prophet Balaam's donkey) (Num. 22:22–35). The prophet's role was special and proved that God was above cultural expectations. Jarena Lee draws on this tradition in her autobiography:

> O how careful ought we to be, lest through our by-laws of church government and discipline, we bring into disrepute even the word of life. For as unseemly as it may appear now-a-days for a woman to preach, it should be remembered that nothing is impossible with God. (36)

Women preachers from the early mystics to the founder of the Salvation Army, Catherine Mumford Booth, drew on the prophet's character in order to preach reform to the people.[16] But among African American women, the call to prophecy is even stronger, dating back at least as early as Maria W. Stewart (Logan, *"We Are Coming"* 31). The role of the prophet takes us back to the fictional women preachers of chapter 1, who were untrained and fundamentally outsiders and whose calls for reform occurred in natural settings, far from the pulpits of institutionalized religion. Reverend Barb was an outsider to Eastside when she preached "By Way of Introduction," and it is from this vantage point that she calls the people to recognition of their status as exiles in a land that does not value them—the black jeremiad. Standing in the small lecture-style pulpit of a converted party house and then later in their midst, she takes a dramatically confrontational stand, draped in the mantle of the prophet. It is, as Proctor suggests, the role often played by the African American preacher, but it is a role especially appropriate for Reverend Barb, whose gender and message place her on the outside of this congregation's struggling sense of itself. But it was risky. After introducing her mission—her narrative vision for Eastside—and rejecting calls to desist from articulating it, Reverend Barb still had work to do to win over her people.

Applying the Old-Time Religion

"By Way of Introduction" suggests Reverend Barb's love and concern for the people but not necessarily her ability to be one of them. But in the months following this sermon, she firmly established the twin themes of intimacy and populism found in Patricia O'Connor's ministry. As a result, her congregation grew steadily. In an interview with Lydia, one of the women leaders who had been with the church from its early days, I learned that Reverend Barb had won over the women as well as the men through her devotion to the children and championing their self-esteem, through her woman-centered approach to ministry and preaching, and through her ability to draw close to the people through her sermons. Lydia was adamant about the difference that it made to have a woman lead the church: "She don't preach like no man in a dress, not like some Margaret Thatcher," she said. Lydia offered examples from the sermons: birth imagery, the difficulties of pregnancy, and problems caused by men. She also said that Reverend Barb disclosed her private life in the pulpit, and normally not "the good stuff," which made her seem more human to her people. Lydia contrasted Reverend Barb's style to a former minister whose personal disclosures were all "boastful," reminding the congregation, for example, that his father was the first electrical engineer in the family.

On August 26, 1990, Reverend Barb preached a sermon titled "Daniel's Story," based on Daniel 6:1–10, which illustrates several of these points. The sermon begins with the invocation, "I'd like for you to pray with me for a few minutes on the subject 'Daniel's Story,'" and then announces the problem: "We are in a crisis all over the world." Working her way through the devastations caused by drugs, poverty, and lack of education in African American neighborhoods around the nation, she announces that these conditions weren't "in the game plan and wouldn't have happened if we had remembered from day one *whose we are.*" Explaining to the congregation the nature of the Old Testament covenant between God and the people, she introduces the core of the sermon by saying, "When you are bad enough to hold onto God's hand and to stand on his promises, then God comes through like you wouldn't believe. Which brings me to Daniel's story."

The next section of the sermon is a dramatic retelling of the rise and fall of Daniel, about fifteen minutes of narration. Storytelling *(energia),* a central feature of African American preaching, was the feature of Reverend Barb's preaching about which she was most proud. Her special method was to map out the psychological aspects of the characters, connecting them to twentieth-century African American culture, and animating the story so that the audience could place themselves into the minds of the characters.[17] Daniel became a *"bad* Negro," "a teacher's pet." King Darius became a dumb old guy who got hung up by his ego:

> And what they did was they went to King Darius and they said, "Oh, King *Dar*-i-us, oh humble *ki*-ing." They really buttered him up. "Darius, we *love* you. And we want *nothing else in this world* but to pay total homage to *you.*" That's called getting him by strok-

ing his ego. "We want you to know, Darius, that we respect you above all other people, and we want everybody to function in that acknowledgment. So we wonder, King Darius, if you would help us have sort of a holiday. For thirty days if you would just sign a decree, what we'll do for those thirty days is we'll give you *everybody* in this kingdom to pay you total homage. Nobody will pray to their god. Nobody will look to the west. Everybody will look to *you*, blessed King Darius. Everybody will look only to you for their salvation." And Darius liked the stroking, and thought, Oh, that sounds pretty good. Needless to say, he wasn't real bright. It never crossed his mind what they were trying to do—but then of course intelligence often does give way to ego stroking. And so Darius went ahead and signed the decree. Well, the entire Babylonian community knew that the decree had been signed, including Daniel. *I just love it!* The Word says that they took the decree to Daniel, and as soon as he knew that it had been signed, he went into his room and he knelt down at his window, which faced Israel, and he started to pray to his God. And the other presidents just sort of smiled. "Well, we've got him now!"

Reverend Barb moved the congregation into this Old Testament world through her animation of the various parts of the story. Her rendition of the presidents' deception of King Darius in fawning voice was very humorous, drawing the congregation in and causing many to laugh. Her ironic commentaries, such as "of course intelligence often does give way to ego stroking," were meant to transform the characters into terms understood by her congregation. They became insiders to this Old Testament story.

Moving through Darius's anguish over Daniel being thrown to lions, Reverend Barb takes the people next to the cave where Darius kept watch, waiting until morning so he could collect the remains of his friend. "Darius was so surprised," she said, "when he walked into the cave that morning and he looked over and he saw first of all the lion just lying down kind of flicking his tail around, kind of looking at Darius like he had lost his mind. 'Come on in now. What took you so long?'" Reverend Barb turns to the main point of the sermon: "That's Daniel's story and I love that story because to me that's talking about the old-time religion." The final section (about ten minutes) applies the theme of this sermon to Reverend Barb herself and to the people. Her first application (told in the midst of the people, on the floor) is to herself:

[That's] the old-time religion that my mother used to tell me about. My mother used to say, "Barbara, God sees every hair on your head," and I believed her. She said, "Barbara, if you tell a lie, God will hear it before I do." "Mommy, what will God do to me?" "I don't know. That's between you and God." Scared me to death. "Barbara, if you don't use your talents, you're not hurting me. Because I didn't make you. God made you so you're hurting his feelings, and you don't want to hurt his feelings." I believe it.

By amplifying her voice to imitate her mother and then herself as a child, Reverend Barb offers the congregation a glimpse of her as a little girl— a woman who is *still* subject to her mother's voice. While Reverend Barb grew up to endorse her mother's beliefs, in this anecdote she offers herself as unsure, even terrified, of her mother's views. She is scared of this God, and by presenting herself this way, she offers her people the chance to see that she is also subject to—and needing—the old-time religion she's talking about.

She reinforces this point in the next personal story, which brings the people into Reverend Barb's life in college:

> I'm glad that I stopped being afraid of saying that Jesus is my personal Lord and Savior. When I was trying to be educated—because I went to the fine schools, you know. And I didn't want anybody to think I was ignorant either, and so when they started talking about all this Jesus, I just kind of stepped back and sat down. I didn't want nobody to know. I wondered what they had but I didn't want to be labeled, but as soon as that day happened, when I found myself saying "Jesus," and as soon as I found myself starting to say, "Thank you, Jesus," I noticed that I wasn't the same person anymore. I was real glad to see that my intelligence was okay, but it didn't make any difference at that point. All I knew was that I felt a whole lot better once I started holding onto God's unchanging hand and not my chemistry books. [Clapping in congregation.] That's what it is. That's what it is, that's what it is. That's what the old-time religion is about. And that's what I want us to have.

In this story, Reverend Barb testifies to her personal relationship with God. While she shows herself doing the right thing, it is interesting to notice that she finds a way to represent herself as a person who fails. She also manages to temper her education—a point that puts distance between her and many congregation members—by asserting that she learned to draw strength not from her chemistry books but rather from her faith, the same faith she has in common with the people. This comment drew strong approval from members of the congregation, who clapped and said, "Yes!" in response. Both stories illustrate a human being in process, not a distant authority.

Near the end of "Daniel's Story," Reverend Barb addresses the men in the congregation, illustrating Lydia's point that Reverend Barb offered a woman's perspective in her sermons, often to the delighted embarrassment of the men.

> Don't you know that when you invite God into your life, when you're getting ready to do something wrong, say you're going to have an affair with Miss Sally—and she's *fine*. And she does for you all the things that your wife don't do, and you have little conversations with her, and she wears just the right clothes, and you say, "Oh, my, my, *my*." [Clapping and laughter in congregation.] And you scheme and you plot to get it all set up. Little dinner, little wine, and a little *you-know-what* afterward. You're all ready for it, but don't you know that if you got that old-time religion, God might let you go on and have a little dinner. God might even let you have a little bit of wine. But as soon as you step over and get ready to do something you know you ain't got no business doin', you'll feel this little tap on your shoulder. God will be *all into* you. You might go ahead and do it, but you'll be so miserable, you'll be so miserable, that he will make you stand up and do right. That's what the old-time religion is all about.

Reverend Barb sided with the women in the congregation here, as she often did in her sermons. During my four months at Eastside, it was not uncommon for her to stop in the midst of the sermon, smile, raise her eyebrows, and say, "Women, you know how our men are!" This sense of private conspiracy with the women was not unappreciated by the men. Lydia said the men "just loved" the fact that Reverend Barb "told them off" in some of her sermons. Reverend Barb said in an interview after another sermon in which she told a "Miss Sally" story, "Last week I was talking about how women can pull men into their clutches. And I went on about how the men never see it. I can remember because I was looking at some of the men and they were just laughing. Because they could see themselves."

Reverend Barb's performance of "Daniel's Story" is a brilliant dance with the congregation. She begins with a prophetic message of African American suffering and loss of identity—a message that made some of the older members uncomfortable—moves into the Old Testament story and narrates it to bring the story into the room "so you could taste the dust in your mouth," and finally applies the point to herself and to everyone in the room. The opening is most controversial, with the greatest potential distance between Reverend Barb and the congregation. She stood in the pulpit for this message. The middle section moves Reverend Barb closer to the congregation. The story is humorous, passionate, and familiar: one could imagine oneself as Darius; one could imagine his surprise upon discovering Daniel standing among the lions, an angel at his side. Daniel's faith is wonderful, unimaginable. Reverend Barb was on the move in this section, stepping out from behind the pulpit and moving in front of it. In the last section, she reaches for the faith of Daniel; she says that she needs it for herself. At this point, she was in the center of the congregation. She has moved from prophet to humble fellow traveler in the course of the sermon. But she has done still more: she has re-centered the Old Testament and its application around the everyday experience of African American men and women. Her use of narrative is *womanist,* for it refocuses biblical stories on African American experience while keeping the gendered *differences* of those experiences at the center of her sermon.

Another sermon that offered this pattern, with even greater success, was a sermon titled "The Prodigal Son." Reverend Barb began this sermon (after her invocation to "pray with me" about the subject) with the question, "Have you ever been mad? I mean, *mad?*" Her text was the parable of the prodigal son, generally used to illustrate the nature of grace, even for the most spectacular sinner. However, Reverend Barb reversed the focus of this parable to the good son who had stayed by and loyally supported his father with no special reward. She renamed the players: the prodigal son became Tyrone; the good son became Leroy. Narrating the story of Tyrone and Leroy for a full fifteen minutes, Reverend Barb drew the picture of a man who had the right to be enraged. He had done all that he needed to do, never straying, but his brother received all the attention and all the rewards when he returned home. As with "Daniel's Story," Reverend Barb used African American dialect and colloquialisms to tell the story, repeating such lines as, "You know how it is when somebody be jumpin' on your last nerve?" The entire congregation was laughing and clapping throughout the narrative. Finally, at the end, she posed a question: "You know, the Bible always says not to be angry, not to let the sun go down on your wrath. But what if you have a reason to be mad? What if you are a perfect Christian and you are wronged? How do you let go of your anger?" After a long pause in the sermon, she answered this question not with an answer but rather with a surprising admission of defeat on this issue. She said, "I don't know the answer, but here is what has happened when I have tried to let go." Drawing from her experiences of being discriminated against for being an African American woman—for instance, having to quit her job as a television journalist for refusing to cut her braids—she offered herself up as an example of a woman who struggled with anger and could do nothing but take her defeat in this area to God. Standing in the midst of the congregation, Reverend Barb and many of the members of the congregation wiped away tears as she finished the sermon and invited visitors to join the church.

Such profound personal disclosure centered on stories of defeat and humility,[18] strategically placed at the end of the sermon,[19] offered to me and to other members of the congregation the strong impression that Reverend Barb was applying the message of the sermon to herself. This practice made not only the message but also Reverend Barb accessible, close, "one of the people." In concert with a prophetic message of African American heritage, one that put her at odds with a few of the older members, this preaching strategy reinforced Reverend Barb's image as a populist, a member of the community, and a humble, courageous leader who quietly and consistently led both children and adults to discover their heritage and recover their self-esteem.

The Story of David and Bathsheba

The most important group to be won over by Reverend Barb in those first three months were the core members—the women. She formed a support group for women called The Sisterhood that met once a week and discussed such difficult issues as domestic abuse. Reverend Barb said her goal with the women was to get them to "stand up to their men," to "have some backbone," and to get over self-hatred. She believed that women didn't get behind themselves enough and, in the process of living, gave up or lost their rights. But in addition, as many members said to me in the course of the fieldwork, she brought a woman's perspective to the pulpit that was new and refreshing to both men and women. Reverend Barb described her mission in this way:

> I think the main thing a woman preacher can do is that she can acknowledge her femininity and not try to be a male. Our perspectives on life are different. You cannot help but have a different perspective on life and on things that happen in life if you're a woman. Men and women think entirely different. I learned that from being married. My husband's a good man, but goodness, Lord! When we, some of the basic things, he looks at me like I'm from left field. I think *perspective*. I mean I've had men come up to me and say, "Oh, I never thought of it like that," or "I thought my wife was the only one who thought that, but now you're helping me to understand that." I think I bring my female perspectives, my prejudices, my strengths as a woman. You know, David and Bathsheba, that story comes differently when I do it as opposed to when a man does it. There's a kind of undercurrent of acceptance of certain things in the Bible, you know. David and Bathsheba, hey, she's a fine woman, and why not do it? The male, he sees it from this undergirding, and he understands. His sexual urges match that of David's, you know? So he could understand it. But you know, a

female looks at it in an entirely different way. And I enjoy bringing that perspective. I enjoy bringing that perspective. And my hope is that with more and more women in the pulpit, there will be a better understanding between males and females. Because they've heard the male perspective for thousands of years. Now, you'll hear it not from your wife whom you don't respect because she doesn't know anything but hear it from some kind of authority figure who you are *learning* to respect. Hear it, and that way see if it doesn't make some differences in your relationship. I think it makes a difference in my own relationship, because I think my husband hears me differently when I preach as opposed to when we talk back and forth.

This passage illustrates the conflicts between men and women in the congregation and the importance Reverend Barb placed on having both sexes hear the point of view of a woman coming out of the mouth of an authority figure, or as Reverend Barb put it, less certainly, "some kind of authority figure who you are *learning* to respect." In the pulpit, she was open about the conflicts she and her husband, Richard, had over household duties and child care. When she mentioned the conflict, she often dramatized it ("So *I* say [. . .], and *he* says [. . .]"). Her openness over her own conflicts with Richard validated the experience of the married couples in the congregation. Several members mentioned this to me in interviews, saying that the men and women in the congregation had conflicts of perspective, and they appreciated the fact that Reverend Barb did not whitewash her own marital troubles.

But perhaps the most remarkable application of women's experience came when Reverend Barb animated the point of view of women in the Bible. Like Pat and many other women preachers, Reverend Barb had preached a "birth" sermon, told from the woman's perspective, of course. Of this sermon, Reverend Barb said, "By the time I was through with that sermon, *I* was hurting! [Laughs.] I didn't want any more babies!" Preached at the large staff church where she started her ministry, the birth sermon was so successful that twenty-two people joined the church that day. In another sermon to the same congregation, she preached on Mary and Joseph, becoming Joseph, to show his perspective, and then becoming Mary, to show hers.

> It really did something to me as I was doing it. When I look back it was deathly quiet in there. And when I was done, everyone was crying. I was crying, too. Because we really understood the miracle of that type of obedience. And love for God at a time when your very humanness would've said, "No!"

In another sermon, preached around Thanksgiving, Reverend Barb offered a letter to God from a woman's perspective. She said, "I preached it from a purely feminine point of view, but it hit the men. It hit the men." More common was Reverend Barb's habit of using her own gendered experiences as brief points of illustration, a practice that underscored the validity of women's perspectives in the congregation. Her hermeneutic was consistent with Cheryl Kirk-Duggan's "Womanist theory," which, when articulated "midst a faith-based curiosity, seeks to observe, analyze, and celebrate the lives and gifts of Black women toward the transformation of themselves, of other African Americans, and of society" (139). Reverend Barb did not use the word "womanist" to describe herself, but it was clear that she drew on this tradition to fashion her distinctive mission to Eastside.

Reverend Barb's status as an outsider—both because of gender and mission—gave her a unique opportunity to revise Eastside's sense of sacred space. One of the epigraphs to this chapter is from de Certeau's *Practice of Everyday Life*. In a chapter titled "Spatial Stories," he distinguishes between the fact and fiction, map and narrative, and suggests that stories have the effect of redrawing boundaries: "[S]tories 'go in a procession' ahead of social practices in order to open a field for them" (125). Reverend Barb worked to redraw boundaries between priest and people through her *sermo corporis*—the speech of her body—during the act of walking the aisle. But she also opened new territories through the narratives she told, narratives that made it possible to rethink relations between men and women, between African Americans and the dominant culture, between parents and children, between the church and the neighborhood. "What the map cuts up, the story cuts across" (de Certeau 129): what she could not demonstrate through the simple act of walking, she could redistribute in the imagination through the act of storytelling.

We can see these principles at work in Reverend Barb's sermon "Defining the Church." One of the tasks Reverend Barb inherited was finishing Eastside's first freestanding church, a building whose construction was halted before she arrived because the contractor went bankrupt. The church was finished soon after my fieldwork ended. But in the meantime, Reverend Barb learned that many people were waiting to join the church until the building was finished. In "Defining the Church," she took on the concept of sacred space, arguing, "Most of us want a church to look like a church" and for everyone in the church to look and act their part.

> I wonder what Jesus would say today if he walked in here, in this place, and we told him we have a church. I guess just as important, I wonder what each of us would say if we were asked what is a church. I've been thinking a lot about this question lately, especially as we have moved closer and closer toward moving into our new facility. I've been immersed in discussions about windows and car-

pets and pews and parking lots and walls and doors and bathrooms and kitchens, and it's all exciting seeing God's temple move from a dream to a reality and it's going to be a high, high day when it's all said and done, but the reality is that that building is not the church. Not in the way I'm thinking. Lots of people think that the building is a church. Lots of people think that that building is a church as opposed to this place, this space. In fact many people, too many, have said as soon as you move down, Reverend Barb, as soon as you move down there I'll be right on down there. The implication and what they are not saying is that you all ain't got no church right now, so when you get serious, when you really get a church, when you get a real church you can count me in.

Among the expectations she dispelled were the need for a male preacher, a preacher who hollered and danced and didn't have too much education, a beautiful building, the right rituals, and clean, fresh-smelling congregants (and none with dreadlocks). She corrected this vision with another, one that emptied out the stuff of sacred space. It was fitting she offered the synoptic Gospel story of Jesus tearing down the money-changers' stalls in the temple. Reverend Barb argued, "When we as preachers bow to the expected form of preaching and ignore pertinent social, cultural, and historical issues, we are killing the church."

Back in the Clearing, Baby Suggs was building up a new church, one that was not distinctly Christian but nevertheless was focused on the social, cultural, and historical needs of her people. On Hayslope Green, Dinah Morris was building a new church, one that was centered outside the walls of the Anglican Church and its hypocritical practices. "This space is not the church," Reverend Barb asserted. "Neither is the space at 1450 Township Road [the new building]." What was the church, she argued, were such actions as the following:

Loving each other when it's hard. That's the church. Talking to your father or your mother when all they've ever done is ignore you, that's the church. Making the effort to understand your spouse. Standing up for the rights of the oppressed people. That's the church. Standing on the promises of Jesus and making sure that nobody messes with our children. That's the church.

By calling her people to think about "church" as occurring beyond the familiar boundaries of wooden and stone structures, Reverend Barb stood with the fictional preachers of Adam Bede and Beloved, as well as other great women African American prophets, in creating sacred spaces in everyday life. But also, as she reminded her congregation, it was only by thinking of church outside the boundaries of denomination that women preachers could ever be heard.

Reverend Barb achieved her goal of acceptance by the congregation by wrapping herself in the mantle of prophet in the tradition of African American women who came before her and by creating an atmosphere of intimacy with the congregation. Eventually, her message of heritage and empowerment, a distinctive characteristic of African American preaching (LaRue; H. Mitchell, *Black Preaching*), was viewed as a populist move. Nevertheless, it was the walk she took beyond the prophetic heights of the pulpit into the heart of the congregation and the stories she told from a womanist perspective that earned her acceptance into the community at Eastside. That her walk was one filled with self-disclosure and evocative of the gendered tensions in the church made her especially beloved of the women at Eastside.

When I returned to Eastside in June 1991, seven months after the end of my fieldwork, the congregation was meeting in their new facility, a simple white clapboard building with steeple, stained glass, and all the trimmings of a traditional Protestant church. Membership had risen to around three hundred members, and approximately one hundred people were in attendance that Sunday, about one-quarter of whom were men. Reverend Barb was preaching from a new pulpit, placed on a platform that raised her up much higher than she had been in the party-house chapel. But as she preached, she stepped down from that pulpit and onto the floor, saying as she walked,

> This pulpit is too high. I need to be down [on the floor] so we can really dialogue. [. . .] [Preaching's] not about being "omnipotent" or, you know, somehow better than anybody else, it's just that God happened to make me a preacher but he made you a so-and-so and we all got to work on this ministry together.

And the people leaned forward in the gleaming new pews and clapped, the intimacy of the party house that Reverend Barb had created very much alive.

5

Disputed Geographies and the Woman Preacher

> The opacity of the body in movement, gesticulating, walking, taking its pleasure, is what indefinitely organizes a *here* in relation to *abroad,* a "familiarity" in relation to "foreignness."
> —Michel de Certeau, *The Practice of Everyday Life*

One Sunday while the Reverend Barbara Hill was invited to preach at another church, her husband, then a seminary student, took charge of the service. Eastside United Church of Christ was still meeting in the party-house chapel, and Richard Hill was pleased to have the opportunity to answer some of his wife's complaints that he didn't do his part in watching their children or seeking to understand her point of view sometimes. The congregation laughed about his opportunity to take revenge and murmured their support at the start of the service. But when Richard Hill rose to give the sermon, the congregation learned that he was a man of logic and reserve; he called his wife "kind of excitable" and said that he liked to base his sermons more on facts. Indeed, Richard stayed behind the pulpit for his sermon, and after a few jokes about his wife, he engaged the people in the biblical text with little emotion. He ended the sermon from behind the pulpit. However, after his "Amen," something interesting happened. Every Sunday when Reverend Barb said, "The doors of the church are wide open. Is there one [who will join the church]?," the choir, seated in three rows of chairs to the left of the pulpit, stood on their feet and began to sing. But on this Sunday, the lead soprano in the choir, a small woman about twenty-five years old, left her station with the choir and walked forward to stand with Richard next to the pulpit. She sang one verse and then another, with the choir joining her at the chorus. Amplifying the emotion in her voice little by little, she walked out from behind the pulpit and down the aisle, singing all the while, until she had reached the center of the church, in the midst of the congregation. Then she lifted up her arms to punctuate the emotion in her voice, the congregation shouting "Amen" and "Yes, *ma'am!*" and some people wiping away a tear. She stood there amidst the "Hallelujahs" and ended the service with the blessing of emotional connection and celebration that Richard Hill had not accomplished that day. Richard had not joined the people with the divine through the placement of his own body, and so a layperson, a woman, had spontaneously transgressed sacred space in order to enact the ritual that Reverend Barb performed each Sunday at Eastside and that he was too reserved to perform.

What is going on here? Throughout this book, I have explored the gender ideologies inherent in preaching theory and the ways in which two women preachers worked to take their place as leaders of their churches, despite the strong preferences of their congregations and the masculine models that haunted their efforts. In the first chapter, I suggested that character is established in location and that novelists, geographers, architects, historians, and philosophers have all noted that we hold in our minds a relationship between "being in the right place" and "having good character." Pulpits are a physical enactment of an idea about the relationship of people to priest. In the second chapter, I illustrated the way in which gender ideologies are enacted and reenacted in rhetorical theory to underscore the relationship between rhetorical performance and gendered behavior. Distance and authority, including global formulations of the audience, are enduring features of preaching theory tied to larger ideas of authority and nationhood.

During the months I spent at St. John's and Eastside, I witnessed Pat and Reverend Barb transgress rhetorical space in order to enact a new relationship with their congregations. Because gender is a complex set of behaviors that shift and change over time in a culture, we can view this study only as a snapshot, a moment in time, in which two women preachers encountered the twin problems of the history of sacred space and the gendered history of their art. My argument is that they enacted a transformation of the art of preaching in two key ways: by transgressing sacred space and by engaging in a local, populist theology. Reverend Barb went further, draping herself in the mantle of prophet, a fundamental outsider, while symbolically walking the aisle of the church in order to bring herself to the center. Both Pat and Reverend Barb occasionally preached what Lawless has called a "woman's sermon," that is, a sermon built upon the foundation of women's experiences ("Weaving"). However, they did so within a larger context: to build their image as populists—women who stand with their congregations and not at a distance from them. This act of walking, of bringing intimacy to the act of preaching, is, as de Certeau suggests, an act of transgression, of being "out of place." Yet this act of transgression accomplishes the purpose of marrying people and priest, the divine and the ordinary, the high and the low. It is an act of intimate dialogue.

When Richard Hill stayed in the pulpit at the end of the sermon, he failed to enact the ritual of intimate dialogue that Reverend Barb enacted each Sunday. He tethered his authority to the pulpit, and although he did engage in some lighthearted banter with the congregation during the sermon, his was a sermon built on *logos,* on foundational truths, and not on a relationship with the people. He offered the three-point sermon. He knew his biblical exegesis. But he did not perform the ritual of intimacy through his delivery. The evidence that Reverend Barb's use of rhetorical space was powerful and had transcended method to become ritual was the fact that a laywoman was moved to enact the ritual when Richard Hill did not. Although she was not a minister, her movement from platform to center of the people served a mimetic function— it simulated that movement of the divine to the people and therefore evoked an emotional response. Durkheim argues that religion is the fundamental separation of the sacred from the profane. In the practice of the women preachers in this study, religion was instead the ritual communion of sacred and profane within rhetorical space. The architectural structures that set off the people from the priest, intended from the earliest moments in Judaism to set off the holiest from the most depraved, with women left in the outer structures, was ritually transgressed each Sunday with the movement of the woman preacher from the pulpit to the pews set aside for the congregation.

In this chapter, I argue that such moves are well suited to women who are defined historically not by the sacred parts of the church but rather by the most profane, through the curse of Eve. Women preachers who embrace a theology of populism and establish intimacy with their congregations are building their status literally on new ground. Nevertheless, it would be misleading for me to draw tidy conclusions, for gender ideology always manifests itself in local, historical contexts and is ever on the move. Therefore, in this chapter I offer a counterexample: a woman appointed to lead a small Methodist church with intractably fractured geographies.

Ritual Transgressions: Delivery, Narrative, Theological Purpose

When we first glimpse the Reverend Theron Ware in Harold Frederic's 1896 novel, *The Damnation of Theron Ware,* Frederic draws a picture of national manhood in its youthful and pious form. Viewed through the perspective of the Methodist Episcopal congregation at Tecumseh, Ware is a

> tall, slender young man with the broad white brow, thoughtful eyes, and features moulded into *that regularity of strength which used*

to characterize the American Senatorial type in those far-away days of clean-shaven faces and moderate incomes before the War. (8, emphasis added)

Meanwhile, Ware's wife is viewed as "bright-faced, comely, and vivacious," a woman whom the congregation "noted with approbation [. . .] knew how to dress" (8). From this brief description at the beginning of the tragedy, we recognize that Frederic draws a connection in the mind of the reader between Ware and the long tradition of white men who have served as national leaders. Because she is neatly dressed and "comely," Mrs. Ware is assigned the national role reserved for presidents' wives: hostess and helpmate. From their first appearance, the preacher and his wife are assigned gender roles that bring with them expectations for behavior and assumptions about their character and relative authority.

As I argue in chapter 2, the connection between preachers and national male leaders was made explicit after 1850 when homileticians began importing precepts drawn from the "cult of manhood" into the training of preachers. It was not enough to "look" the part, as Frederic seems to suggest in his novel; homileticians argued that one must also prove oneself "manly" through a complex (and somewhat contradictory) set of character traits: one must be self-restrained but also forceful; one must be pious but also vigorously "of the world"; one must be at home in libraries but also in the public sphere. These masculine characteristics are considered necessary to be a good preacher and come to stand in place of earlier maxims about being a "good man," by which pre-Victorian homileticians simply meant a pious man—a man of God. In *Damnation,* Frederic suggests that Ware is tragically flawed because he proves himself to be without the appropriate manly characteristics, and he takes a tragic fall in the course of the narrative. A preacher must not just be a man—he must also be a "manly" man.

The "place" of a manly man is in the pulpit; the "place" of a manly man is in the Senate; the "place" of a manly man is in the White House. When in the public spaces where politics and religion are practiced, the "place" of woman has been in the pews, the balconies, the galleries, or in fact outside the walls of these locations. The most famous proclamation of the second-generation feminist movement may have been "A woman's place is everywhere," because it called attention to the restrictive gender ideologies that tied women with domestic and secondary spaces in the geographies of public life. Nowhere do local communities and their leaders enforce these boundaries more than in American religious institutions, including, once again, many churches in the Southern Baptist Convention. Little wonder that in the opening months of her ministry, Reverend Barb preached a sermon redefining the nature of sacred space, in which she argued that all the micro-adjustments that make up "church," including prohibitions on the sex of the preacher, "do not a church make."

Using de Certeau's theory of the act of walking, I have called Pat and Reverend Barb's rhetorical performances "ritual transgressions." Pat and Reverend Barb both articulated that transgressing sacred space was an explicit part of their art. Pat came down from the pulpit after the masculine head of the church left for a summer-long sabbatical, offering her the opportunity to explore a different relationship with the congregation. She learned to preach from notes and moved to the floor to preach. She reported that her congregation reacted enthusiastically. Such a spatial arrangement allowed her to look her parishioners in the eye when she spoke and to engage them in dialogue in the midst of the sermon. Likewise, as she moved down to the floor to be close to her congregation, Reverend Barb said that the pulpit was "too high" and that the act of preaching is "not about being 'omnipotent' or, you know, somehow better than anybody else." She moved physically to be with the people as she applied the lesson of the sermon to herself and therefore, by extension, to everyone.

Both Pat and Reverend Barb also sought a rearrangement of the relationships among members of the community. In their sermons, they preached a theology of populism, arguing that their churches were themselves communities, communities that had obligations to the members within as well as people in the neighborhoods surrounding the church. For St. John's Lutheran Church, a large church with a strong economic base and a congregation full of professionals, "community" was a challenging concept; religion was a commodity for many of the members—organized into a church, religion meant a youth ministry, a coffee hour, and a place to go to meet other young couples with children. Pat entered into dialogue with the congregation on Sunday mornings in order to introduce them to the people in the community, to help them learn to think of themselves as the church. Members of Eastside United Church of Christ already thought of themselves as part of the ministry; the church was small and had been built from the summer lunch program and youth ministry. Most everyone who was a member participated in the life of the church. But Reverend Barb asked them to enlarge the scope of their vision, to become a part of the solution to chronically low self-esteem in the African American community. Nevertheless, as we saw in her sermon "Defining the Church," Reverend Barb also needed to challenge the people to enlarge their vision of what the church could be; in one part of the sermon she reported a conversation in which she suggested to a new member that her husband, a man with dreadlocks, might not be welcomed at Eastside because he would not fit into the normative assumptions of what was acceptable to wear in that space. Through their stories, Pat and Reverend Barb rearranged relationships and heralded new social practices.

Several studies of women preachers suggest that their message of social liberation has the potential to change the nature of the Protestant churches (Nesbitt; Lawless, *Women Preaching;* C. Smith, *Weaving*). But no study explores how rhetorical performance enacts this message. What Pat and Reverend Barb were attempting to do was to open the people to a sense of themselves as a community—to reorganize their sense of identity. As they did so, they transgressed comfortable spaces. Pat and Reverend Barb offered the people a vision of themselves as a community, all the while standing close by, illustrating that they spoke in terms that were experience-near, not experience-far. If we go back to the scene of Dinah Morris's apple cart or Baby Suggs's rock, we can comprehend the quiet but important power that comes from delivery that demonstrates intimacy and a message that communicates solidarity with the common people.

Theologically, Pat and Reverend Barb were attempting to break with a pattern of worship exemplified by Rev. Harold Mosely in which the minister set himself apart from the congregation and preached to the members of the church as individuals, each working toward a private relationship with God. A long-standing pattern in the art of preaching, preaching for the salvation and regeneration of individuals creates a sense of churches not as communities but rather as atomizing institutions, such as schools, where the goal is not to build up a society but rather to build up individuals for their place in postindustrial life. Pat and Reverend Barb preached inclusion and tolerance of diversity, but their larger goal was to reconnect the individuals in their congregations to local contexts. The tensions in Reverend Barb's church whorled around the conflict between faith as private experience and faith as praxis/liberation (naming and resisting oppressive social relationships). The resistance that Pat felt to her message was more passive: her congregation was welcoming of the changes she made to the sermon but had not yet fully acted on her message.

In *Preaching as Local Theology and Folk Art,* Leonora Tubbs Tisdale suggests that the best preaching is a "contextual" act in which the language, form, and theology of the sermon arises from the theology, ethos, and ritual life of a congregation. In rhetorical terms, she suggests that the preacher carefully assess the rhetorical situation in order to choose the best forms for preaching. In many ways, we can conclude that Pat and Reverend Barb were successful preachers in Tisdale's terms because their congregations did approve of the choices they made in their sermons most of the time. Reverend Barb drew her congregation to the threshold of discomfort by warning them away from measuring themselves through the eyes of "white" or dominant culture. Nevertheless, she was sensitive to all the moves expected in an African American context (drawing attention to the ways in which she did not meet them, as in the case of "hollering") and did use local idioms and made culturally specific references within her narratives. Tisdale breaks from homiletic tradition in the extent to which she recommends shaping the sermon form, content, and purpose around the local congregation. But she does not account for one important feature of the rhetorical life of women preachers: character. Like Craddock and others, Tisdale assumes that the preacher is a generic creature without race, gender, or sexual orientation; the preacher's rhetorical choices are shaped around the congregation without regard to the factors that shape the preacher herself, including the congregation's fears, hopes, and expectations of her because of her gender.

Pat and Reverend Barb addressed the character issue by transgressing ritual boundaries between people and priest and in doing so bringing intimacy and a sense of the wisdom of common people to their preaching. These ritual transgressions illustrated a movement away from deductive preaching styles, in which the wisdom of the priest is part of the ritual separation between him and the people. Nevertheless, as both Pat and Reverend Barb said in remarkably similar terms, they both had "a kind of authority" (different from the men they knew, but powerful nevertheless) and that the people were "learning to respect" them on their own terms. This power was built upon the character that comes from those leaders who pay attention to the geographies that separate them from others and who work those boundaries, drawing respect from the people because the people's position had not been acknowledged in quite these terms before. The magic of these transgressions is illustrated in the fact that a laywoman felt compelled to "walk the aisle" to fulfill Reverend Barb's ritual crossing of the divine/human divide when she was not there to perform it. We cannot claim these are exclusively "women's moves," for certainly Henry Ward Beecher acknowledged the power of removing oneself from the pulpit in order to have more direct contact with the congregation. But we can acknowledge the rhetorical fit of these "spatial strategies" for women in congregations in which their character is an open question and in a historical moment when the institutional roads to good character offered to boys and men are closed to them, roads that give white clergymen in their context and black clergymen in theirs the habitual approval of congregations. For white clergymen, these institutional roads (military, Boy Scouts, sports) also bring them into the company of national manhood, an even more powerful source of cultural capital.

Spatial strategies that acknowledge the divide between pulpit and pew, podium and chair are often thrilling and surprising to an audience. At a recent conference, a prominent scholar shared a podium on a high platform with a former gang member and new graduate student who served as a research assistant during the scholar's study of gang life. The graduate student's role was to explain gang symbols as a literacy form to the room packed with over four hundred people. When he stood up to speak, he stopped and said, "You know, it's too high up here. I'm going to come on down to the floor to talk with you all," and his move was electrifying because it transgressed a boundary in that ballroom, with its chandeliers and deep plush carpet. Once he repositioned himself with microphone near the front row of chairs, the audience seemed more powerfully with him, because he chose to be more powerfully "with them" by seeking greater intimacy.

Elizabeth Dole counted on this rhetorical effect at the 1996 Republican National Convention when she gave the nomination address for her husband, Senator Robert Dole. Rhetorically, her job was to make Senator Dole more human, for he was widely considered by pundits to be too remote for American voters. To accomplish this task, she took a wireless microphone, left the podium and teleprompters, and gave her speech while walking the aisles of the convention center, arguing that she wanted the audience to know the "Bob Dole I know." Far more calculated and obviously ineffective than the spontaneous move of the graduate student (Dole lost by a wide margin to President Clinton), Elizabeth Dole's transgression of long-held boundaries nevertheless was a rhetorical strategy that drew the interest of the audience and pundits. Moving into the audience to give the speech was a rare gesture for a politician speaking on national television, but while this spatial strategy made Elizabeth Dole appear warmer and more accessible, the effect did not transfer to her husband, which was her goal.

In Dole's case, and in the case of the graduate student, moving toward the audience was a welcomed strategy. Those attending the Republican National Convention seemed especially welcoming of Elizabeth Dole's speaking from the floor. Likewise, the congregations at St. John's Lutheran Church and Eastside United Church of Christ welcomed their ministers into their midst. However, these strategies assume a situation in which the speaker is not barred from breaking down the boundaries of sacred space. Populism fails if the common people reject the values in the speaker who seeks to draw near to them. Another way to put this is that the preacher may not be invited into the spaces the congregation members occupy. As David Harvey suggests, "Popular understandings of places are organized through the elaboration of [. . .] all manner of personal or collective hopes and fears" (321). The collective map of sacred space elaborated by the congregation may be one of the issues over which the minister and the congregation (or groups within the congregation) are struggling for control. To understand how such a rhetorical situation is handled by a preacher without the "American senatorial" features bestowed by national manhood, let us turn to the final case study, which is, like the novel by Harold Frederic, about a Methodist preacher.

Power and Place in an Urban Neighborhood Church

Imagine that you have attended a small church in a working-class neighborhood for your entire life: you were married there, raised a family there, and now, in your retirement years, are one of its core members. You are white and conservative. Every six years, the United Methodist Church sends you a new minister. You don't have any choice about who they have sent you; it is a system built upon the itinerant preaching of the early Wesleyan movement, when ministers and their families moved frequently. One year the United Methodist Church sends you a woman preacher, a woman young enough to be your daughter. She is a feminist, or so you have heard. She avoids calling God "Father," except in the Lord's Prayer. She speaks a little too softly. Although you don't like these features of your new minister, you forgive them. You know she'll be gone in a few years, anyway. What will remain is the church, with its core members, the annual chicken noodle dinner, and the aging but well-tended building. These are the features that define the church for you.

But this minister is liberal. She preaches about "diversity" and "community" almost every Sunday. She believes in an "inclusive" church. One day three strangers show up in the church. They are young and somewhat bohemian-looking. They look like a lot of the younger people moving into the neighborhood, fixing up the old brownstones. Someone stops you after church and whispers that the visitors are homosexuals. You are theologically and culturally opposed to homosexuality, but you know that visitors come and go. Nothing to worry about. But the next Sunday they come back. The new minister talks to them for a long time after the service. The following Sunday they bring some friends. After awhile, one of "them" is playing the organ on Sunday mornings. They don't hide their sexuality. They talk about it. Then you hear that the minister has started a new Bible study group, and you hear that "they" go to it. You dig in for a long fight.

This was the point of view of some of the older members of Victory Hills United Methodist Church, a two-hundred-member church located in an urban neighborhood undergoing profound demographic changes. Once a white, working-class area with strong ethnic identity, the neighborhood was becoming home to young professionals and a growing gay and lesbian community, a diverse group who were renovating many of the brownstones and other historic buildings that had decayed through years of neglect and lack of capital investment. Victory Hills was primarily a working-class church with an aging adult membership—certainly not a growing church. The area of town in which it was located was on the border between the renovated and decayed sections of a historic district. On the south border next to the church, urban blue collar families (mostly white) lived. On the north border, one block away, the beautiful restored brownstones began. Two blocks to the north was a park lined with brownstones where a summer Shakespeare company put on plays for the public. However, Victory Hills served the poorer neighbors; the church operated a learning center for neighborhood children struggling in school. In 1987, the Reverend Janet Moore (known as "Pastor Janet" to her people) was the associate pastor of a suburban church, her first position after graduating from the Methodist Theological School in Chicago. That year, the bishop chose her to lead Victory Hills, a church that was in trouble financially and losing members. She was the first woman to pastor this church. When I arrived at her office on October 2, 1990, three years into her appointment, Pastor Janet, as she was known to her people, was involved in a boundary struggle whose fault line extended beyond the walls of the church to the neighborhood beyond.

The youngest of the three ministers I studied (she was thirty-one at the time of the study), Pastor Janet grew up in huge Methodist churches where her father served as the minister of music. Influenced both by his choice of career and the environment in which he served, Pastor Janet was a music major in college before she decided to go to seminary. She described the churches of her childhood as traditional, formal, and decidedly patriarchal, reporting, like Pat and Reverend Barb, that the men she heard preach often had a "forbidding" style, with sermons focused on the depravity of human beings that produced tremendous guilt. She was skeptical of authority figures because she had been betrayed by one as a child: a trusted adult molested her for several years, and she had been too frightened and confused to report him. These experiences informed her theological purpose, which was to create a community of Christians dedicated to peace, social justice, and diversity. Pastor Janet was the only minister of the three I studied who called herself a feminist; she used inclusive language except when leading the congregation in the Lord's Prayer, and in her sermons espoused a God with both masculine and feminine qualities. She admitted that in her private devotions, she prayed to a feminine God and that doing so was essential to her faith. In our interviews, she suggested that women needed to hear more about self-esteem than about sin, for their levels of guilt were already too high; in her sermons, God was a source of comfort, not a source of judgment and fear.

While Pat's and Reverend Barb's congregations had some choice about whom they would "call" to be their minister, Pastor Janet's congregation did not. Pastor Janet and others with whom I spoke noted that this system has had both positive and negative implications for women preachers: on the one hand, the system gets women in the door of churches that might otherwise have rejected them outright on the basis of sex, but it also makes it harder for them to be accepted once they step foot inside the door. Pastor Janet's gender and youth were strikes against her from her congregation's perspective, but she did not experience real opposition until her ministry began to draw gay and lesbian members from the neighborhood. The congregation was a long-standing one, with retired members who had attended the church all their lives. On a given Sunday, nearly one-third of the members appeared to be of retirement age or older. The rest of the members included middle-aged members, a few young families, and the young single members (gay and lesbian). This church, like Reverend Barb's church, contained a few families who were quite economically disadvantaged. The original members of the church were working class, while the new members, most gay or lesbian, were more likely to be professionals. Therefore, both lifestyle and class issues were dividing the church.

The Geographies of Victory Hills

At the nexus of the controversy at Victory Hills was rhetorical space, both in Code's sense of the word, that is, the control over whose perspective could be uttered, and in my own, that is, the ordering of people and objects within the physical location of the church. The older members guarded the territories they could control; since they were long used to a turnover in leadership, their spatial strategies were well honed and designed to preserve tradition. In response, Pastor Janet preached sermons that challenged strategies of preservation in the congregation and formed new constituencies among the members that supported her own theological vision for the community. She used many of the rhetorical strategies that Pat and Reverend Barb used, with one important exception: she did not leave the pulpit during the service except to offer the pastor's prayer. It is my contention that this important difference in a ministry otherwise so similar to those of the other two women ministers came about because the movement of priest to people suggested in the sermons was being refused by a significant number of the congregation members. She was not invited into their space.

In an interview, I asked Pastor Janet when the problems with her congregation began. She traced the onset of conflicts to a Mother's Day

sermon earlier in the year (May 13, 1990) in which she refused to preach
what she called "the traditional Mom and apple pie" sermon honoring
mothers. Instead she focused on community and social justice, trying
to meet head-on the hostility of a few of the members toward the openly
gay and lesbian visitors who were at that time just beginning to attend.

> *Pastor Janet:* One of the first challenges that was put to me was
> surrounding a sermon on Mother's Day. Well, the text was the
> stoning of Stephen. So I talked about dealing with conflict. And
> how it harms all the church, and we don't always deal with it real
> well in relationships. And they wanted to hear fluff and flowers.
> *Roxanne:* What did they say to you about it?
> *Pastor Janet:* Oh, well, "disgusting sermon." Uh-huh. One woman
> wrote a letter to that effect. She wrote a letter to the pastor/par-
> ish relations committee. Well, after that happened, there were a
> couple other people, like her sister, who had walked out in the
> middle of it [and remained] really mad about it. And I said, "Now,
> you look at this. You tell me if this is disgusting, if this is con-
> trary to Scriptures." And so I sent her a copy of the sermon. We
> didn't talk about it any further. [. . .] It's an authority question.

The conflict was over the new gay and lesbian members, particularly
of Calvin, the first openly gay man to join the church, a man whom
Pastor Janet hired to play the organ during Sunday morning services.
More gay and lesbian members joined soon after. A few of the existing
members were spreading hostility toward these new members; they
"wormed up the basket," as Pastor Janet put it, creating a toxic environment. At issue was whether or not openly gay and lesbian Christians
could join the church; for the homophobic members policing the borders of the church, they were the *noa,* or unclean ones. But Pastor Janet
welcomed them, and they were becoming a new base for her ministry.
She called them "vital"—the most "enthusiastic" members of the church.

The sermon she preached on Mother's Day was called "No Popu-
larity Contest." Pastor Janet generally preached from the lectionary,
and indeed, the Scripture for that day was Acts 7:54–60, the stoning
of Stephen.

There is a myth in our society that parenting is easy. You grow up, get
married, have kids, work hard, and you will be happy. Parenting isn't
quite that way.

In our television society, people have seen parents as the Cleavers, the
Bradys, the Huxtables. On *Leave It to Beaver,* the challenge of the parents was to get someone to take out the garbage and to keep the boys
from fighting. On *The Brady Bunch,* the issues got a little more diffi-

cult, but they still weren't too realistic. I remember one where there was a slumber party. The issues were who to invite and how to deal with the boys who put itching powder in the sleeping bags. *The Cosby Show* seems to deal with more realistic issues: making choices about college, the military, work; how to overcome disappointment when you are hurt; dating; even sexuality.

But in all these shows we rarely see, if ever, real anger (either the parent or child), or the frustration of not knowing what to do when communication breaks down completely. I may not be a parent, and correct me if I'm wrong, but I've seen enough frustrated parents and children to know that parenting is not as it appears on television. Oftentimes parents feel/children feel as if they are living in the midst of a war zone. No matter what they do, it isn't right. It may be easy to become a parent, but parenting is anything but easy.

Another myth in our society is that Christians are always happy. Television may not deal with this issue as readily as parenting, but it is still instilled in us. God loves us, we have been saved, we should be happy. Like new parents who have a rude awakening when they bring a child home, so new Christians (and sometimes lifetime Christians) have a rude awakening when they discover that their problems have not gone away. Living out their faith isn't easy. Christians don't always agree.

This reading from Acts is difficult for us to hear, for it confronts us with a struggle between Christians that was not resolved easily or happily. It confronts us with the reality of unhappy times in the lives of the early Christians.

After Jesus died, the disciples knew that they needed more people and selected other followers of Jesus to be apostles and to spread the gospel. Stephen was one of those. In the readings up to what we heard Cynthia share today, Stephen had spoken to the people about how God's people had not been faithful and turned from God in the time of Noah and Moses. If hearing those words hadn't angered the people, his next words did. He called the people "stiff-necked," resistant to the Holy Spirit, and betrayers and murderers of Christ. In anger at the words Stephen said, the verbal stoning which they felt they had received, the people stoned him, physically, to death.

As with parenting, it may be easy to go through the motions to become a Christian, but being a Christian is anything but easy.

Like the mother who does the hardest thing and says "no" to her daughter who has come home drunk again, so Christians have disagreements, too, and sometimes have to take difficult and unpopular stances. While Stephen's words to the early Christians were hard to hear, no doubt, he said them for a reason. No doubt they needed to hear them.

And without a question the people were changed as a result of what they heard that day and what they experienced in his killing, his martyrdom.

There are going to be conflicts, folks, between spouses, friends, parents, and children, Christians, you and me. There are going to be times of disagreement. We, like a parent or child, we, like Stephen and the early Christians, are bound to have conflicts, different ways of looking at the same thing, and resolving the conflicts doesn't happen as easily as on *Leave It to Beaver, The Brady Bunch, The Cosby Show.* But neither do people have to be stoned in the process.

In First Peter, we are reminded to "put away all malice, guile, insincerity, envy, and slander" and to "remember that we are God's people and that we have received God's mercy."

The real tragedy of what happened between Stephen and his people is that their conflict, their verbal and physical stoning, caused them to be unable to see what they had in common. Here they were, God's people, recipients of God's mercy through Jesus Christ, called to spread the gospel to others, but they couldn't experience love for each other. All they could do was "slander" each other.

This happens all too often between parents/children. This is what divides us as Christians.

There are going to be differences of opinion. There are going to be conflicts. There will be stands that we take at home, at work, at church, that are unpopular. But if we are open to hear each other, if we speak honestly with each other, if we remember "that we are God's people and that we have received God's mercy through Jesus Christ" (like Peter said), then there will be no more stonings. Then we will resolve our differences, peacefully, with respect and with love. And God will be evident in our lives and in our relationships. Then the risen Christ will be known in and through and because of us. Amen.

This is a very interesting sermon. Pastor Janet refers to the Jewish Freedmen who brought Stephen to the high priest in Jerusalem as "early Christians," when in fact the author of the Acts of the Apostles identifies those who stoned Stephen as Jewish non-Christians. Because the conflict she was calling to her congregation's attention was based on prejudice (against the gay and lesbian members), this clever renaming of a Jewish-Christian conflict allowed her to recast the turmoil as an internal one. It also allowed her to avoid the anti-Semitism ignited historically when the issue of the martyrdom of early Christians in Jerusalem is raised.[1] Nevertheless, the sermon suggests that someone is being stoned at Victory Hills—perhaps Pastor Janet and others who support the new members. In the sermon, she compares herself to the mother who must confront her daughter when she comes home drunk. The parallels in the conflict seem clear.

This sermon is not the kind that promotes movement between people and priest. The rhetoric of relationship here is one of proclamation, of a call for change. Standing at the pulpit, three steps above the congregation, Pastor Janet stood in her appointed place and called for the congregation to rethink the mappings of the church. She did not move toward the people in a gesture of populism—an affirmation of their common wisdom—because she did not agree with them, nor could she imagine herself acting as they had. The application of the sermon to herself, a gesture that Reverend Barb made almost every week, was not available here, because Pastor Janet was asking, in a sense, for the people to stop throwing stones, to stop passing slander about her (and/or the unpopular new members). She would have to admit to throwing some stones herself in order to reverse the logic of the sermon and meet them halfway. She uses inclusive pronouns throughout the sermon, but the sermon was directed at the "worms in the basket"; the inclusive pronouns softened but did not redirect the message of the sermon.

Pastor Janet had won the right to a few territories in the church: groups that she was required to lead and groups that she formed herself. For example, when I asked her what changes she had brought to the congregation, she mentioned a Thursday night Bible study that offered good fellowship both for her and for the small group that attended. Up to that point, she said, the church did not have Bible studies—the ones that had been tried failed for lack of interest. But this group was strong and active and, it seemed, reflected her own values. At least two gay members had joined, and they seemed to be a source of friendship for her and cohesion for the group. Other groups that she was required to lead, including the church board, seemed to be respecting her, especially since she solved three troublesome issues for them: raising funds, balancing the budget, and streamlining church operations. These were Pastor Janet's territories: the board and the finances of the church and the groups that she started, including the Thursday night Bible study group. The other territories in the church were controlled by the core members. Pastor Janet was expected to attend church events organized by these members, but she was not invited to participate in their organization or leadership. One of those events was a chicken noodle dinner—a key fund-raiser for the church.

Victory Hills' chicken noodle dinner was an annual event that benefited a ladies auxiliary group in the church, a group that used the funds for its own largesse, though they periodically made donations to the church's general fund. It had been going on for as long as anyone could remember, with one elderly couple attending the dinner for over forty years. Pastor Janet reported, "Some members have attended [the dinner] all their adult lives. [. . .] They're real proud of it." The dinner occurred during the first week of November, with the women making noodles in the church kitchen and the men helping with the preparation of the meal. Each Sunday I was there, the announcement period and the time immediately following the service was taken up with communications about this event. Pastor Janet said that although it was an important event in the life of the church, the proceeds for the dinner did not benefit the church as a whole. When Pastor Janet discussed this event, her pronoun usage told the story: the chicken noodle dinner was something "they" were doing; she was excluded from all planning for the event though was expected to attend and pay for her meal. She never aligned herself with these members through the use of inclusive language—she never said "we."

In many ways, the tensions of urban life were in microcosm at Victory Hills: Pastor Janet was a young urban professional herself; she aligned herself with the younger, newer members, many of whom were outcasts in this church but were in fact the center of economic renewal for this neighborhood. The fault line between the older, established white residents, whose working-class conservatism formed the core of the membership, and the new urban professionals who were remodeling brownstones and moving into the neighborhood ran down the center of Victory Hills. There were territories belonging to each group: from the point of view of the older members, Calvin's presence behind the organ at the front of the church and Pastor Janet's sermons urging justice and peace ceded the sanctuary (that is, the platform) to new members. Even though the new members had begun sitting together in the third row just below the pulpit, the nave and the kitchen belonged to the older members.

Preaching Across the Divide

In many ways, Pastor Janet had taken more risks in her preaching than had Pat and Reverend Barb, for in her first year as a pastor at Victory Hills, she disclosed from the pulpit her slow recovery from being molested during her childhood. Echoing Pat, she argued that "the preacher has to be present in the pulpit [. . .]; they themselves have to be sharing from themselves, or it doesn't seem authentic." And like Pat, she worked to choose stories that illustrated her own struggles, not her own generosity or authority. One week she narrated the story of how she and her husband tried to help a homeless woman who came into the church seeking help. The theme of the sermon was having a vision, so she offered the story to illustrate that "Wilma didn't really have a vision for what she wanted in life." Pastor Janet worked to tell the story in terms of her own struggle rather than her generosity. She ended the narrative by saying, "When she left she was no better off than when she had come: a few new pieces of clothing, a cold behind her, but economically, emotionally, physically without resources. I struggled with what 'I' had done wrong."

Despite the indirect confrontation in the Mother's Day sermon, Pastor Janet was not a confrontational person. She was of medium build with sandy-blond hair, a woman who was confident in a shy sort of way. She did not disclose much about herself in the pulpit, did not use humor much, and talked through her sermons gently. While I had no trouble hearing her, some members of the congregation complained to me that they sometimes couldn't hear her sermons. Pastor Janet laughed when I told her about this complaint and said, "I don't know how many times when I first got here, they're like 'We can't hear you!' It's just that they're not used to listening to a woman." In fact, Pastor Janet did not indicate that she had changed her style to accommodate them but rather that they learned to "crane forward," as she put it, to listen to her. Had she left the pulpit to preach nearer them—that is, if she had moved toward them rather than asking them to lean toward her—she might have resolved this problem. But in another conversation about her style of delivery, she mentioned that although she'd like to preach from the floor, it was "too scary." Her conflicts with the congregation, while not consciously connected with this rhetorical choice, loomed large in her mind at the time I interviewed her. The risks she mentioned involved learning to preach from notes, but it was clear to me that to do so would, as both Pat and Reverend Barb both indicated, change the nature of her relationship with the people. Pastor Janet was conflicted about moving closer to the people. *She wanted the people to move closer to her.* This movement of the people toward the priest/divine is the normal, preordained motion in mainline Protestant church life: in liturgical churches the people go forward to receive communion; in evangelical churches they walk to the altar to confess their sins. With some members of the congregation openly hostile toward gay and lesbian members, Pastor Janet's insistence that the people move closer to her position of love and acceptance was inherently moral and justified.

The one exception to Pastor Janet's use of sacred space involved the pastor's prayer. On Sunday mornings, she stayed in or near the pulpit, except for the pastor's prayer, in which she invited members of the congregation to share their needs and ask for prayers. For that moment, Pastor Janet descended to the altar and kneeled, facing the front of the church with her back to the congregation, in order to be near the people and to pray on their behalf. The older members with whom I spoke said that they preferred a man's preaching to a woman's, but they did like the way Pastor Janet prayed. Of this portion of the service, Pastor Janet said, "Even though sometimes it [the pastor's prayer] can go on too long, it's really proven to be very significant for people. There's just a sense of connection with God in personal needs and in connection with the community." One morning, Calvin asked for prayer for a friend of his dying from AIDS; at that moment I could see the potential of the pastor's prayer to re-map the geographies of the church around common beliefs and concerns. The pastor's prayer was a rare bridge over troubled waters—one of the few bridges I saw at Victory Hills.

Like Pat and Reverend Barb, Pastor Janet was not greatly influenced by her homiletics professors in seminary; in fact, she said, "I can't even remember what he [my homiletics professor] taught me. He was real egotistical, too, and I really struggled with that." She developed her style on her own and so was pleased to see that style reinforced by Fred B. Craddock, whose two-week seminar she took after seminary.

> Fred Craddock is a very petite man with a very high-pitched voice. And he had to learn to overcome those obstacles [. . .]. I mentioned to him that he seemed to have a style I could really relate to, and he said, "Yeah, oftentimes women really can" and that "there's a lot of parallels." He doesn't tell the traditional sports stories; he tells real-life stories [. . .]. He's very much a storyteller.

Indeed, Pastor Janet preached inductively almost every Sunday, using a series of stories to build her point. She called this approach "pulling the point through like a thread." The metaphor is apt, for each section of her sermons was linked together associatively, with the theme repeated after each story and the resolution at the end of the sermon. In one sermon, "Never Enough Time," Pastor Janet linked four stories together: the story of Wilma, the woman she tried to help; the story of U.S. energy policy, which led to the Persian Gulf War; the story of Moses, who wandered in the desert and died without seeing the Promised Land; and the story of a vital woman who died at sixty-six years of age having lived a vibrant life. The thread, repeated after each story, was "To live without a vision is to walk and to not know where you are going." The first two stories were about a lack of vision; the second two were about living with a vision. She ended the sermon with the main point: "God wants us to live life with a vision, a vision for where the journey of life can take us, but where even if we aren't able to realize our dreams like Moses, [. . .] our hopes, our dreams, keep us going, give our lives a sense of purpose."

Craddock argues that this style is less authoritative and more appropriate for congregations filled with Christians who no longer accept deductive sermons of the style that Broadus and other homileticians recommended. Rather than speaking from a position of truth, the minister allows the congregation to draw their own conclusions, conclusions built, of course, upon stories that strongly imply the message. Christine M. Smith has called this method "weaving" and the result feminist preaching, especially when one or more of the stories are built upon women's experience (*Weaving* 40). But let us return to the problem stated in chapter 2: In what way can such sermons exhibit the *character* of the preacher? If character has been built upon a certain forcefulness in the preacher, a certain dynamic quality that comes in part from his association with powers external to the church, how can a preacher build *ethos* while simultaneously evacuating himself from the sermon?

By comparing her own style with Craddock's, Pastor Janet called attention to Craddock's body, to his physical characteristics. She said that he is "a very petite man with a very high-pitched voice," which she called an *obstacle* to him as a preacher. Similarly, Pastor Janet was a feminine presence in the pulpit who was challenged (unfairly, in my view) to strengthen her speaking voice. She attributed a quiet, inductive preaching style to a *feminine body*—both hers and Craddock's. Pastor Janet had character issues at Victory Hills: she was not accepted in all its geographies. And her approach to preaching did not allow her to transgress boundaries: she preached in a way that was designed to bring the congregation along with her to her conclusions. Her quiet and stationary preaching, performed safely in the pulpit, sheltered her from the turmoil in the congregation. She preached community and peace but maintained a distance with her congregation during the sermon. She had been neither called nor invited to lead Victory Hills United Methodist Church, and despite important successes, she had not yet (and perhaps could never) overcome the geographical boundaries that separated her and core members of the congregation. Whether she might have done so—whether she might have felt *invited* to do so—in time is unclear. Having tired of the conflicts within her congregation, in 1991 she left Victory Hills to pursue a different kind of ministry.

Character and the Woman Preacher

In her study of clergywomen in two mainline Protestant denominations in America—Episcopal and Unitarian Universalist—over a sixty-year period, Paula D. Nesbitt suggests that while the influx of clergywomen into the liberal churches has increased, there is still a strong bias for male leadership. Clergywomen tend to be clustered in small rural churches and in part-time and/or gender-segregated positions (such as youth minister). Nesbitt argues that

> such shifts resemble a series of mirrors whereby shapes of occupational and organizational change ripple across the face of many

denominations at once, all the while belying the apparent intransigence of "women's place" within each of these illusions. (161)

Celebrations of women's entrance into the churches occur in isolated pockets of denominational organizations, while most clergywomen continue to experience the reassertion of traditional gender roles or outright resistance. Churches where women have won over their congregations are relatively rare; movement from smaller to larger churches over time, the traditional path of clergymen's ministries, is rarer still.

At the same time, young men are no longer entering the ministry in the liberal churches in strong numbers, a process of feminization that has tended to downgrade the prestige of the profession (Reskin and Roos). In citing this data, Nesbitt writes:

> As long as greater social esteem resides with male gender attribution, and where religious organizations do not have a surplus of economic resources, membership likely will remain politically hesitant to entrust women with positions of power and leadership, despite historical and contemporary evidence that women have capably built congregational memberships and improved their financial circumstances. (164)

Pastor Janet and Reverend Barb both greatly improved the financial health of their churches, and Reverend Barb also increased membership more than tenfold. Pat now leads her own small church, where she has maintained a steady membership. Nevertheless, in the larger context, Nesbitt argues, preference for male leadership of churches is an intractable structural problem: "While the exodus of young men from the ordained ministry and priesthood has been strongly lamented over the last decade [1980–90], nowhere has the arrival of [. . .] women clergy been celebrated" (105). Indeed, no celebration attended the arrival of Pat, Reverend Barb, and Pastor Janet: they were not the first choice of their congregations.

Indeed, gender lies at the nexus of culture and personal identity, making changes in structural conditions a threatening prospect for both religious organizations and individual parishioners. Given generations of backlash against women preachers, it is not surprising that as more women seek ordination, religious organizations such as the Southern Baptist Convention and the Episcopal Church are breaking or weakening protections against gender discrimination in the local churches.[2] As Nesbitt points out, liberation theologies (including feminist, womanist, and *mujeristas*) challenge the nature of authority, including the link between male status and clerical authority (170). But real transformation will not come until this link has been broken. Until then, "women remain either exploited or expendable" in religious organizations (171).

Traditionally, rhetoric has dealt with questions of authority through the concept of *ethos,* a word whose Greek roots are "habit," "custom," and "character" (N. Reynolds, "Ethos" 327). S. Michael Halloran argues, "To have *ethos* is to manifest the virtues most valued by the culture to and for which one speaks" ("Aristotle's Concept" 60). But as Nedra Reynolds warns, "We must remember that in classical Greece and Rome, slaves and women were not welcome to share in the public space of experiences and ideas" from which men gained their *ethos* ("Ethos" 329). In other words, if *ethos* suggests the haunts or spatial locations of men in power, what claims to character or *ethos* do women and others have? Of course, *ethos* has now become interchangeable with *zeitgeist,* or spirit of an era (327), and is applied to any behavior attributed to a speaker or writer. Reynolds combines the old and new definitions to argue for a more fluid, postmodern sense of *ethos* that accounts for those who speak from the margins.

However, in preaching theory, *ethos* has been interchangeable with "character," which in turn is grounded in gender and status. Character is "embodied" in the speaker in the act of preaching. In his book *Preacher and Cross: Person and Message in Theology and Rhetoric,* André Resner Jr. traces the concept of *ethos* from classical Greek to contemporary homiletic theory, noting that Aristotle's equation of *ethos* with embodied moral character survives throughout centuries of homiletic theory. In a sense, homiletic theory from Augustine on strengthens the connection between embodiment, location, and morality, insofar as the preacher is presumed to speak for God and therefore must be the appropriate vessel. Resner found only two homileticians who argued against an emphasis on the character of the preacher in preaching theory: P. T. Forsyth and Clyde E. Fant. Both argued, in the words of Forsyth, "'No man has any right in the pulpit in virtue of his personality or of manhood itself [. . .]. The church does not live by its preachers, but by its Word'" (qtd. in Resner 73). Resner fails to note that Forsyth's assumption is that manhood is not sufficient, but it is, certainly, necessary. A conservative homiletician, Resner concludes:

> [One] implication of this study for homiletics concerns the need for homileticians to be clearer about what preaching's message is [. . .]. My claim that the theology of the cross undergirds our understanding of the gospel has significant implications for how one conceives the relationship of the preacher to the preaching. For, understood this way, the message of preaching makes claims on both the "real" preacher as a person who stands before God's judgment, and on the "perceived" preacher as a person who stands before human judgment. (183)

He goes on to suggest that the extent to which the preacher reveals the "self" in the pulpit has much to do with the purpose for preaching. In this sense, *ethos* is related to the separation of the sacred (those who believe the gospel and have experienced personal salvation) from the profane (those who have not). While Resner's conservatism no doubt prevents him from acknowledging the difficulties of gender, race, and sexual orientation that Reynolds brings to our attention, he does, nevertheless, offer an important point: the *purpose for preaching,* the ideological base upon which the preacher stands, determines how he or she will approach the question of *ethos.* Yet the connection between purpose and the presentation of the self has been fundamentally neglected by homiletic theory.

Pat, Reverend Barb, and Pastor Janet each revised the purpose for preaching to focus not on the regeneration of *individual souls* but rather on the regeneration of *communities.* They were interested in congregations in their "organic relations" and therefore haunted the spaces between the pulpit and the pew. A theology based in truth and individual salvation places a greater emphasis on the personal piety and authority of preachers. Such a theology, especially as practiced in the growing conservative evangelical Protestant denominations, is more invested in the preacher as spokesman for God and far more concerned with delineations of power and male status. As this study shows, a preacher who is interested in *relations* among members engages in a different rhetorical task: creating intimacy and affirming the divinity in everyday spaces. Such a task was not without moments of forcefulness: when their theology clashed with their congregations' values, all three ministers in this study preached prophetically, calling on the congregation to reconsider the nature of their common life. By transgressing space both physically (Pat and Reverend Barb during the sermon; Pastor Janet during the pastor's prayer) and discursively, these three women preachers embodied the theology they preached.

Women preachers throughout history have fought against the presumption of male authority and status in Christian life by claiming that God was not bound by human institutions and could speak through anyone. Nevertheless, even churches founded by women (for example, International Church of the Foursquare Gospel, by Aimee Semple McPherson) eventually discouraged women's ordination, usually after the death of their founders (Nesbitt 108). Women preachers in most Protestant denominations have few models of successful clergywomen to emulate. But, in addition, the wider culture in America has not built a system of support for girls equivalent to that offered to boys to take their place in national life. America has not invested in the idea that civilization can be built around women leaders.

Nesbitt argues that secular organizations that have been "feminized," that is, have been evacuated by men and populated by women, quickly lose status, so that even after their occupational presence has become accepted, women do not receive the respect and economic benefits that once accrued to their male counterparts. Such has been the case with teaching (Schell; Connors, "Overwork/Underpay"). Pastor Janet argued that women ministers bring a more nurturing approach to their work; all three ministers suggested that women are more "real," more "down-to-earth" in their preaching and in their work. If status is equated in part with distance, these three women were not interested in building a ministry upon status—at least not in traditional terms. Instead, they worked toward intimacy and populism; they employed spatial strategies that decreased the distance between themselves and their congregations. Their "character" or *ethos* was established through a rearrangement of sacred space, wherein they attempted to move across boundaries, bringing what status they had as ordained ministers ("a *kind* of authority," as Pat put it) to the people. They were admired for their transgressions—Pastor Janet was a hero to the new members—and for preaching as women, not as "a man in a dress."

Will such changes in theological purpose and rhetorical strategy alter the male status associated with ordained ministry? Those who study gender and culture find the connection between masculinity, leadership, and national life intractable. Indeed, Johnson asks, poignantly, "[H]ow long [will] history be willing to placate the cultural anxiety that would speed [the woman speaker] safely home again?" (*Gender* 172). Feminists and womanists who have studied women ministers are optimistic that their increased presence will begin to transform the association of white heterosexual manhood and the public sphere. I would argue that since religion has been the foundation upon which character—including instrumental assumptions about gender roles—has been built, women ministers have an important opportunity to redefine cultural assumptions that make "a good man" someone to emulate and "a good woman" someone to marry. Women preachers have much to teach us about alternative models for theological purpose, audience construction, and rhetorical performance; they also offer us a glimpse into the movements available to a rhetor whose place has not been inscribed in sacred space.

Geographies of Rhetoric

Maps are a persistent metaphor in feminist, womanist, and *mujeristas* treatises, including feminist treatments of rhetoric (Glenn, "Remapping"). So it is perhaps appropriate in a book about rhetorical space in a series on feminist rhetoric to end with some thoughts about the geographies of rhetoric. The relationship between personal virtue and religious rhetoric has been so persistent in American history that the casual use of religious references in politics, both local and national, is still ubiquitous. Male preachers (black and white) continue to appear with politicians, and to become politicians, with regularity. Religious rhetoric is a critically important part of national life and identity, and yet it is a neglected area of rhetoric studies.

Religious rhetoric primarily filters through the nation's public and private spaces through oral discourse, and it is for this reason, I contend, that it has largely fallen off the map of contemporary rhetoric. Literate spaces are more filtered, secular spaces, where the influence of religion on public life has been sifted and reshaped into code words: "family," "character education," "virtue." Literate spaces are familiar sites for analysis and therefore are the rhetorician's habitus. Nevertheless, religious rhetoric deserves consideration in studies of rhetoric, the public sphere, and gender, and I hope this study will serve as an invitation for more feminist rhetoricians to spend time in these everyday spaces, where discourses of religion and spirituality are vitally alive and (re)shaping the national agenda. One example is the national debate over the place of gay men in the Boy Scouts, which involves, once again, the assigning of good character to masculine heterosexuality. Another example is the religious discourse that emerges even in otherwise secularized feminist discourse. For example, in her largely neglected work on women's spiritual autobiographies, Virginia Lieson Brereton points out that conversion narratives are common in the discourse of otherwise secular second-wave feminists. Finally, cultures rich in oratory, such as many African American communities, are awash in religious rhetoric. Unless rhetoricians attend to religious rhetoric, especially as it is performed in everyday spaces, a significant aspect of American rhetorical culture will remain beyond our borders.

There is also need for further study of women preachers. The neglect of women preachers is a significant oversight in feminist studies across the humanities. Long before women were invited to speak about secular subjects to promiscuous audiences, they were preaching, exhorting, testifying, and prophesying. The vast majority of these women are only now being recuperated. Vicki Tolar Collins's work on Methodist preachers is an important example within the field of rhetoric. The women preachers featured in this book are vital and dynamic feminists who are working in their small spheres of influence to change national life. There are women preachers in many denominations and religious traditions (women rabbis, for example) around the nation whose rhetorical performances deserve our attention. Because of the relentlessly heterosexist nature of Protestant culture, the rhetorical performance of gay, lesbian, and bisexual clergy urgently warrants our study and appreciation.

The study of physicality and space, especially in studies of rhetorical performance (formal or informal), is a promising area of research that offers important opportunities for feminists. Attention to bodies, material culture, and space has been a hallmark of feminist cultural study (including geography), influencing such feminist rhetoricians as Maureen Daly Goggin, who is studying the communicative properties of quilts. Attention to physicality and space within rhetorical performance enhances textual analysis by bringing the temporal aspects of rhetoric (space, movement, audience) into focus. Such studies offer feminists a way to counter the universalizing tendencies of rhetorical theory, which occlude specific, gendered/raced bodies and their extraordinary oratorical performances.

Finally, because the body is a central feminist concern, rhetoricians might use the concept of rhetorical space to re-center feminist theories of rhetoric around the canon of delivery. What might that mean? Delivery involves space, the body, and the place of both in the social imaginary. Delivery involves historical concepts of the public and private spheres. As an art, delivery is creative, progressive, active, mobile; it promotes and reflects relationships; it both embodies the word and is the word. Delivery is based in and on cultural norms and the breaking of those norms. Feminists desire realignment of rhetorical space, both linguistic and material. Orators accomplish an alignment of the world each time they speak, whether behind pulpits or on the streets. Perhaps it is in this neglected canon that feminist rhetoricians will find a theoretical home.

Epilogue

An Ethnography of Relations

We "know" the Other is within us and affects how we evolve [. . .].
Rimbaud's "I is an other" is literal in terms of history. In spite of
ourselves, a sort of "consciousness of consciousness" opens up and
turns each of us into a disconcerted actor in the poetics of Relation.
　　　　　　　　　—Édouard Glissant, *Poetics of Relation*

Epilogues are for loose ends, and this one is no exception. In it I want
to say something about the poetics of Relation, to borrow a lovely
phrase from ethnographer Édouard Glissant, who uses it to describe the
language of lived experience in Martinique among New World Africans.
But "poetics of Relation" is also a good description for ethnography,
which is an "approximate truth," as Glissant writes, "given in a narrative" that attempts to render something of the Relation between the
ethnographer and "the Other" (27). The ethnographer is the "disconcerted actor" that Glissant describes in the epigraph for this chapter, a
Being who must write about the Other while "the Other is within,"
affecting how she evolves (27). Some theorists have reduced this insight
by arguing that all ethnography is autobiographical. And perhaps it is.
But what happens to the ethnographer in the field is not a mere footnote to her life story—what the Other gives does, in fact, influence one's
evolution. Therefore, I feel some responsibility to speak to this aspect
of my fieldwork, acknowledging, of course, that these are partial truths.

When I was a young girl, it seemed patently unfair that all the heroes
available to me were men. Nevertheless, bravery, physical strength and
agility, knowledge of the natural world, and oratorical power were the
qualities I craved, so in my world of make-believe, I was a boy. Even as
my body dragged me reluctantly toward puberty, I imagined myself as
an orphan named Aubrey who immigrated to America on a boat and
could wrestle sharks to save passengers thrown overboard. I was rarely
a girl during playtime, for to be a girl would be to acknowledge my
identity as the passive and uninteresting character in the real American

tale that was my life. One day I was watching *Speed Racer,* a TV cartoon about another boy-hero with whom I desperately identified. Speed Racer was rescuing his girlfriend, Trixie, from yet another brush with death when it suddenly hit me: *I* am Trixie. I *cannot* be Speed Racer. If I were to become a lesbian instead of just a shy tomboy, all my fantasies to this point would have made sense. I could love Trixie and be her hero. But I was not—I was just a straight white girl living in a two-bedroom urban house in the Midwest where girls took gymnastics or dance lessons. My evangelical pastor had taught me all about Trixie's role: she should be submissive to her man. "Femininity is [. . .] not the product of a choice," Judith Butler writes, "but the forcible citation of a norm" (*Bodies* 232). As long as I focused on being Speed Racer, I could avoid dealing with being a girl. But on the eve of puberty, I realized I could no longer delude myself: I was Trixie. The preacher meant *me.*

After this revelation, I spent much of my time focusing on the inequities between the sexes. In high school, I declared to my family that it was unfair for God to have sent a man to save the world. But I did not question the rightness of the values associated with masculine heroes in American culture: I only protested that those same values were not recognized in women. Feminism taught me more complex lessons, but my upbringing nevertheless caused in me what Donna Haraway calls a "split and contradictory self" (586). Of course, this is the condition of our existence in postmodernity, but gender ideologies within religious contexts cause a special kind of "splitting" because they can be so extreme in their absolutism. As Angela A. Aidala has argued, "Religious movements typically differ from their secular counterparts in offering a morally absolute set of definitions and rules to follow concerning women, men, and their relations" (288). That I would define myself first as Speed Racer and then later as his loyal but weak girlfriend was all but guaranteed by my upbringing. Issues of race and sexual orientation were not on my radar screen then, but as I grew up I became strongly oriented toward issues of justice, and these issues finally propelled me out of institutional religious belief. I did not set out to study women preachers: I only wanted to understand the relationship between gender and the rhetorical arts. Nevertheless, my fieldwork immersed me in my childhood again in very surprising ways. Two issues stood out for me personally: religion can be powerfully redefined when a woman preaches, and the racial segregation that still marks American life is even more troubling than I knew.

In my first field site, I became aware that Pat was a woman who was at home with an athletic femininity. She was petite yet full of energy and humor—and power. A reader pointed out to me that my description of Pat in chapter 3 reveals this perception: "She reminded me of a tomboy, a woman more at home in Converse sneakers than skirts"; she "plopped on the floor and illustrated a biblical principle using cartoon characters" and "played co-ed basketball in seminary." She was brave, athletic, and resilient; at the same time, she was unapologetically female and believed that her experiences as a woman gave her opportunities to change the nature of the church. She was the first preacher I ever saw leave the pulpit to preach from the floor or stop in the midst of a sermon to speak with individuals in the congregation. In my childhood (and in much popular culture), boys are given the character traits of bravery, athleticism, and resilience, whereas girls are nurturing and interested in cultivating relationships. Pat embodied all these character traits. The reader who pointed out my androgynous descriptions also noted that the pseudonym I chose for this preacher, "Pat," although the shortened form of "Patricia," could also be the nickname for "Patrick." Because of the groundbreaking work of transgender researchers and activists, we know that gender traits are fluid constructions; but because they are so strongly tied to ideology and nation-state, Pat's construction of self was a delightful surprise. To put it another way, Pat got to be Trixie *and* Speed Racer. I am not invested in the idea of the unified self; nevertheless, Pat's *character* as a living strategy was news to my twelve-year-old self.

I am well aware of critics who will say that the rhetorical strategies exhibited by the women in this study have nothing to do with gender. Over the years, Catholics have argued with me that after Vatican II, many priests across the United States left their pulpits, never to return; they preached their homilies from the floor or just behind the altar. Their act was an effort to bring the people closer to the divine. In chapter 1, I offer evidence that Henry Ward Beecher left the pulpit to engage his congregation more fully (and manfully). In the question-and-answer session following the lecture in which Beecher makes these comments, he suggests that the model for Protestant preaching ought to be a conversation of a few of the faithful around a fire. Pat suggested that this dialogue of the faithful was for her modeled in the early church, which she envisioned in terms equivalent to Beecher's fireside chat. The issue is intimacy: the *simulacrum* of simple conversation among like-minded individuals in sacred space.

A fair question here might be, What preacher would *not* want to enact the conditions of the early church in his or her sanctuary? In the way that rhetoricians view the Greek *polis* with nostalgia, Protestants regard this image of the early church as the perfect condition for Christian teaching and worship. The evangelical church I attended from around age twelve until graduation organized *koinenia,* or small groups, so that the growing church might maintain the intimate feeling of community that is thought to have been present in the house churches of early

Christendom. Nevertheless, as we saw in the first chapter, the basilica is based on the floor plan of homes of wealthy patriarchs or on the courthouse; religious life is entwined with the values of nation and therefore with hierarchy and gender hegemony. Just as women and slaves were not invited to the polis, so women were excluded from full participation in the early churches after nation and religion were married in third-century Rome. Beecher's fireside chat does not include women; and the Catholic Church, while encouraging of androgyny among its priests, excludes women from ordination.

What does Pat's rhetorical performance have to do with gender? For her and for me, in the context of late-twentieth-century mainline Protestant Christianity, most everything. That is, in the context of long-standing traditions that have excluded women and embraced atomizing notions of religion as existing for individual salvation—as well as in the local context of St. John's—Pat's performance is a ritual transgression of sacred space well suited for her to make as a woman preacher. Her spatial strategies included storytelling, dialogue, and personal disclosure as well as leaving behind the safety and authority of the pulpit. Certainly men have made such moves, but not, I would argue, in the name of feminizing sacred space. Indeed, it is not uncommon in African American churches for clergymen to leave the pulpit during the sermon; for this reason, when I asked Reverend Barb about what she brought to the ministry as a woman, she emphasized the content and self-disclosure evident in her stories and not her habit of walking the aisle on Sunday mornings. Nevertheless, it makes a difference that at the end of her walk, she stood with the congregation and applied the message of her sermon to herself. It made a difference for this congregation that no clergyman had walked the aisle at Eastside.

For Pastor Janet, who named herself a feminist and was in the process of transforming Victory Hills into a congregation that would not only tolerate but also welcome gay and lesbian parishioners, being a woman preacher was all about preaching justice and inclusion; it was about being a nurturing presence. That she did not feel welcomed to bridge the geographical divide in her delivery did not mean that she neglected the larger goal of transforming relationships within the church. And while she was not the most powerful preacher I studied, she was the woman with whom I most related: she was open with me and with her congregation about being broken by hierarchies in the church and in the larger culture. Her sense of God was feminine and poetic; her sense of loyalty and friendship to the besieged gay and lesbian community was remarkable and, in the context of her church, very brave. Pastor Janet had not yet embodied populism in her delivery, but she had begun to create a kind of intimacy through the use of narrative and in the pastor's prayer. In the context of her church, which in many ways rejected her message, Pastor Janet perhaps transgressed as many boundaries as she was able.

But I digress. As important as it was for my twelve-year-old self to see a woman embodying a full range of human traits and therefore redefining for me what it meant for a woman to have "character," more important was what I learned as an adult about white culture. At Eastside United Church of Christ, where I was the only white person in the congregation for most of my time there, I was embraced and welcomed into the community at a level I did not know was possible in a Protestant church—of any ethnic makeup. While conceding the dangers of romanticizing this fieldwork site, I nevertheless want to acknowledge that I was moved by Reverend Barb's preaching and by the sense of community at Eastside at a very deep level. What was happening each week in this church? Reverend Barb believed that a service must include an emotional release from the burdens of living in the dominant culture. The tears I sometimes shed with the congregation were not so much for a transcendent religious experience (although perhaps) but for the relief of having the difficulties of human life acknowledged in a context in which justice and liberation were the starting point for religious belief. Needless to say, I was not the primary audience for the sermons. But I was conscious that in crossing this cultural divide (an artificial divide, as I discovered—I was invited to join the church formally), I was privileged to glimpse not only the crushing limitations of the religion of my childhood but also the opportunities for re-envisioning what a spiritual/communal life beyond the dominant culture might look like. It has also led me to ask questions in other life contexts: for example, what forms of expression do schools privilege, and what do these forms of written and verbal expression *do* to students (Mountford, "Let Them Experiment")? It is one thing to acknowledge diversity and quite another to be blown away by the limitations inherent in the institutional and cultural settings one haunts. I would not have had these insights, however, if the people of Eastside had not extended themselves to me in friendship. Would I have continued attending Eastside had I stayed in that city? I'd like to think I would have.

In the final line of a book full of depressing statistics about clergy-women in America, Nesbitt writes,

> A conscious reconstitution of gender understanding, done concurrently with close exegetical and theological reflection, can open new directions for fresh understandings of commonality and appreciation for diversity that facilitate a functional religious, as well as cultural, pluralism in a global community. (177)

This study is an effort to uncover the gender ideologies at work in the art of preaching, one of the most ancient of the rhetorical arts. It also offers a glimpse into the nature of rhetorical space and the relationship of space to gender. My hope is that this study will reinforce efforts by feminists to explore the impact of national manhood on American life. But through the portraits of three women preachers I present here, I also hope to offer a glimpse into the difference it makes when women engender the word.

Notes

Works Cited

Index

Notes

Introduction
Gendered Bodies, Feminism, and Rhetorical Performance

1. It is important to note that the history of preaching (that is, the study of major preachers and their sermons) and the history of the art of preaching are not the same. The art of preaching, like all arts of rhetoric, is, as John F. Genung describes, a body of knowledge "made efficient by skill [. . .], the working-rules of an art" (5). The rules of preaching—the discipline of homiletics—have guided educated preachers for almost two millennia.

2. Edward Hall identifies nonverbal (bodily) communication as "the silent language." His perception is especially apt when considered within the academic field of rhetoric, which has largely neglected the body as a system of signs since Whately's time.

3. A religious manifestation of this belief system is Christian Science (Church of Christ, Scientist), a Bible-based system of spiritual healing founded by Mary Baker Eddy. Christian Scientists believe physical healing can be affected by faith and adherence to a set of spiritual laws.

4. Lisa Ede, Cheryl Glenn, and Andrea A. Lunsford argue that all five canons of rhetoric must be reconsidered from a feminist perspective. In their discussion of delivery, they suggest that it is the rhetoric of inclusion that marks the distinction between feminist and traditional oratory. Their focus is not so much on the body as on an orator's choice of words and subject.

5. Women participated fully in the life of the early Christian church, holding offices as deaconesses and prophets (Torjesen, *When Women Were Priests*). Their images are painted in catacombs, sculpted in reliefs on tombs, and tiled in mosaics (Torjesen, "Early Christian *Orans*" 42). The Gospel of Mary (Magdalene) is a playful reminder that the early centuries of Christianity were marked by tension between men and women but not by the outright repression that followed. By the third century, as the church hierarchy was being established under male rule, patricians such as St. Ambrose began to restrict women's participation in church life. Ambrose interpreted John 20:17, in which the recently risen Christ forbids Mary Magdalene to touch him, as proof that Paul's admonitions against women teaching or holding authority over men (1 Cor. 14:34–35; 1 Tim. 2:12) were correct. This logic was extended to women handling the sacraments, vestments, or incense; baptizing; teaching; and preaching. Gratian, Pope Innocent III, Gregory IX, and Thomas Aquinas repeated this doctrine (Jansen 67–68). The grounds for excluding women from the sacred spaces was their perceived uncleanness. See chapter 1 for further discussion of

the gendering of sacred space. For theory on women's place in the public sphere in general, see Landes, "Public," and Elshtain.

6. Here is a sampling of ordination dates (that is, the first year a woman was ordained) for mainline Protestant denominations: Congregationalists, 1853; American Unitarian Association, 1871; Disciples of Christ, 1888; Assemblies of God, 1935; Methodist Church, 1956; United Presbyterian Church, North America, 1958; Southern Baptist Convention, 1964 (revoked, 2001); Christian Methodist Episcopal Church, 1966; Lutheran Church in America, 1970; Mennonite Church, 1973; Episcopal Church, 1976; Reformed Church in America, 1979 (Chaves 16–17).

7. Throughout this book, the names of the ministers, their parishioners, their churches, and others connected to them (e.g., their children and husbands) have been changed.

1. On Gender and Rhetorical Space

1. Lloyd Bitzer defines the rhetorical situation as "a natural context of persons, events, objects, relations, and an exigence which strongly invites utterance" (5). By "objects," Bitzer has in mind "documents," not elements of a physical location (8). Bitzer's definition was challenged by Vatz in 1973 for being too narrow but has nevertheless been engaged and extended by such scholars as Richard L. Larson, Consigny, Jamieson ("Generic"), Hunsaker and Smith, Biesecker ("Rethinking"), Garret and Xiao, and Gorrell. It is presented by Crowley and Hawhee as a standard category of rhetorical analysis in the 1999 edition of *Ancient Rhetorics for Contemporary Students* (12–13).

2. Of course, the material is interpreted through language and does not escape the power of naming. For an especially rich exploration of this point, see Kolodny's *The Land Before Her: Fantasy and Experience of the American Frontiers, 1630–1860*.

3. June Hadden Hobbs illustrates this point through an analysis of hymn-writing, which, she argues, shows that religious men, even when embracing the "softened" Calvinism identified by Douglas, still wrote hymns that embraced patriarchal views of Christianity. She writes, "[M]ale and female uses of the language of [. . .] 'evangelical domesticity' represent a struggle between two kinds of authority. [. . .] From this gendered contest emerge distinctly male and female models of spirituality" (78). Women hymnists wrote hymns with imagery of motherhood, love between friends, or erotic love. Men, on the other hand, used war or chivalric imagery, especially in depicting Christian mission. Spirituals offer yet another cultural touchstone for understanding American Christian history (see Kirk-Duggan's *Exorcising Evil*).

4. One of my readers suggests that the rock could be considered "monolithic"—not unlike Father Mapple's pulpit. As a metaphor within Christian literature, a rock represents strength and also the nature of God, as in the refrain of the evangelical hymn "The Solid Rock": "On Christ, the solid rock, I stand, / All other ground is sinking sand." However, the context for this rock in the Clearing is not distinctively Christian, and Morrison draws the reader's attention to the fact that this spirituality, created by an escaped slave for other ex-slaves and their descendants, is the pulpit of the "unchurched" (87). It is the

pulpit of a loving woman who speaks, perhaps, for a more elemental, matriarchal deity.

5. All biblical references are to *The New Oxford Annotated Bible.*

6. The authorship of the two letters to Timothy are disputed; some scholars attribute them to Paul, while others suggest that they are the work of an unknown author who used Paul's name as a pseudonym (*New Oxford Annotated Bible* 300).

7. Of course, this insight led George Fox to invite women to preach. See Rebecca Larson's 1999 book *Daughters of Light: Quaker Women Preaching and Prophesying in the Colonies and Abroad, 1700–1775* for an outstanding history of Quaker women preachers in England and the Colonies.

8. See especially Brekus on American women preachers through 1845 and Rebecca Larson on Quaker women in the colonial period.

9. In the story by the Associated Press, the chairman of the drafting committee is reported to have said, "'Southern Baptists, by practice as well as conviction, believe leadership is male'" (Lieblich).

10. For an ethnographic exploration of the *mechitzah,* see Manning's *God Gave Us the Right,* 105–9.

11. The one exception to the gender ideology at work was status: women of high rank could assume political leadership if they were first-born in a royal family. After contact with the West called into question the function of the system, a woman leader overthrew the *kapu* in 1819 (Ortner 163–71).

12. According to the logic of the space, if the gospel is associated with the women's side of the church, the words of Christ are feminized in some way. However, to this day in Catholic churches, a woman may not read the gospel (that is, from the four Gospels, Matthew, Mark, Luke, and John); it must be read by a priest, who may not, by definition, be a woman.

13. It is important to note that associations of geographies with one sex or the other do not always imply a hierarchy. For example, Diné (Navajo) people understand the sexes to be in balance with each other, not in a hierarchical relationship (*Sa' ah Naaghaai Bik'eh Hozhoon,* the Diné worldview, contains the idea of the balance of all life, including male and female). Sacred locations, shapes, geographical directions, and colors are associated as male or female, but as in many cultures, both sexes are assumed to have both male and female qualities (for example, one's right side is female and associated with healing, while one's left side is male and associated with protection). Men and women perform separate ceremonies for the people—for example, women perform the Blessingway while men perform the Enemyway. The sexes do not commingle in sacred places such as sweat lodges, but for reasons other than gender hierarchy. One can see the principle of balance at work in Diné distinctions between "gender" and "sex": while there are two sexes recognized, there are five genders, with men and women able to assume each other's roles. My thanks to Irvin Morris, my Diné colleague and friend, for sharing with me his lecture on this subject.

14. For something to have "a place," it must have existed first in undifferentiated "space." Jonathan Z. Smith turns to social geographer Yi-Fu Tuan to explain out how "space" becomes "place," as in when a physical structure becomes a "place" we know. For Tuan, such a transformation occurs when

"abstract space" becomes endowed with meaning; only after this semiotic transformation can "space" become "place" (J. Smith 28).

15. The desk refers to the pulpit. Since the pulpit is descended from the ambo, or lectern, naming it a "desk" is historically accurate.

16. And, in fact, Davis argues that while women may indeed receive the call to preach, they should not become pastors: "It is not my intention, to advocate Female Pastors; but a woman may express her views in public, by way of exhortation &c.;—without taking upon herself the care of a church" (13). Therefore, when a woman is found in a pulpit, it is for a special circumstance.

17. Jacqueline R. Devries uncovered the 1913 annual report of the Women's Social and Political Union, the British suffragist group founded in 1903 by Emmeline Pankhurst and her daughters (320). In the report, the WSPU declares a war against the Church for siding with the government in blocking women's right to vote. After this declaration, suffragists boycotted, staged walk-outs, and disrupted sermons in their own churches. In the period April through July 1914, Devries found references in the British national press or the *Suffragette* to more than fifty acts of arson or bombings, including not only churches and chapels but also synagogues (326).

18. Grenz puts the date at 1993: "In November 1993, the General Synod of the Church of England voted overwhelmingly to allow women to be ordained priests" (19). The difference may be semantic—1994 would have been the year in which women were actually ordained.

19. And for Melville, the design and placement of the pulpit and its meaning are vitally connected. In the concluding paragraph to his chapter on Father Mapple's pulpit, he writes of the pulpit's design:

> What could be more full of meaning?—for the pulpit is ever this earth's foremost part; all the rest comes in its rear; the pulpit leads the world. From thence it is the storm of God's quick wrath is first descried, and the bow must bear the earliest brunt. From thence it is the God of breezes fair or foul is first invoked for favorable winds. Yes, the world's a ship on its passage out, and not a voyage complete; and the pulpit is its prow. (43–44)

20. In many nonliturgical Protestant churches, the "sanctuary" is the entire worship area.

21. White writes:

> The basilican arrangement, which has been preserved in a number of ancient churches, has become of interest to church builders in our own time. Scholars are not of one mind about the ultimate origins of the basilica, but evidently it came into prominence as the usual form for the Roman law courts. The design was derived from the Greek temple, which in turn was derived from the private houses of Greeks. (56)

22. The footnote to this passage is very amusing:

> Preaching from this pulpit one Lent evening in the [1880s], when it was the use to bring the choir-boys into the nave nearly facing

the pulpit, I noticed a youthful pair of choristers, as my sermon drew to a close, leaning forward and staring most earnestly at the lion on the stairway below me. On subsequent inquiry, I was told that it was the custom of the senior choristers to "green" the novices by assuring them that the lion opened its mouth and yawned if the preacher exceeded half-an-hour! (J. Charles Cox 48n.2)

23. Revelation 5:5 refers to the risen Christ (as opposed to the crucified Christ, depicted as a lamb) as "the Lion of the tribe of Judah."

24. According to White, this design prevailed by the early seventeenth century (111). As is well known, the Quakers maintained absolute separation of men and women in their services, even going so far as to build separate entrances for the sexes and a removable partition so that the sexes could meet separately. The practice ended in the nineteenth century. The Mennonites also had this tradition; my research assistant, Marta Brunner, recalls that in her childhood, Mennonites of her parents' generation sat wherever they pleased, but the older members voluntarily seated themselves on separate sides of the church, men on the left (the traditional south side) and women on the right.

25. In the question-and-answer session that follows this lecture, Beecher is asked whether or not architects should be hanged, presumably for placing the pulpit too far away from the congregation. Beecher responds by offering the example of a prayer meeting that is "very dull and very stiff and very proper" but is followed by the informal gathering of "brethren [. . .] around the stove." A deacon asks the minister a question about a sermon and goes on to enact the portion of the sermon he refers to with an outstanding—and animated—little oratory. The minister answers, and others join in. "Around the stove was the real meeting," Beecher writes. "The other was the mere *simulacrum* of a meeting" (*Lectures on Preaching* 75).

26. See C. Clark's excellent biography as well as Ryan's scholarly treatment of Beecher's oratory.

2. The Manly Art of Preaching

1. See chapter 4 for Rev. Barbara Hill's views on the many ways in which the ideologies of race impact African Americans—particularly children.

2. Nineteenth-century preaching manuals were meant to be complete textbooks addressing all aspects of sermon preparation and delivery. For example, in the preface to the first edition of *A Treatise on the Preparation and Delivery of Sermons,* John Broadus writes that his textbook is meant to be used by instructors, by preachers who had not studied homiletics in college or had not attended college, and by experienced preachers looking for "a fresh stimulus" (viii–x).

3. Bederman notes that the Victorian ideal of "manhood" equated masculinity with self-restraint and piety. She argues that it is not until the early twentieth century that more primitive ideals of masculinity permeate the cultural landscape. Bederman uses the word "manliness" to describe the gender ideology of the Victorian period and "masculinity" to describe the gender ideology of the early twentieth century. However, as she notes, these ideologies coexist well into the twentieth century. In the religious literature that concerns us here,

we can see both ideals at work in such early treatises as Edwin H. Chapin's *Christianity, the Perfection of True Manliness* (1854). For this reason, I will preserve "masculinity" as the generic term for gender ideologies surrounding men's behavior. The distinction that will be most important for us is the move from "manliness" to "muscular Christianity," the latter of which is a more secular and middle-class movement associated with the Social Gospel Movement.

4. During his presidential campaign, John F. Kennedy's Catholicism invoked whispers that the Vatican would gain control of America. When Al Gore chose Joseph Lieberman as his running mate in the 2000 presidential campaign, he played up Senator Lieberman's moral character (Lieberman was one of the first to condemn President Clinton for his affair with Monica Lewinsky and was widely considered a moral compass in the Senate). Since Lieberman was not a Christian, his morality needed to be established through other symbolic means. Other presidents, including Clinton, could simply be seen holding a Bible or coming out of church in order to establish their "morality."

5. Historian Allen Warren writes:

> From its opening pages there is a direct association between manliness and the life and training of the military scout, trapper and colonial frontiersman [in *Aids to Scouting*]. These are the "real men," who do their duty to the King and their countrymen and who form part of a heroic national tradition stretching back to the knights of King Arthur and Richard I and including Raleigh, Drake and Captain Cook. For boys the exemplar is Kipling's character Kim, the model young scout training himself in personal health and for public service. But the scout is no superman and the first class scout has relatively modest qualities—he is able to read and write, he has sixpence in the savings bank and he has taken an oath to honour God and the King. The Scouts' laws enjoin him to be honourable, loyal, useful, friendly, courteous in his dealings, kind to animals, to obey orders with a smile and to look after his money in a thrifty fashion. (201)

6. In a press release dated June 28, 2000, the Boy Scouts of America states:

> We are very pleased with the U.S. Supreme Court's decision in the Dale case. This decision affirms our standing as a private association with the right to set its own standards for membership and leadership.
>
> This decision allows us to continue our mission of providing character-building experiences for young people, which has been our chartered purpose since our founding.
>
> For more than 20 years, the Boy Scouts of America has defended its membership standards. We went to the highest court in the land, the U.S. Supreme Court, in order to do so. The Boy Scouts of America, as a private organization, must have the right to establish its own standards of membership if it is to continue to instill the values of the Scout Oath and Law in boys. Thanks to our legal victories, our standards of membership have been sustained.

We believe an avowed homosexual is not a role model for the values espoused in the Scout Oath and Law. ("Boy Scouts of America Sustained")

7. Bederman argues that Darwin's influence on the cult of manhood brought more emphasis on physical strength and raw power and less emphasis on piety and civic duty. Nevertheless, the Boy Scouts of America as well as other organizations continue to maintain a dual emphasis on physical training and moral and civic duty.

8. The Promise Keeper oaths:

1. A Promise Keeper is committed to honoring Jesus Christ through worship, prayer and obedience to God's Word in the power of the Holy Spirit.

2. A Promise Keeper is committed to pursuing vital relationships with a few other men, understanding that he needs brothers to help him keep his promises.

3. A Promise Keeper is committed to practicing spiritual, moral, ethical, and sexual purity.

4. A Promise Keeper is committed to building strong marriages and families through love, protection and biblical values.

5. A Promise Keeper is committed to supporting the mission of his church by honoring and praying for his pastor, and by actively giving his time and resources.

6. A Promise Keeper is committed to reaching beyond any racial and denominational barriers to demonstrate the power of biblical unity.

7. A Promise Keeper is committed to influencing his world, being obedient to the Great Commandment (see Mark 12:30–31) and the Great Commission (see Matthew 28:19–20). ("Seven Promises")

9. In the year 2000, the Promise Keepers planned twelve "conferences" in stadiums.

10. John Springhall writes:

The YMCA, started in 1844 by George Williams, a former apprentice draper and evangelical Sunday School teacher, was essentially an attempt to bring Christianity down to the level of the average Victorian by showing him that religion was not really about what was perceived as "feminine" piety and incense but was instead a robust and manly affair in the Kingsley mould. As the century wore on, the YMCA became progressively more secular and more of a vehicle by which manliness was to reach the aspiring lower middle class, especially clerical and office workers in the large cities. In the 1880s the movement had a total membership of over 80,000 but, although it had started out with the aim to "influence religious young men to spread the Redeemer's Kingdom amongst those by whom they are surrounded," the YMCA came gradually—under the influence of "muscular Christianity"—not to represent anything in particular, except an emphasis on the all-round spiritual and physical development of young men. (53–54)

11. In his thirteenth-century preaching manual *De eruditione praedicatorum,* Humbert of Romans forbids women from preaching on the following grounds:

(1) [W]omen are lacking in sense; (2) they are bound by a subject condition; (3) if women preach, they provoke lust, just as the *Glossa (ordinaria)* says; and finally (4) in memory of the foolishness of the first women, Bernard said, "she taught [just] once and subverted the whole world." (qtd. in Jansen 68)

12. Wilkins became an influential advocate of "plain style." His fifth chapter, on "expression," contains concepts of clarity and simplicity more commonly found in the eighteenth century. "Obscurity in the Discourse," he writes, "is an Argument of Ignorance in the mind. The greatest learning is to be seen in the greatest plainness" (199).

13. Campbell is the author of *The Philosophy of Rhetoric,* read widely in Britain and North America. Thirty editions were printed in America alone. Campbell began a trend in rhetoric still popular in the twenty-first century: the classification of discourse by its primary "aim" or psychological effect. In George Kennedy's view, four separate approaches to rhetoric cohabit in the eighteenth century. The first approach was simply the continuation of a technical, Ciceronian rhetoric. The second approach was the Elocutionary Movement, with its emphasis on the development of refined taste and correct speech. Thomas Sheridan was one of the movement's founders. The third was a Platonic, philosophical approach, calling for a return to Greek rhetoric and the work of the early church fathers (Fénelon was this movement's most famous apologist). The fourth, which Kennedy calls a reaction or contrast to the third, is the so-called new rhetoric of Campbell and others, who based their discussions of rhetoric on the new logic and faculty psychology of the day (227–28).

14. Rebecca Sullivan writes:

The Second Great Awakening promoted evangelism and the secularization of religion in the service of nation building. The Plan of Union [evangelism efforts by Timothy Dwight and Lyman Beecher] was launched to build Protestant Churches across the west. Both efforts were aimed at counteracting the slow process of clerical disestablishment that had been initiated by Presidents Jefferson and Madison. (218)

In effect, once disestablished from the state, Protestant leaders worked to argue for the relevance of religion to national life, an argument they have largely won. See also Douglas.

15. In fact, since women won the argument for coeducation in the nineteenth century, it is probable that they would also have won entrance into seminaries and ordination rights far sooner if it were not for the pervasive influence of the cult of manhood on religion in America.

16. The *Dictionary of American Biography: Authors Edition* describes Storrs

as "a leading citizen, rivaling in influence and public esteem his contemporary, Henry Ward Beecher" ("Storrs" 18:101).

17. See especially Edward W. Said's *Orientalism* (1978) and *Culture and Imperialism* (1993).

18. Popular in the United States, "Onward Christian Soldiers" was originally written by Sabine Baring-Gould while he was curate of Horbury, Yorkshire (Church of England). Intended as a processional for children, the hymn was set to the now-traditional tune "St. Gertrude" by Sir Arthur Sullivan in 1871. For more on Baring-Gould, see Purcell's biography.

19. For example, even the Promise Keepers are charged with taking back their families and restoring Christian brotherhood across racial lines, more modest (though no less controversial) fulfillments of this heroic ideal.

20. Russell Hirst has described Phelps as a conservative, but in fact his treatises are very much in the mainstream of preaching manuals, including John Broadus's *Treatise on the Preparation and Delivery of Sermons* (1870) and Daniel Kidder's *Treatise on Homiletics* (1864); alternatively, Nan Johnson suggests that Broadus, Phelps, and Kidder can all be described as "New Rhetoricians," that is, rhetoricians in the Scottish tradition who adapted neoclassical rhetoric to contemporary understanding of psychology (*Nineteenth-Century Rhetoric* 98; 274n.15). Johnson argues that they "adhere to the epistemological assumption that moral character and sincerity conjoin to create a natural path of communication from mind to mind" (223).

21. It is for this reason that Hirst classifies Phelps as "conservative."

22. Here Phelps foretells the effect of televangelism on religious life.

23. Broadus writes:

> Eloquence is so speaking as not merely to convince the judgment, kindle the imagination, and move the feelings, but to give a powerful impulse to the will [. . .]. Augustine says, *Veritas pateat, veritas placeat, veritas moveat,* "Make the truth plain, make it pleasing, make it moving." (4–5)

3. *Sermo Corporis*

1. Of course, in one sense, the Catholic tradition has encouraged a view of its priests as asexual by requiring their celibacy.

2. As is well known, gender is the sociological aspect of sex. The complexity of the relationship between "sex" and "gender" is famously recounted in Anne Fausto-Sterling's "Five Sexes" and in Emily Martin's *Woman in the Body.* Even biological arguments about sex are discursively imbricated with gendered (cultural) assumptions and stereotypes. My argument is that while women's bodies have been historically associated with sexuality, in the nineteenth century, men's bodies came under similar scrutiny, a trend that continues (see Bordo, *The Male Body*).

3. *Evangelicals on the Canterbury Trail: Why Evangelicals Are Attracted to the Liturgical Church* includes the stories of six ex-evangelicals who, like Webber, were troubled by the doctrines and plastic worship of evangelicalism. Webber was a graduate of Bob Jones University, a Baptist school made famous

in 1999 when presidential candidate George W. Bush stopped there to speak and was subsequently questioned about the university's stance against mixed-race relationships.

4. Rhetoricians believe that stories allow groups to form a sense of common experience or purpose that is necessary for a sense of belonging. Also called "fantasy themes," these everyday stories can create a powerful sense of purpose necessary for group action. In their study of union negotiation of teachers' contracts, researchers found that consensus was reached through shared characterizations on both sides of the negotiating table over the perceived incompetence of the lawyers hired by the union and school district (Putnam, Van Hoeven, and Bullis). Kenneth Burke argues that psychoanalysts work at the level of root metaphors (which are, at base, what stories are based on) to effect conversions in their patients. They begin to tell new stories about their lives once they have accepted a new metaphor to describe themselves (*Permanence and Change* 125).

5. This movement involves finding feminine names for God, rewriting liturgies to eliminate sexist language, and looking for areas of worship to emphasize women's experiences. Begun in earnest in the 1970s, the movement was highly controversial and continues to be a sore subject in many churches.

6. Of course, this model preserves normative heterosexuality.

4. Engendering the Black Jeremiad

1. Strong women parishioners (sometimes called "mothers") are an important part of the black church, and they can either rally for or against women ministers. In *Black Metropolis,* St. Claire Drake and Horace Cayton note that when Pentecostal, Holiness, and Spiritual churches banned women preachers, those denominations became more popular with women laity, who had unchallenged power in secondary roles in the church structure (30). Nevertheless, Higginbotham argues:

> Research on women preachers, while of great value, does not capture the more representative role of the majority of women church members. Left obscured is the interrelation between the rising black churches in the late nineteenth and early twentieth centuries and the indefatigable efforts of black women's organizations. Left unheard are women's voices within the public discourse of racial and gender self determination. In short, the focus on the ministry fails to capture adequately the gender dimension of the church's racial mission. (3)

Gilkes, a sociologist and ordained minister, argues that women have been the backbone of the black church in America from the beginning. She calls the network of support provided by women slaves to their communities "a third institution that, together with the institutions of church and of family, fostered the physical and psychic survival of black people during slavery" (34). Gilkes argues that women have held the black church together.

2. Glenn prefers the word "re-gender" to "engender," out of recognition

that the rhetorical tradition has always already been "gendered." I prefer "engender" because feminist/womanist preachers so often begin by calling attention to the way in which the tradition has been "gendered," though the gendering has become normative and therefore invisible.

3. See Logan for analysis of Stewart's rhetoric (*With Pen and Voice* 1–5; "*We Are Coming*" 23–43).

4. Cleophus J. LaRue calls the Exodus story one of the central motifs in African American preaching:

> No single symbol has historically captured more clearly the distinctiveness of African American Christianity, and subsequently its preaching, than the Exodus. The story of the exodus speaks especially to blacks, for it recounts the activity of God in the life of a degraded and marginalized people forcibly held against their will in the land of their captors. (46)

5. While there are clear parallels between the problems faced by European American women and African American women in the fight for ordination, womanist theologians and religious historians draw sharp distinctions between these groups. Gilkes argues, "[T]he world view of African slaves did *not* exclude women from religious and political authority. The realities of slavery guaranteed, furthermore, that black women were *never* treated as white women were" (75). The stereotype of the European American woman—that she was weak, frivolous, and intellectually inferior—could not be applied to African American women, whose labor, in effect, made it possible for wealthy Southern white women to fulfill the stereotype of their gender. African American women were punished for their capacity to work, for failing to fulfill mainstream (white) standards of femininity. Under the Johnson administration, black women were blamed for weakening the status of black men because they so effectively led not only their own families but also a variety of community organizations. For all these reasons, as well as the persistent, dehumanizing experience of legal and social discrimination, the women's movement of the 1960s and 1970s did not attract the widespread support of black women. African American women (as well as other women of color, including Native Americans) have experienced institutionalized racism as a tripartite structure: "economic exploitation, political exclusion, and cultural humiliation" (Gilkes 199).

6. For example, the AME Church extended the right of ordination to women in 1960, the Christian Methodist Episcopal Church in 1966 (Chaves 16–17). Of course, African American women preachers have had distinguished careers in the twentieth century despite the obstacles. The roll call is long, and the following are only a few highlights: Mary L. Tate founded the Church of the Living God, the Pillar, and the Ground of Truth Church in 1908. Mother Leafy Anderson founded the Church of the Redemption in Chicago in 1915 and the Eternal Life Spiritual Church in New Orleans between 1918 and 1921. Ida B. Robinson founded Mt. Sinai Holy Church in 1924 and served as a bishop of her denomination. Phyllis Edwards was ordained as a deaconess in the Episcopal Church in 1965. In 1977, Pauli Murray was the first African American woman ordained an Episcopal priest. In 1984, Barbara C. Harris was conse-

crated as the first woman bishop of the Episcopal Church, and Leontine J. Kelly was consecrated the first African American woman bishop of the United Methodist Church. In addition to Reverend McKenzie, several other women hold significant positions in the AME Church as presiding elders of districts and conferences (McKenzie 37–38).

7. This phrase was made famous by Dr. Martin Luther King Jr., who may have heard a version of it from Benjamin E. Mays, King's mentor (Colston 18).

8. This singsong quality is also found in white folk preaching and is called the "chanted sermon" (Raboteau 46).

9. According to Raboteau, in the first 120 years of slavery, only Anglican missionaries (part of the Society for the Promulgation of the Gospel in Foreign Parts) and a few Puritans and Quakers preached to slaves and free blacks in the Colonies (16). Raboteau suggests that the First Great Awakening reached the Southern Colonies in 1739. The revivalists were resisted by many Southern slaveholders, who in turn drove many slave churches underground to secret cabins, woods, or "hush harbors" (42).

10. Cheryl A. Kirk-Duggan defines a womanist as "a Black feminist who takes seriously the experience and oppression related to gender as well as race and class."

> Womanist theory arises out of a "least-of-these" theology, a call to love, be concerned for, and provide uplift for Black women and for all people experiencing oppression and marginalization because of labels and categories used to separate and control those who are different. (138–39)

Jacquelyn Grant adds that a womanist is "a strong Black woman [. . .] who has developed survival strategies in spite of oppression of her race and sex in order to save her family and her people" (205).

11. "Trampin'" is an old spiritual, categorized by Marylou I. Jackson in 1935 as a "spiritual of determination." Like many spirituals, the verses and refrain are changed by individual singers, but the refrain as sung at Eastside each Sunday is as follows: "I'm trampin', trampin', try'n to make heav'n my home, / I'm trampin', trampin', try'n to make heav'n my home." For interesting variations of this spiritual (both in musical arrangement and text), see Bolton and Burleigh; Jones and Smith (for The Southernaires, 1935); and Anderson (arranged by Edward Boatner, recorded by Anderson in 1941, and re-released in 1999).

12. There was one white man who occasionally attended church at Eastside but had stopped attending by the end of my fieldwork.

13. The sermon is lightly edited where the quality of the recording rendered some words inaudible.

14. I was not present for this sermon since it occurred before I began fieldwork at Eastside. This tape was provided to me by the church.

15. Sharon Crowley and Debra Hawhee offer the following example of *parrhesia*: "The university administration has tolerated hate speech on this campus, and so to some extent they are to blame for its widespread use" (252). A rarely discussed figure of thought in rhetoric related to the rhetor's relationship to the audience, *parrhesia* might be considered a central or founding fig-

ure of thought for womanist orators and preachers. For example, McKenzie argues the "biblical womanist theological perspective [. . .] speaks of surviving in the struggle, of being in charge, courageous, assertive, and *bodacious*" (42, emphasis added). She argues, "*Womanist* bespeaks of the 'Daughters of the Conference,' Jarena Lee, Amanda Berry Smith, and other contemporary clergywomen who have had to be forthright, courageous, and assertive in order to respond to God's call" (43).

16. See P. Walker; King; Glenn, *Rhetoric Retold;* and Hardesty. An early example of an apologetics of women's preaching centered around the "call" to be a prophet occurs in Fannie McDowell Hunter's *Women Preachers* (1905). For the use of prophetic utterance by African American women speakers, see Logan, *"We Are Coming."*

17. *Energia* (also spelled *enargeia*) is a rhetorical method of description in which the orator paints a scene for the audience with words that is so vivid and compelling that the audience can almost see it (Lanham 64; Crowley and Hawhee 154–56). In this sermon, Reverend Barb also engaged in *ethopoiia,* or the animation of one of the characters. Lanham describes this form of *energia* as a moment of "acting" in which the rhetor pretends to be a character he or she is describing (71).

18. Beverly J. Moss notes in her dissertation that African American congregations expect to hear the testimony of their pastors in the pulpit (166), suggesting that some form of self-disclosure is required of men as well. The distinction made by congregation members at Eastside was of degree and type of disclosure: Reverend Barb was far more "intimate" in her choices of detail and far more likely to talk about her failures than the former pastors of Eastside.

19. The placement of this self-disclosure in the ending of the sermon is interesting, since the application section of sermons normally is focused on the congregation. In one famous nineteenth-century African American sermon, John Jasper includes his testimony at the beginning of the sermon, designed to illustrate how he learned to read and to show his overall lack of education outside biblical truths (131). Such self-disclosure sets up his *ethos* as undereducated but able to speak for God. Self-disclosure at the end of a sermon suggests that the sermon is preached as much to the preacher as to the congregation, and this is a point that Reverend Barb acknowledged. In an interview, she said, "The most powerful sermons are the ones you are really preaching to yourself."

5. Disputed Geographies and the Woman Preacher

1. The author of the Acts of the Apostles reports that many of those present at the stoning, including Saul of Tarsus (later to become St. Paul), were later converted. Stephen is falsely accused of preaching "against this holy place and the law"; the witnesses at Stephen's trial reportedly say that he prophesied that "Jesus of Nazareth will destroy this place and will change the customs that Moses handed on to us" (Acts 6:13–14). Just as Stephen is falsely accused of "destroying this place" and changing the customs, so also is Pastor Janet accused of bringing conflict to Victory Hills by welcoming openly gay and lesbian members.

2. In 1994, the U.S. Episcopal Church recognized "the theological legitimacy of those who either explicitly oppose or support women's ordination," a resolution that had the effect of allowing local congregations to discriminate on the basis of gender (Nesbitt 109).

Works Cited

Aidala, Angela A. "Social Change, Gender Roles, and New Religious Movements." *Sociological Analysis* 46 (1985): 287–314.

Allen, Arthur. *The Art of Preaching*. New York: Philosophical Library, 1943.

Anderson, Marian. "Trampin'." *Spirituals*. Arr. Edward Boatner. New York: RCA Victor Red Seal, 1999.

Andrews, Dee E. *The Methodists and Revolutionary America, 1760–1800: The Shaping of an Evangelical Culture*. Princeton: Princeton UP, 2000.

Andrews, William L. Introduction. W. Andrews 1–22.

———, ed. *Sisters of the Spirit: Three Black Women's Autobiographies of the Nineteenth Century*. Bloomington: Indiana UP, 1986.

"Attempt to Burn a Church: Suffragist Leaflets Tied to Tombstones." *Times* 23 Mar. 1914: F12.

Augustine, St., Bishop of Hippo. *De doctrina christiana*. Trans. D. W. Robertson Jr. Indianapolis: Bobbs-Merrill, 1958.

Bachelard, Gaston. *The Poetics of Space*. 1958. Trans. Maria Jolas. Boston: Beacon, 1994.

Bakhtin, Michel. "Discourse in the Novel." *The Dialogic Imagination: Four Essays*. Ed. Michael Holquist. Trans. Caryl Emerson and Michael Holquist. Austin: U of Texas P, 1981. 259–422.

Ballif, Michelle. *Seduction, Sophistry, and the Woman with the Rhetorical Figure*. Carbondale: Southern Illinois UP, 2001.

Balmer, Randy. Introduction. Claussen, *The Promise Keepers* 1–5.

Barrie, Thomas. *Spiritual Path, Sacred Place: Myth, Ritual, and Meaning in Architecture*. Boston: Shambhala, 1996.

Bauman, Richard, and Donald Braid. "The Ethnography of Performance in the Study of Oral Traditions." *Teaching in Oral Traditions*. Ed. John Miles Foley. New York: MLA, 1998. 106–22.

Bederman, Gail. *Manliness and Civilization: A Cultural History of Gender and Race in the United States, 1880–1917*. Chicago: U of Chicago P, 1995.

Beecher, Henry Ward. *Lectures on Preaching*. New York: Ford, 1872.

———. *Popular Lectures on Preaching*. London: Simpkin, Marshall, 1872.

Behar, Ruth. *Translated Woman: Crossing the Border with Esperanza's Story*. Boston: Beacon P, 1993.

Bieler, Andre. *Architecture in Worship: The Christian Place of Worship*. Philadelphia: Westminster, 1965.

Biesecker, Barbara A. "Coming to Terms with Recent Attempts to Write Women into the History of Rhetoric." *Philosophy and Rhetoric* 25 (1992): 120–61.

——. "Rethinking the Rhetorical Situation from Within the Thematic of *Differánce.*" *Philosophy and Rhetoric* 22 (1989): 110–30.

Bitzer, Lloyd F. "The Rhetorical Situation." *Philosophy and Rhetoric* 1 (1968): 1–14.

Bizzell, Patricia. "Feminist Methods of Research in the History of Rhetoric: What Difference Do They Make?" *Rhetoric Society Quarterly* 30.4 (2000): 5–17.

Blackwood, Andrew Watterson. *The Preparation of Sermons.* New York: Abingdon, 1948.

Blair, Carole. "Contemporary U.S. Memorial Sites as Exemplars of Rhetoric's Materiality." Selzer and Crowley 16–57.

Bolton, Dorothy G., and Harry Burleigh. *Old Songs Hymnal: Words and Melodies from the State of Georgia.* New York: Century, 1929.

Bordo, Susan R. *The Male Body: A New Look at Men in Public and in Private.* New York: Farrar, 1999.

——. *Unbearable Weight: Feminism, Western Culture, and the Body.* Berkeley: U of California P, 1993.

"Boy Scouts of America Sustained." *Boy Scouts of America Home Page.* 10 Mar. 2003 <http://www.scouting.org/media/press/000628/index.html>.

"Breadsall Church Destroyed." *Times* 6 June 1914: A8.

Brekus, Catherine A. *Strangers and Pilgrims: Female Preaching in America, 1740–1845.* Chapel Hill: U of North Carolina P, 1998.

Brereton, Virginia Lieson. *From Sin to Salvation: Stories of Women's Conversions, 1800 to the Present.* Bloomington: Indiana UP, 1991.

Britt, Elizabeth C. *Conceiving Normalcy: Rhetoric, Law, and the Double Binds of Infertility.* Tuscaloosa: U of Alabama P, 2001.

Broadus, John. *A Treatise on the Preparation and Delivery of Sermons.* 1870. New York: Harper, 1926.

Brody, Miriam. *Manly Writing: Gender, Rhetoric, and the Rise of Composition.* Carbondale: Southern Illinois UP, 1993.

Bulwer, John. *Chirologia: or the Natural Language of the Hand. And Chironomia: or the Art of Manual Rhetoric.* 1644. Ed. James Cleary. Carbondale: Southern Illinois UP, 1974.

Burke, Kenneth. *Permanence and Change: An Anatomy of Purpose.* 3rd ed. Berkeley: U of California P, 1984.

Butler, Judith. *Bodies That Matter: On the Discursive Limits of "Sex."* New York: Routledge, 1993.

——. *Excitable Speech: A Politics of the Performative.* New York: Routledge, 1997.

Buttrick, David. *A Captive Voice: The Liberation of Preaching.* Louisville: Westminster/John Knox, 1994.

Campbell, George. *Lectures on Systematic Theology and Pulpit Eloquence.* Ed. Henry J. Ripley. Boston: Lincoln and Edmands, 1832.

Campbell, Karlyn Kohrs. *Man Cannot Speak for Her.* Vol. 1. New York: Greenwood, 1989.

Carpenter, Delores C. *A Time for Honor: A Portrait of African American Clergywomen.* St. Louis: Chalice, 2001.

Chapin, Edwin H. *Christianity, the Perfection of True Manliness.* New York: Henry Lyon, 1854.

Chaves, Mark. *Ordaining Women: Culture and Conflict in Religious Organizations.* Cambridge: Harvard UP, 1997.

Chilcote, Paul Wesley. *John Wesley and the Women Preachers of Early Methodism.* Diss. Duke University, 1984. ATLA Monograph Series 25. Metuchen, NJ: American Theological Library Assn., 1991.

Cintron, Ralph. *Angels' Town:* Chero *Ways, Gang Life, and Rhetorics of the Everyday.* Boston: Beacon, 1997.

Clark, Clifford E. *Henry Ward Beecher: Spokesman for a Middle-Class America.* Urbana: U of Illinois P, 1978.

Clark, Gregory. "Writing as Travel, or Rhetoric on the Road." *College Composition and Communication* 49 (1998): 9–24.

Claussen, Dane S., ed. *The Promise Keepers: Essays on Masculinity and Christianity.* London: McFarland, 2000.

———, ed. *Standing on the Promises: The Promise Keepers and the Revival of Manhood.* Cleveland: Pilgrim, 1999.

Code, Lorraine. *Rhetorical Spaces: Essays on Gendered Locations.* New York: Routledge, 1995.

Collier-Thomas, Bettye. *Daughters of Thunder: Black Women Preachers and Their Sermons, 1850–1979.* San Francisco: Jossey-Bass, 1998.

Collins, Vicki Tolar. "Walking in Light, Walking in Darkness: The Story of Women's Changing Rhetorical Space in Early Methodism." *Rhetoric Review* 14 (1996): 336–54.

Colston, Freddie C. Introduction. *Dr. Benjamin E. Mays Speaks: Representative Speeches of a Great American Orator.* Ed. Freddie C. Colston. Lanham, MD: UP of America, 2002. 1–28.

Connors, Robert J. *Composition-Rhetoric: Backgrounds, Theory, and Pedagogy.* Pittsburgh: U of Pittsburgh P, 1997.

———. "Overwork/Underpay: Labor and Status of Composition Teachers since 1880." *Rhetoric Review* 9 (1990): 108–25.

Consigny, Scott. "Rhetoric and Its Situations." *Philosophy and Rhetoric* 7.3 (1974): 175–86.

Cox, J. Charles. *Pulpits, Lecterns and Organs in English Churches.* London: Oxford UP, 1915.

Cox, James W. *Preaching: A Comprehensive Approach to the Design and Delivery of Sermons.* San Francisco: Harper, 1985.

Craddock, Fred B. *As One Without Authority.* Nashville: Abingdon, 1979.

———. "Is There Still Room for Rhetoric?" *Preaching from the Brink: The Future of Homiletics.* Ed. Martha J. Simmons. Nashville: Abingdon, 1996. 66–74.

———. *Overhearing the Gospel.* Lyman Lecture Series. Nashville: Abingdon, 1978.

Crowley, Sharon. "Afterword: The Material of Rhetoric." Selzer and Crowley 357–64.

———. *The Methodical Memory: Invention in the Current-Traditional Rhetoric.* Carbondale: Southern Illinois UP, 1990.

Crowley, Sharon, and Debra Hawhee. *Ancient Rhetorics for Contemporary Students*. 2nd ed. Boston: Allyn, 1999.

Davies, Horton. *Varieties of English Preaching, 1900–1960*. Englewood Cliffs, NJ: Prentice-Hall, 1963.

Davis, Almond H. *The Female Preacher; or, Memoir of Salome Lincoln*. 1843. New York: Arno, 1972.

Davis, D. Diane. *Breaking up [at] Totality: A Rhetoric of Laughter*. Carbondale: Southern Illinois UP, 2000.

de Certeau, Michel. *The Practice of Everyday Life*. Trans. Steven Rendall. Berkeley: U of California P, 1984.

DeRemer, Bernard R. "Teacher of Preachers: The Life of John Albert Broadus." *Christianity Today* 13 Apr. 1962: 22–23.

Devries, Jacqueline R. "Transforming the Pulpit: Preaching and Prophecy in the British Women's Suffrage Movement." Kienzle and Walker 318–33.

Douglas, Ann. *The Feminization of American Culture*. 1977. New York: Noonday, 1998.

Drake, St. Clair, and Horace R. Cayton. *Black Metropolis: A Study of Negro Life in a Northern City*. New York: Harcourt, 1945.

Durkheim, Emile. *The Elementary Forms of the Religious Life*. 1915. Trans. Joseph Ward Swain. New York: Free P, 1965.

Ede, Lisa, Cheryl Glenn, and Andrea A. Lunsford. "Border Crossings: Intersections of Rhetoric and Feminism." *Rhetorica* 13 (1995): 401–41.

Eliot, George. *Adam Bede*. 1859. Ed. Beryl Gray. London: Everyman, 1994.

Elshtain, Jean Bethke. *Public Man, Private Woman: Women in Social and Political Thought*. Princeton, NJ: Princeton UP, 1981.

Enders, Jody. *Rhetoric and the Origins of Medieval Drama*. Ithaca, NY: Cornell UP, 1992.

Enos, Richard Leo. "Viewing the Dawns of Our Past Days Again: Classical Rhetoric as Reconstruction Literacy." *Defining the New Rhetorics*. Ed. Theresa Enos and Stuart C. Brown. Newbury Park, CA: Sage, 1993. 8–21.

Faludi, Susan. *Stiffed: The Betrayal of the American Man*. New York: Morrow, 1999.

Farrell, Thomas B. *Norms of Rhetorical Culture*. New Haven: Yale UP, 1993.

Fausto-Sterling, Anne. "The Five Sexes: Why Male and Female Are Not Enough." *Sciences* 33 (Mar.–Apr. 1993): 20–24.

Foote, Julia A. J. "A Brand Plucked from the Fire: An Autobiographical Sketch." W. Andrews 161–234.

Foucault, Michel. *Discipline and Punish: The Birth of the Prison*. 1977. New York: Vintage, 1979.

———. "Of Other Spaces." *Diacritics* 16 (Spring 1986): 22–27.

Fredal, James. "The Language of Delivery and the Presentation of Character: Rhetorical Action in Demosthenes' *Against Meidias*." *Rhetoric Review* 20 (2001): 251–67.

Frederic, Harold. *The Damnation of Theron Ware*. 1896. Ed. Everett Carter. Cambridge: Harvard UP, 1960.

Garret, Mary, and Xiaosui Xiao. "The Rhetorical Situation Revisited." *Rhetoric Society Quarterly* 23.2 (1993): 30–40.

Gates, Henry Louis, Jr., ed. *"Race," Writing and Difference*. Chicago: U of Chicago P, 1986.

Genung, John F. *The Working Principles of Rhetoric: Examined in Their Literary Relations and Illustrated with Examples*. Boston: Ginn, 1900.

Gilkes, Cheryl Townsend. *"If It Wasn't for the Women . . .": Black Women's Experience and Womanist Culture in Church and Community*. Maryknoll, NH: Orbis, 2001.

Glenn, Cheryl. "Remapping Rhetorical Territory." *Rhetoric Review* 13 (1995): 287–303.

———. *Rhetoric Retold: Regendering the Tradition from Antiquity Through the Renaissance*. Carbondale: Southern Illinois UP, 1997.

Glissant, Édouard. *Poetics of Relation*. Trans. Betsy Wing. Ann Arbor: U of Michigan P, 1997.

Goffman, Erving. *The Presentation of Self in Everyday Life*. New York: Doubleday, 1959.

Goggin, Maureen Daly. "An *Essamplaire Essai* on the Rhetoricity of Needlework Sampler-Making: A Contribution to Theorizing and Historicizing Rhetorical Praxis." *Rhetoric Review* 21 (2002): 309–38.

González, Justo L., and Catherine G. González. *The Liberating Pulpit*. Nashville: Abingdon, 1994.

Gorrell, Donna. "The Rhetorical Situation Again: Linked Components in a Venn Diagram." *Philosophy and Rhetoric* 30 (1997): 395–412.

Gospel of Mary. *The Gnostic Gospels*. Ed. Elaine H. Pagels. New York: Vintage, 1979.

Grant, Jacquelyn. *White Women's Christ and Black Women's Jesus: Feminist Christology and Womanist Response*. Atlanta: Scholar's P, 1989.

Grenz, Stanley J. *Women in the Church: A Biblical Theology of Women in Ministry*. Downers Grove, IL: InterVarsity, 1995.

Grimké, Sarah. "Letters on the Equality of the Sexes and the Condition of Woman, Letters III, IV, and XIV." *The Rhetorical Tradition: Readings from Classical Times to the Present*. Ed. Patricia Bizzell and Bruce Herzberg. Boston: Bedford, 685–96.

Grosz, Elizabeth. *Volatile Bodies: Toward a Corporeal Feminism*. Bloomington: Indiana UP, 1994.

Hall, Edward. *The Silent Language*. Garden City, NY: Doubleday, 1959.

Halloran, S. Michael. "Aristotle's Concept of *Ethos*, or If Not His, Somebody Else's." *Rhetoric Review* 1 (1982): 58–63.

———. "Rhetoric in the American College Classroom: The Decline of Public Discourse." *Pre/Text: A Journal of Rhetorical Theory* 3 (1982): 245–65.

Haraway, Donna. "Situated Knowledges: The Science Question in Feminism and the Privilege of the Partial Perspective." *Feminist Studies* 14 (1988): 575–99.

Hardesty, Nancy. *Your Daughters Shall Prophesy: Revivalism and Feminism in the Age of Finney*. Chicago Studies in the History of American Religion 5. Brooklyn, NY: Carlson, 1991.

Harvey, David. *Justice, Nature, and the Geography of Difference*. Cambridge, MA: Blackwell, 1996.

Hedahl, Susan K. "The Model Preacher: Ethos and the Early American Pulpit." *Dialog* 29 (3): 183–88.

Herskovits, Melville J. *The Myth of the Negro Past.* New York: Harper, 1941.

Hess, Margaret Ballard. "Women's Ways of Preaching: Development of Self, Mind, and Voice in Women Preachers." Diss. Andover Newton Theological School, 1994.

Higginbotham, Evelyn Brooks. *Righteous Discontent: The Woman's Movement in the Black Baptist Church, 1880–1920.* Cambridge: Harvard UP, 1993.

Hirst, Russell. "The Sermon as Public Discourse: Austin Phelps and the Conservative Homiletic Tradition in Nineteenth-Century America." *Oratorical Culture in Nineteenth-Century America: Transformations in the Theory and Practice of Rhetoric.* Ed. Gregory Clark and S. Michael Halloran. Carbondale: Southern Illinois UP, 1993. 78–109.

Hobbs, June Hadden. *"I Sing for I Cannot Be Silent": The Feminization of American Hymnody, 1870–1920.* Pittsburgh: U of Pittsburgh P, 1997.

hooks, bell. *Black Looks: Race and Representation.* Boston: South End, 1992.

Hunsaker, David, and Craig Smith. "The Nature of Issues: A Constructive Approach to Situational Rhetoric." *Western Speech Communication* 40 (1981): 148–52.

Hunter, Fannie McDowell. *Women Preachers.* Dallas: Berachah, 1905.

Hurston, Zora Neale. *Dust Tracks on a Road: An Autobiography.* 1942. Urbana: U of Illinois P, 1984.

Jackson, Marylou I. *Negro Spirituals and Hymns, Arranged for Women's Choruses and Quartettes.* New York: Fischer, 1935.

Jamieson, Kathleen Hall. *Beyond the Double Bind: Women and Leadership.* Oxford: Oxford UP, 1995.

———. "Generic Constraints and the Rhetorical Situation." *Philosophy and Rhetoric* 6 (1973): 162–70.

Jansen, Katherine Ludwig. "Maria Magdalena: *Apostolorum Apostola.*" Kienzle and Walker 57–96.

Jarratt, Susan. *Rereading the Sophists: Classical Rhetoric Refigured.* Carbondale: Southern Illinois UP, 1991.

Jasper, John. "The Sun Do Move." LaRue 131–37.

Johnson, Nan. *Gender and Rhetorical Space in American Life, 1866–1910.* Carbondale: Southern Illinois UP, 2002.

———. *Nineteenth-Century Rhetoric in North America.* Carbondale: Southern Illinois UP, 1991.

Jones, Clarence, and Homer Smith. *Spirituals, Traditional Melodies, and Messages of True Faith: As Presented by the Southernaires.* New York: Frances Rockefeller King, 1935.

Kates, Susan. *Activist Rhetorics and American Higher Education, 1885–1937.* Carbondale: Southern Illinois UP, 2001.

Kennedy, George. *Classical Rhetoric and Its Christian and Secular Tradition from Ancient to Modern Times.* Chapel Hill: U of North Carolina P, 1980.

Kerferd, G. B. *The Sophistic Movement.* Cambridge: Cambridge UP, 1981.

Kienzle, Beverly Mayne. "The Prostitute-Preacher: Patterns of Polemic against Medieval Waldensian Women Preachers." Kienzle and Walker 99–113.

Kienzle, Beverly Mayne, and Pamela J. Walker, eds. *Women Preachers and Prophets Through Two Millennia of Christianity.* Berkeley: U of California P, 1998.

King, Karen L. "Prophetic Power and Women's Authority: The Case of the Gospel of Mary (Magdalene)." Kienzle and Walker 21–41.

Kirk-Duggan, Cheryl A. *Exorcising Evil: A Womanist Perspective on the Spirituals.* Maryknoll, NY: Orbis, 1997.

Kirsch, Gesa. *Women Writing the Academy: Audience, Authority, and Transformation.* Carbondale: Southern Illinois UP, 1993.

Kolodny, Annette. *The Land Before Her: Fantasy and Experience of the American Frontiers, 1630–1860.* Chapel Hill: U of North Carolina P, 1984.

Krueger, Christine. *The Reader's Repentance: Women Preachers, Women Writers, and Nineteenth-Century Social Discourse.* Chicago: U of Chicago P, 1992.

Landes, Joan B. "The Public and the Private Sphere: A Feminist Reconsideration." *Feminism, the Public, and the Private.* Ed. Joan B. Landes. Oxford: Oxford UP, 1998.

———. *Women and the Public Sphere in the Age of the French Revolution.* Ithaca, NY: Cornell UP, 1988.

Lanham, Richard A. *A Handlist of Rhetorical Terms.* 2nd ed. Berkeley: U of California P, 1991.

Laqueur, Thomas. *Making Sex: Body and Gender from the Greeks to Freud.* Cambridge: Harvard UP, 1990.

Larson, Rebecca. *Daughters of Light: Quaker Women Preaching and Prophesying in the Colonies and Abroad, 1700–1775.* New York: Knopf, 1999.

Larson, Richard L. "Lloyd Bitzer's 'Rhetorical Situation' and the Classification of Discourse: Problems and Implications." *Philosophy and Rhetoric* 3 (1970): 165–68.

LaRue, Cleophus J. *The Heart of Black Preaching.* Louisville, KY: Westminster/ John Knox, 2000.

Lawless, Elaine J. *Handmaidens of the Lord: Pentecostal Women Preachers and Traditional Religion.* Philadelphia: U of Pennsylvania P, 1988.

———. "Weaving Narrative Texts: The Artistry of Women's Sermons." *Journal of Folklore Research* 34 (1997): 15–43.

———. *Women Preaching Revolution: Calling for Connection in a Disconnected Time.* Philadelphia: U of Pennsylvania P, 1996.

———. "Writing the Body in the Pulpit: Female-Sexed Texts." *Journal of American Folklore* 107 (1994): 55–81.

Lee, Jarena. "The Life and Religious Experience of Jarena Lee." W. Andrews 25–48.

Lefebvre, Henri. *The Production of Space.* Cambridge, MA: Blackwell, 1984.

Lehman, Edward C., Jr. *Gender and Work: The Case of the Clergy.* SUNY Series in Religion, Culture, and Society. Albany: State U of New York P, 1993.

Lévi-Strauss, Claude. *The Savage Mind.* Chicago: U of Chicago P, 1966.

Lieblich, Julia. "Southern Baptists Retreat on Allowing Female Pastors." *Arizona Daily Star* 15 June 2000: A6.

Lincoln, C. Eric. Foreword. H. Mitchell, *Black Preaching* 5–8.

Logan, Shirley Wilson. *"We Are Coming": The Persuasive Discourse of Black Women*. Carbondale: Southern Illinois UP, 1999.

———, ed. *With Pen and Voice: A Critical Anthology of African American Women*. Carbondale: Southern Illinois UP, 1995.

MacKenzie, John M. "The Imperial Pioneer and Hunter and the British Masculine Stereotype in Late Victorian and Edwardian Times." Mangan and Walvin 176–98.

Maitland, Sara. *A Map of the New Country: Women and Christianity*. Boston: Routledge, 1983.

Mangan, J. A., and James Walvin. Introduction. Mangan and Walvin 1–6.

———, eds. *Manliness and Morality: Middle-Class Masculinity in Britain and America, 1800–1940*. Manchester, UK: Manchester UP, 1987.

Manning, Christel J. *God Gave Us the Right: Conservative Catholic, Evangelical Protestant, and Orthodox Jewish Women Grapple with Feminism*. New Brunswick, NJ: Rutgers UP, 1999.

Martin, Emily. *Flexible Bodies: Tracking Immunity in American Culture from the Days of Polio to the Age of AIDS*. Boston: Beacon, 1994.

———. *The Woman in the Body*. Boston: Beacon, 1992.

Mattingly, Carol. *Appropriate[ing] Dress: Women's Rhetorical Style in Nineteenth-Century America*. Carbondale: Southern Illinois UP, 2002.

McKenzie, Vashti M. *Not Without a Struggle: Leadership Development for African American Women in Ministry*. Cleveland: United Church P, 1996.

McLoughlin, William G. *Billy Sunday Was His Real Name*. Chicago: U of Chicago P, 1955.

Melville, Herman. *Moby-Dick*. 1851. Ed. Harrison Hayford and Hershel Parker. New York: Norton, 1967.

Mitchell, Henry H. *Black Preaching*. Philadelphia: Lippincott, 1970.

———. *Black Preaching: The Recovery of a Powerful Art*. Nashville: Abingdon, 1991.

Mitchell, W. Fraser. *English Pulpit Oratory from Andrewes to Tillotson: A Study of Its Literary Aspects*. New York: Macmillan, 1931.

Morrison, Toni. *Beloved*. New York: Plume, 1987.

Moss, Beverly J. "The Black Sermon as a Literacy Event." Diss. U of Illinois at Chicago, 1988.

———. *A Community Text Arises: A Literate Text and a Literacy Tradition in African-American Churches*. Creskill, NJ: Hampton, 2001.

Mountford, Roxanne. "Engendering Ethnography: Insights from the Feminist Critique of Postmodern Ethnography." *Ethics and Representation in Qualitative Studies of Literacy*. Ed. Gesa Kirsch and Peter Mortensen. Urbana, IL: NCTE, 1996. 205–27.

———. "Let Them Experiment: Accommodating Diverse Discourse Practices in Large-Scale Writing Assessment." *Evaluating Writing: The Role of Teachers' Knowledge about Text, Learning, and Culture*. Ed. Charles Cooper and Lee Odell. Urbana, IL: NCTE, 1999. 366–96.

Muir, Elizabeth Gillan. *Petticoats in the Pulpit: The Story of Early Nineteenth-Century Methodist Women Preachers in Upper Canada*. Toronto: United Church, 1991.

Nelson, Dana D. *National Manhood: Capitalist Citizenship and the Imagined Fraternity of White Men.* Durham, NC: Duke UP, 1998.

Nesbitt, Paula D. *Feminization of the Clergy in America: Occupational and Organizational Perspectives.* New York: Oxford UP, 1997.

The New Oxford Annotated Bible with Apocrypha. Ed. Bruce M. Metzger and Roland E. Murphy. New York: Oxford UP, 1991.

Norén, Carol M. *The Woman in the Pulpit.* Nashville: Abingdon, 1991.

Okonjo, Kamene. "Aspects of Continuity and Change in Mate-Selection among the Igbo West of the River Niger." *Journal of Comparative Family Studies* 13.3 (1992): 339–60.

Ong, Walter J. *Fighting for Life: Context, Sexuality and Consciousness.* Ithaca, NY: Cornell UP, 1981.

Ortner, Sherry B. *Making Gender: The Politics and Erotics of Gender.* Boston: Beacon, 1996.

Outram, Dorinda. *The Body and the French Revolution.* Trans. Elborg Forster. Cambridge: Cambridge UP, 1981.

Patai, Daphne. "Sick and Tired of Scholars' Nouveau Solipsism." *Chronicle of Higher Education* 23 Feb. 1994: A52.

Pence, Owen E. *The Y.M.C.A. and Social Need: A Study of Institutional Adaptation.* New York: Association P, 1939.

Pestana, Carla Gardina. "The City upon a Hill under Siege: The Puritan Perception of the Quaker Threat to Massachusetts Bay, 1656–1661." *New England Quarterly* 56 (1983): 323–53.

Phelps, Austin. *English Style in Public Discourse with Special Reference to the Usages of the Pulpit.* New York: Scribner's, 1883.

———. *Men and Books; or Studies in Homiletics.* 1882. New York: Scribner's, 1892.

———. "The Theory of Preaching: An Oration Before the Porter Rhetorical Society of the Theological Seminary at Andover." Andover, MA: Draper, 1857.

———. *The Theory of Preaching: Lectures on Homiletics.* 1881. New York: Scribner's, 1894.

Phelps, Elizabeth Stuart. *Austin Phelps: A Memoir.* London: Nisbet, 1891.

Porter, Ebenezer. *Lectures on Homiletics and Preaching, and on Public Prayer; Together with Sermons and Letters.* Andover, MA: Flagg, Gould and Newman, 1834.

Pratt, M. Bruce. "Identity: Skin Blood Heart." *Yours in Struggle: Three Feminist Perspectives on Anti-Semitism and Feminism.* Ed. Elly Bulkin, Minnie Bruce Pratt, and Barbara Smith. New York: Long Haul, 1984. 9–63.

Proctor, Samuel D. "Prophetic Preaching Now." *Preaching on the Brink: The Future of Homiletics.* Ed. Martha J. Simmons. Nashville: Abingdon, 1996. 154–63.

Purcell, William Ernest. *Onward Christian Soldier: A Life of Sabine Baring-Gould, Parson, Squire, Novelist, Antiquary.* London: Longmans, Green, 1957.

Putnam, Linda L., Shirley A. Van Hoeven, and Connie A. Bullis. "The Role of Rituals and Fantasy Themes in Teachers' Bargaining." *Western Journal of Speech Communication* 55 (1991): 85–103.

Quintilian. *Institutio oratoria.* Trans. H. E. Butler. 4 vols. London: Loeb Classic Library, 1953.

Raboteau, Albert J. *Canaan Land: A Religious History of African Americans.* New York: Oxford UP, 2001.

Rader, Benjamin G. "The Recapitulation Theory of Play: Motor Behaviour, Moral Reflexes and Manly Attitudes in Urban America, 1880–1920." Mangan and Walvin 123–34.

Ratcliffe, Krista. *Anglo-American Feminist Challenges to the Rhetorical Traditions: Virginia Woolf, Mary Daly, Adrienne Rich.* Carbondale: Southern Illinois UP, 1996.

Reagles, Steven. "One Century after the 1889 Yale Lectures: A Reflection on Broadus' Homiletical Thought." *Preaching* 5 (Nov.-Dec. 1989): 32–36.

Reskin, Barbara S., and Patricia A. Roos. *Job Queues, Gender Queues: Explaining Women's Inroads into Male Occupations.* Philadelphia: Temple UP, 1990.

Resner, André, Jr. *Preacher and Cross: Person and Message in Theology and Rhetoric.* Grand Rapids, MI: Eerdmans, 1999.

Reynolds, John Frederick, ed. *Rhetorical Memory and Delivery: Classical Concepts for Contemporary Composition and Communication.* Hillsdale, NJ: Erlbaum, 1993.

Reynolds, Nedra. "Composition's Imagined Geographies: The Politics of Space in the Frontier, City, and Cyberspace." *College Composition and Communication* 50 (1998): 12–35.

———. "Ethos as Location: New Sites for Understanding Discursive Authority." *Rhetoric Review* 11 (1993): 325–38.

Rhetorica ad Herennium. Trans. Harry Caplan. Loeb Classical Library. Cambridge: Harvard UP, 1981.

Rice, John R. *Bobbed Hair, Bossy Wives and Women Preachers: Significant Questions for Honest Christian Women Settled by the Word of God.* Wheaton, IL: Sword of the Lord, 1941.

Robert of Basevorn. *Forma praedicandi. Rhetoric in the Middle Ages: A History of Rhetorical Theory from St. Augustine to the Renaissance.* By James R. Murphy. Berkeley: U of California P, 1974. 344–55.

Rose, Gillian. *Feminism and Geography: The Limits of Geographical Knowledge.* Minneapolis: U of Minnesota P, 1993.

Royster, Jacqueline Jones. *Traces of a Stream: Literary and Social Change among African American Women.* Pittsburgh: U of Pittsburgh P, 2000.

Ruddick, Susan M. *Young and Homeless in Hollywood: Mapping Social Identities.* New York: Routledge, 1996.

Ryan, Halford R. *Henry Ward Beecher: Peripatetic Preacher.* Great American Orators 5. New York: Greenwood, 1990.

Said, Edward W. *Culture and Imperialism.* New York: Knopf, 1993.

———. *Orientalism.* New York: Pantheon, 1978.

Schell, Eileen E. *Gypsy Academics and Mother-Teachers: Gender, Contingent Labor, and Writing Instruction.* Portsmouth, NH: Boynton/Cook, 1997.

Schiess, Betty Bone. Foreword. Schmidt ix–xii.

Schmidt, Frederick W. *A Still Small Voice: Women, Ordination and the Church.*

Women and Gender in North American Religions. Syracuse, NY: Syracuse UP, 1996.

"Scouting's Values." *Boy Scouts of America Home Page.* 10 Mar. 2003 <http://www.scouting.org/boyscouts/resources/34307/values.html>.

Selzer, Jack. "Habeas Corpus: An Introduction." Selzer and Crowley 3–15.

Selzer, Jack, and Sharon Crowley, eds. *Rhetorical Bodies.* Madison: U of Wisconsin P, 1999.

"Seven Promises of a Promise Keeper." *PK Online: Official Website of Promise Keepers.* 19 July 2000 <http://www.promisekeepers.com/faqs/core/faqscore24.html>.

Sheridan, Thomas. *A Course of Lectures on Elocution.* 1796. Delmar, NY: Scholars' Facsimiles and Reprints, 1991.

Smith, Christine M. "Preaching as an Art of Resistance." *The Arts of Ministry: Feminist-Womanist Approaches.* Ed. Christie Cozad Neuger. Louisville, KY: Westminster/John Knox, 1996. 39–59.

———. *Weaving the Sermon: Preaching in a Feminist Perspective.* Louisville, KY: Westminster/John Knox, 1989.

Smith, Jonathan Z. *To Take Place: Toward Theory in Ritual.* Chicago: U of Chicago P, 1987.

Soja, Edward W. *Thirdspace: Journeys to Los Angeles and Other Real-and-Imagined Places.* Cambridge, MA: Blackwell, 1996.

Southern, R. W. *Western Society and the Church in the Middle Ages.* New York: Penguin, 1970.

Springhall, John. "Building Character in the British Boy: The Attempt to Extend Christian Manliness to Working-Class Adolescents, 1880–1914." Mangan and Walvin 52–74.

Sterling, Dorothy, ed. *We Are Your Sisters: Black Women in the Nineteenth Century.* New York: Norton, 1984.

Storrs, Richard S., Jr. "Character in the Preacher: A Discourse Delivered Before the Porter Rhetorical Society of the Theological Seminary, Andover, Mass., Aug. 5th, 1856." Andover, MA: Draper, 1857.

"Storrs, Richard S., Jr." *Dictionary of American Biography: Authors Edition.* Vol. 18. New York: Scribner's, 1935.

Stott, John R. W. *Between Two Worlds: The Art of Preaching in the Twentieth Century.* Grand Rapids, MI: Eerdmans, 1982.

Sullivan, Rebecca. "A Wayward from the Wilderness: Maria Monk's *Awful Disclosures* and the Feminization of Lower Canada in the Nineteenth Century." *Essays on Canadian Writing* 62 (1997): 201–23.

Tisdale, Leonora Tubbs. *Preaching as Local Theology and Folk Art.* Minneapolis: Fortress, 1997.

Torjesen, Karen Jo. "The Early Christian *Orans:* An Artistic Representation of Women's Liturgical Prayer and Prophecy." Kienzle and Walker 42–56.

———. *When Women Were Priests: Women's Leadership in the Early Church and the Scandal of Their Subordination in the Rise of Christianity.* San Francisco: HarperCollins, 1995.

Vatz, Richard E. "The Myth of the Rhetorical Situation." *Philosophy and Rhetoric* 6 (1973): 154–61.

Walker, Alice. *The Temple of My Familiar.* New York: Pocket, 1989.

Walker, Pamela L. "A Chaste and Fervid Eloquence: Catherine Booth and the Ministry of Women in the Salvation Army." Kienzle and Walker 288–302.

Warren, Allen. "Popular Manliness: Baden-Powell, Scouting, and the Development of Manly Character." Mangan and Walvin 199–219.

Webber, Robert E. *Evangelicals on the Canterbury Trail: Why Evangelicals Are Attracted to the Liturgical Church.* Waco, TX: Word, 1985.

Webber, Thomas. *Deep Like the Rivers: Education in the Slave Quarter Community, 1831–1865.* New York: Norton, 1978.

Welch, Kathleen. *The Contemporary Reception of Ancient Rhetorical Theory: Appropriations of Ancient Discourse.* Hillsdale, NJ: Erlbaum, 1990.

———. "Reconfiguring Writing and Delivery in Secondary Orality." J. Reynolds 17–30.

West, Michael Lee. *She Flew the Coop.* New York: HarperPerennial, 1994.

Whately, Richard. *The Elements of Rhetoric, Comprising an Analysis of the Laws of Moral Evidence and of Persuasion, with Rules for Argumentative Composition and Elocution.* 1846. Landmarks in Rhetoric and Public Address. Ed. Douglas Ehninger. Carbondale: Southern Illinois UP, 1963.

White, James F. *Protestant Worship and Church Architecture: Theological and Historical Considerations.* New York: Oxford UP, 1964.

Wilkins, John. *Ecclesiastes, Or a Discourse Concerning the Gift of Preaching as It Falls under the Rules of Art.* London: Samuel Gellibrand, 1646. *Early English Books, 1641–1700.* Ann Arbor, MI: UMI, 1976. 421 620:10.

Wollestonecraft, Mary. *A Vindication of the Rights of Women: With Strictures on Political and Moral Subjects.* Ed. Ulrich H. Hardt. Troy, NY: Whitson, 1982.

Zikmund, Barbara Brown, Adair T. Lummis, and Patricia Mei Yin Chang. *Clergy Women: An Uphill Calling.* Louisville, KY: Westminster/John Knox, 1998.

Index

abolition, 58, 86, 97, 99

actio. See delivery

Adam Bede (Eliot), 18–19, 20, 21–23, 25, 26, 28, 33, 37–38, 51, 126, 133

African American preaching, 42, 63, 96–127, 128–30, 131–34, 137–38, 142, 143, 144, 145, 147, 149, 156, 170n.1, 170n.2, 171nn.4–6, 172n.7, 172n.15, 173nn.16–19

African Americans: children, 20, 44, 102–3, 105, 107, 110, 111, 112, 114, 118, 120, 123, 125, 126, 165n.1; churches of, 12, 13, 19, 96–130, 132–34, 135, 151, 156, 157, 170n.1, 172n.9, 172n.11, 172n.12, 173n.18; general history of, 7, 8, 12, 13, 40, 63, 96–101, 171n.4, 172n.7, 172n.9, 172n.11, 173n.19; men, 20, 40, 97–102, 104, 107, 110–14, 116, 118, 120–21, 123–24, 125–26, 128–30, 151, 156, 172n.7; women, 7, 8, 12, 13, 20–21, 23, 26, 31, 33, 37, 68, 70, 96–99, 100, 102–27, 117–18, 120–22, 127, 128–29, 142, 143, 144, 145, 147, 149, 156, 157, 165n.1, 170n.1, 170n.2, 171n.3, 171n.5, 171n.6, 172n.10, 172n.15, 173nn.16–19

African Methodist Episcopal (AME) Church, 12, 13, 19, 97–99, 102, 171n.6

African Methodist Episcopal Zion Church, 12, 98

architecture: of churches, 3, 14, 17–23, 24, 25–26, 28–39, 48, 65–66, 71–73, 79–80, 82–83, 96, 102–4, 125–27, 128, 130, 131–32, 134–35, 136–37, 138, 144, 146, 149, 155–56, 163n.12, 164nn.15–17, 164nn.19–22, 165n.24, 165n.25; of cities, 23–25, 136–37, 143; of other spaces, 24, 25, 28, 30–31, 33, 135, 163n.13. *See also* geography; pulpit; sacred spaces; space

Aristotle, 16, 64, 69, 148

artes praedicandi. See art of preaching

art of preaching: defined, 2, 161n.1; history of, 2–3, 14, 38, 40–42, 47–64, 66–70, 77–78, 79–80, 94–95, 96–102, 116, 129, 131, 133–34, 145–46, 148–49, 161n.1, 165n.2, 168nn.11–13, 168n.15, 168n.16, 169nn.20–23; literary treatment of, 17–23, 25, 26, 32–33, 37–38, 164n.19; and space, 3–4, 17–39, 65–66, 70–73, 74–75, 79–83, 85, 93–95, 96, 102–4, 105–8, 121–23, 125–27, 128–30, 132–35, 144–46, 149–50, 155–56, 164n.16, 164n.19, 164n.22, 165n.25; women's, 4, 9–14, 18–23, 26, 27–28, 32–33, 34, 37–39, 51, 63–64, 65–66, 70, 72–95, 96, 100, 102–27, 128–30, 131–47, 149–50, 154–58, 165n.1, 172n.15, 173nn.17–19. *See also* homiletics; preaching; rhetoric

audience: characteristics of, 14, 73–75, 100–108, 136–38, 157; for preaching manuals, 3, 40–42, 47–64, 100; and rhetorical performance, 4, 5–7, 9–13, 17–23, 27, 32–33, 36–39, 48–49, 51, 55, 58, 64, 65–70, 72–95, 96, 100–127, 128–30, 132–36, 138–39, 142–46, 150–52, 154–57, 173n.18, 173n.19; and space, 17–23, 25–27, 31–39, 65–66, 75, 79–83, 85, 93–95, 96–97, 102–4, 105–8, 121–23, 125–27, 128–30, 132–35, 138, 143–46, 149, 165n.25; treated in literature, 17–23, 25, 32–33, 37–38, 130–31; treated in rhetoric, 41, 47–64, 66–69, 77–78, 80, 96–97, 129, 133–34, 145–46, 148–49, 172n.15, 173n.17

Roxanne Mountford is an associate professor of English at the University of Arizona, where she teaches courses in women's studies, rhetorical theory, and research methods in rhetoric and composition. She has published numerous essays on gender, rhetoric, and research methods in edited volumes and journals, including *JAC, Rhetoric Review,* and *Rhetoric Society Quarterly.*

Studies in Rhetorics and Feminisms

S tudies in Rhetorics and Feminisms seeks to address the inter-disciplinarity that rhetorics and feminisms represent. Rhetorical and feminist scholars want to connect rhetorical inquiry with contemporary academic and social concerns, exploring rhetoric's relevance to current issues of opportunity and diversity. This interdisciplinarity has already begun to transform the rhetorical tradition as we have known it (upper-class, agonistic, public, and male) into regendered, inclusionary rhetorics (democratic, dialogic, collaborative, cultural, and private). Our intellectual advancements depend on such ongoing transformation.

Rhetoric, whether ancient, contemporary, or futuristic, always inscribes the relation of language and power at a particular moment, indicating who may speak, who may listen, and what can be said. The only way we can displace the traditional rhetoric of masculine-only, public performance is to replace it with rhetorics that are recognized as being better suited to our present needs. We must understand more fully the rhetorics of the non-Western tradition, of women, of a variety of cultural and ethnic groups. Therefore, Studies in Rhetorics and Feminisms espouses a theoretical position of openness and expansion, a place for rhetorics to grow and thrive in a symbiotic relationship with all that feminisms have to offer, particularly when these two fields intersect with philosophical, sociological, religious, psychological, pedagogical, and literary issues.

The series seeks scholarly works that both examine and extend rhetoric, works that span the sexes, disciplines, cultures, ethnicities, and sociocultural practices as they intersect with the rhetorical tradition. After all, the recent resurgence of rhetorical studies has not so much been a discovery of new rhetorics; it has been more a recognition of existing rhetorical activities and practices, of our new-found ability and willingness to listen to previously untold stories.

The series editors seek both high-quality traditional and cutting-edge scholarly work that extends the significant relationship between rhetoric and feminism within various genres, cultural contexts, historical periods, methodologies, theoretical positions, and methods of delivery (e.g., film and hypertext to elocution and preaching).

Queries and submissions:
Professor Cheryl Glenn, Editor
  E-mail: cjg6@psu.edu
Professor Shirley Wilson Logan, Editor
  E-mail: Shirley_W_Logan@umail.umd.edu
Studies in Rhetorics and Feminisms
  Department of English
  142 South Burrowes Bldg
  Penn State University
  University Park, PA 16802-6200